# WUNDT'S ETHICS

Vol. I  Introduction; and the Facts of the Moral Life
Vol II  Ethical Systems
Vol III. The Principles of Morality; and the Departments of the Moral Life.

# TRANSLATOR'S PREFACE

AS in the two preceding volumes of the English translation of Professor Wundt's *Ethik*, the references have been given in English, so far as possible, and the editions brought up to date

Throughout the section on Legal Norms (pp. 160–192) much of the significance of the discussion rests on the fact that the German word *Recht* means both 'law' and 'right' The difficulty thus presented to the English reader has been somewhat lessened, it is hoped, by translating the phrase *subjektives Recht* 'subjective law, or right,' and *objektives Recht* 'objective right, or law'

The translator wishes, as before, to acknowledge her indebtedness to Professor E. B Titchener for a number of suggestions and for a revision of the proofs

# CONTENTS

## PART III.

## The Principles of Morality

### CHAPTER I

#### THE MORAL WILL.

1 Will and Consciousness—      PAGE
- (a) The Fact of Consciousness     3
- (b) The Conception of Will     5
- (c) The Motives and Causes of Will     9
- (d) The Development of Will Heterogenetic and Autogenetic Theories     12
- (e) The Forms of Voluntary Activity     14

2 The Individual Will and the Social Will—
- (a) The Ego and Personality     20
- (b) The Relation of the Individual to the Whole     22
- (c) Individualism and Universalism     24
- (d) Ethical Atomism and the Pyschological Theory of Substance     29
- (e) The Individual Will and the Social Will in the Light of the Theory of Actuality     32

3 The Freedom of the Will—
- (a) General Characteristics of Freedom     37
- (b) The Causality of Will     39
- (c) Indeterminism and Determinism     41
- (d) Psychical and Mechanical Causality     44
- (e) The Causality of Character     55

# Contents

λ

**4** Conscience—

      PAGE

|  |  |
|---|---|
| (*a*) The Various Conceptions of Conscience | 59 |
| (*b*) The Origin of Imperative Motives | 64 |
| (*c*) The Imperatives of Constraint | 67 |
| (*d*) The Imperatives of Freedom | 68 |
| (*e*) The Religious Form of Moral Imperatives | 72 |

### CHAPTER II.
#### MORAL ENDS

| | | |
|---|---|---|
| 1 | The Principal Forms of Moral Ends | 75 |
| 2 | Individual Ends | 77 |
| 3 | Social Ends | 79 |
| 4. | The Ends of Humanity | 84 |
| 5. | Immoral Ends | 91 |

### CHAPTER III
#### MORAL MOTIVES

| | | |
|---|---|---|
| 1 | The Principal Form of Moral Motives | 94 |
| 2 | Motives of Perception | 95 |
| 3 | Motives of the Understanding | 99 |
| 4 | Motives of Reason | 104 |
| 5. | Immoral Motives— | |

|  |  |
|---|---|
| (*a*) The General Conditions of Immoral Volition | 108 |
| (*b*) Individual Forms of Immorality | 112 |
| (*c*) The connection of Immoral Motives | 116 |
| (*d*) Theories of Punishment . | 118 |
| (*e*) The Essential Nature of Punishment | 123 |

### CHAPTER IV
#### THE MORAL NORMS.

1. The General Significance and Classification of Moral Norms—

|  |  |
|---|---|
| (*a*) Fundamental and Derivative Norms | 130 |
| (*b*) Positive and Negative Norms | 132 |
| (*c*) The Conflict of Norms . | 137 |
| (*d*) The Relation of Moral Norms to the Concepts of Duty and Virtue | 143 |
| (*e*) The General Classification of Moral Norms | 150 |

## Contents

XI

| | PAGE |
|---|---|
| 2 Individual Norms | 152 |
| 3 Social Norms | 154 |
| 4 Humanitarian Norms | 156 |
| 5 Legal Norms— | |
| (*a*) The Natural Law Theory and the Historical Theory of Law | 160 |
| (*b*) The Protective Theory and the Theory of Constraint | 167 |
| (*c*) Subjective Law, or Right | 172 |
| (*d*) Objective Right, or Law | 175 |
| (*e*) General Definition of Law | 176 |
| (*f*) Justice | 179 |
| (*g*) Fundamental and Auxiliary Legal Norms | 182 |
| (*h*) Fundamental Norms of Law | 187 |
| 6 The Norms and the Departments of Moral Life | 192 |

## PART IV

## The Departments of the Moral Life

### CHAPTER I
#### THE INDIVIDUAL PERSONALITY

| | |
|---|---|
| 1. Property | 197 |
| 2 Occupation | 201 |
| 3 Civic Position | 206 |
| 4 Intellectual Cultivation | 211 |

### CHAPTER II
#### SOCIETY

| | |
|---|---|
| 1. The Family | 225 |
| 2 Social Classes | 234 |
| 3. Associations | 245 |
| 4 The Community | 255 |

### CHAPTER III
#### THE STATE

| | |
|---|---|
| 1. The State as a Financial and Economic Community | 258 |
| 2 The State as a Legal Community | 261 |
| 3 The State as a Social Unit | 269 |
| 4 The State as an Association for the Advancement of Culture | 272 |

xii                    *Contents*

## CHAPTER IV.

### HUMANITY.

|   |                                          | PAGE |
|---|------------------------------------------|------|
| 1 | The Economic Intercourse of Nations      | 286  |
| 2 | The Law of Nations                       | 288  |
| 3 | The Association of Civilised States      | 295  |
| 4 | The Common Intellectual Life of Humanity | 298  |

### INDEX

| Index of Names and Subjects | 305 |
|-----------------------------|-----|

# PART III

## THE PRINCIPLES OF MORALITY.

433]

# CHAPTER I

## THE MORAL WILL.

### I. WILL AND CONSCIOUSNESS.

#### (a) The Fact of Consciousness

A LONG course of physiological experiment and logical reflection has gradually made us aware that our conception of the external world is influenced in many and various ways by the nature of our sense organs, the structure of our nervous system, and, finally, by the peculiarities of our modes of representation and thought. But that our perception of the *inner* world is influenced in the opposite way, that our tendency is ever to transfer into the system of inner experiences the images produced in us by the course of events in external nature—this is a fact which, as a rule, we tend to overlook. Yet it is well adapted to have a disturbing effect on the accuracy with which we observe our inner life, not only because it makes us confuse our own conceptions with their objects, but because these conceptions themselves become intermingled with foreign elements.

Since in the case of external objects the conditions under which we know the outer world have led us to abstract from the feelings that accompany the representation of those objects, we think we can do the same thing when we are considering these representations as purely subjective states in our own minds Further, since we combine with the

4        *The Moral Will*        [434

external object of a representation the notion of a permanently persisting thing, we are led to transfer this notion also to the representation as it exists in us; to think of it as appearing and disappearing, like external things, independently of ourselves. Finally these supposed changes on the part of objects need a stage on which to take place; and so we create the notion of an *internal space*, which we call *consciousness*, analogous to the external space in which the drama of external nature is played. Feelings, desires, and volitions do not, of course, have external objects corresponding to them, as representations do. Hence in their case, we give up the attempt to regard each individual process as an independent thing. Instead, each class of these inner states is made an independent existence, influenced in its behaviour by representations, and occasionally exerting influence upon them in its turn.

All these fictions vanish if, instead of dealing with abstractions derived from the objects of external perception, we reverse the procedure and leave the relation of inner perceptions to external things wholly out of account at the outset Representations will then be not objects but processes, phenomena belonging to a ceaseless inner stream of events Feelings, desires and volitions will be parts of this stream, inseparable in actuality from representations, and, like them, the expressions of no independent existences or forces; rather possessing reality only as individual feelings, desires or volitions. Nay, the distinctions between these processes themselves are ill-defined; we call a certain stirring of our inward nature Feeling, when the active element that characterises our conception of will remains in the background, we call it Desire, when this active element becomes noticeable, but exerts as yet no direct power to change the course of inner events; we speak of a Volition, when to our inner state there is added the perception of self-

# *Will and Consciousness*

activity, and the influence which this exercises in changing either our internal processes or such of our mental states as have outward reference  Finally, from this point of view consciousness is an abstraction, without even the shadow of independent reality  When we abstract from the particular processes of our inner experience, which are its only real elements, and reflect upon the bare fact that we do perceive activities and processes in ourselves, we call this abstraction Consciousness  The term thus expresses merely the fact that we have an inner life; it no more represents anything different from the individual processes of this life than physical life is a special force over and above the sum of physiological processes.  As a matter of fact, the hypostatised notion of consciousness stands on a par with the 'vital force' of the older physiology  This is not to deny that we may continue to make good use of the rectified conception; just as physiology would find it difficult to get on without the notion of life.

## *(b) The Conception of Will.*

The attempt to erect into substantial entities not merely our inner perceptions themselves, but even the various aspects which they offer to our conceptual thought, has nowhere wrought more confusion than in the conception of will.  A division of the feelings into certain classes was suggested by their obvious relation to ideas.  But in the case of the will there was not even this motive for adopting an individualising method of treatment  On the contrary, the fact that all distinctions between volitions might be successfully referred to the accompanying feelings and desires gave the more warrant for the view that the will itself was a substantial force, which at most presented occasional differences in intensity, but in general stood distinct from the varied

## 6 *The Moral Will* [435-6

residue of conscious content as one and the same *Deus ex machina.* Even such vague differences as that of pleasantness and unpleasantness were lost in the case of will True, the will might occasionally be accompanied by a feeling of pleasantness or unpleasantness, by a desire or aversion, but in its essence it remained indifferent to these extraneous accompaniments Whether its decisions were impelled by pleasure and passion, whether it was a cold spectator, or whether, as Kant required, it acted in direct opposition to inclination, it was still the same will, the pure abstraction of activity substantialised into a real force.

If we discard prejudice and make up our minds to consider the facts as they show themselves to be, apart from any conceptual scheme, these creations of an imaginative power that gives life to the abstractions of its own thought will vanish They assume the form which they may rightfully claim—that of points of view chosen with more or less regard to their practical utility, from which we may look at the series of inner events , or, if one prefers the expression, that of various aspects which this series furnishes to our consideration Every act of will presupposes a feeling with a definite and peculiar tone : it is so closely bound up with this feeling that, apart from it, the act of will has no reality at all. The two share throughout that concrete and definite character which in strictness makes every single act of our psychical life different from every other. On the other hand, all feeling presupposes an act of will , the quality of the feeling indicates the direction in which the will is stimulated by the object with which the feeling is connected We speak of effort or desire when the transition from will to action is checked by some kind of internal resistance , for example, by opposing impulses. Thus will becomes desire when such resistance arises , desire becomes will when the resistance disappears Hence these distinctions are purely conceptual .

the flow of conscious life is not concerned with them Not infrequently it is less the fact itself than the way in which we choose to look at the fact that decides what term we shall use. Voluntary activity, however, is always present when a feeling is followed by an alteration in conscious content corresponding to the direction of the feeling, and, under certain conditions, by the associated external act It is thus the feeling, which precedes and stands in immediate relation to the given change in consciousness, that alone distinguishes voluntary activity from other conscious processes Precisely on account of its dependence upon subjective excitation, we regard an alteration in the course of our ideas, occasioned by a feeling of pleasantness or unpleasantness, as the characteristic expression of self-activity. We call such a process active, spontaneous, or willed, terms which have exactly the same meaning , and we contrast with these active processes all others as merely passive experiences.[1]

So far as we know them in introspection and can infer them from external perception, consciousness and will are inseparably united. But will is not merely a function which sometimes accrues to consciousness and is sometimes lacking it is an integral property of consciousness Thus, will has its share in the development of consciousness. Perhaps it would be better to say that this development is in its most essential parts a development of will Hence a principal manifestation of the growing wealth of inner experience is to be found in the forms of voluntary activity. Thereby the will gains an ever greater complexity of internal structure Various currents of volitional excitation run side by side and intermingle, and so the act of will itself becomes an increasingly complex product of elementary processes alike in kind.

---

[1] *Cf.* on this point my *Grundzuge d physiologischen Psychologie*, 4th ed , ii , pp. 255, 577 ff , *Essays*, pp. 199 ff., 286 ff , and *Philos. Studien*, vi , pp. 373 ff

8                    *The Moral Will*                    [437-8]

Earlier impressions, which, under the form of ideas, have lost their power to affect consciousness, can still exert an influence upon the voluntary act, especially if they are combined with other elements that belong to the immediate present   Such excitants of the will as these, which fail to reach their full effectiveness, but which precede and accompany the individual action, remain in the stage of feeling   Since, however, even those stimuli which pass over into an active alteration of consciousness are perceptible as feelings before they bring about their result, the feelings may be treated as, generally speaking, the most immediate conditions of voluntary activity.   In so far as they anticipate the voluntary act by their general quality and direction, they serve as the immediate motives of volition.   The only way in which any other kind of conscious state can operate on the will is by becoming a state of feeling   in itself it may be a mediate but not a direct motive of volition.   Every feeling is, on the other hand, an immediate motive ; every feeling of pleasure marks a striving towards the object that excites the pleasure ; every unpleasant feeling a striving against its object, and the effort towards or away from the object becomes voluntary activity whenever it is not checked by opposing feelings   This direct relation between feeling and action seems, at first sight, less clear in the case of many feelings, such as those belonging to the intellectual and æsthetic classes. Really, however, it is only more easily overlooked here because of the forms assumed by the voluntary act under such circumstances.   A person lost in contemplation of a work of art is striving to preserve his perception of it, and his will offers a powerful resistance to other and distracting impressions.   Intellectual activity requires a very high degree of internal tension on the part of the will, and this tension is brought about through the strong affective motives of interest and satisfaction.

### (c) The Motives and Causes of Will.

Since our introspection shows us that an affective motive is the indispensable antecedent of the voluntary act, it is natural to assume that the causal determination of will is wholly comprehended in this relation to the feelings that precede or accompany volition. The very terms 'motive' and 'ground of action' indicate an assumption of this sort, which, moreover, finds support in the notion, described above, of psychical activities as separated and split off from each other. Such a conception makes it peculiarly difficult to understand how psychical forces that are wholly different in nature can operate on each other; and this difficulty is, as a rule, a welcome opportunity to the upholders of a substantial will "Of course," we are now told, "motives cannot be the determining causes of will, for only things of the same kind can stand in a true causal connection. It follows that motives are merely the *conditions* under which the decision of the will occurs, the *cause* of this decision can be nothing but the will itself." We shall meet this truly scholastic course of reasoning again when we come to consider the problem of freedom. It is so evidently an ontological artifice that we need not pause long over it. The abstraction of a will without content and separated from all its real relations is first transformed into a substantial thing, and then it is discovered that the thing is in reality as empty as the concept to which it corresponds. To allow this would involve too glaring a contradiction of experience; and so the theory ends by admitting, under the name of conditions, as much as is necessary of the real relations in which the will exists, and separating off, under the title of true causes, as much as seems desirable for other reasons.

However, if such ontological inventions as the one just described do not suffice to free the will from the empirical

10  *The Moral Will*  [439

causality of the feelings, there is another and a weightier reason why we should not regard the immediate affective motives as the true or complete causal determinants of the will. This reason is found in the very fact that the will is not, as the above theory represents it, something foreign and opposed to the feelings, but forms with them a single coherent process, and cannot be separated from them except by a process of abstraction that is not even always definite as regards its limits. If, as we have seen, the feelings are themselves merely undeveloped volitions, they can be said to share in causing the will only as each stage in the course of any process depends upon the preceding stage. Hence, in the total complex of the causal conditions of will, the immediate affective motives are effects far more than they are causes. This is especially true of those decisive motives which really determine the action in accordance with their quality and direction. In so far as they precede the decision of the will and are among the forces most active in the strife between various motives, they form, it is true, a specially important part of the causes of volitions. In so far, however, as they accompany the action, or even its results, they are integral parts of the effect itself. But all the feelings that motivate an action presuppose other causal conditions just as much as the motives that finally decide it  Feelings and desires are thus simply the last members of a causal series that is only to a very limited extent accessible to our intro-spection, since it ends by taking in the whole previous history of the individual consciousness and the sum total of the conditions which originally determined the latter  And so we see that every voluntary act, even the simplest, is the end of an infinite series, of which the last links alone are open to our observation.

But the term motive in its wider significance means not merely the feelings that immediately indicate the direction and quality of the voluntary act which they precede it includes the ideas with which these feelings are associated. Although, when considered in their true nature, feeling and idea form inseparable parts of one and the same process, in the present instance the feeling element seems to become more intense in proportion as it assumes the character of a force acting on the will Thus the less powerful motives are those which are weaker in feeling-tone : the element of will is there, but it is too weak to prevail over other and stronger motives

From this point of view we are led to draw certain distinctions which have their importance in the consideration of voluntary actions. Those motives which actually operate upon the will we shall call *actual* motives; those which as conscious elements of weaker feeling-tone remain ineffective we shall designate as *potential* motives When an actual motive involves the idea of the effect of the corresponding action it is a *purpose* or *final* motive And if the final motive anticipates in idea the ultimate result of the action it is the *leading* motive, as distinguished from *incidental* motives, which involve ideas of effects that either precede the most important result of the act or form inessential accompanying features If, in the former case, the incidental results are regarded as conditions of the ultimate result, they are called *means* Such incidental and auxiliary results may, especially in the case of the more complex voluntary acts, have an influence on the nature of the action not less important than that of the final result itself. They may vary, however, while the latter remains identical Any given leading motive may be accompanied by different combinations of incidental motives, and the *total purpose* or *aim* of the action is determined by the sum of all these motives. But since motives form only a part of the causal determinants of will ; since, moreover, external influences may intervene

12                    *The Moral Will*                    [440-1

in the course of the action, to help or hinder, it is self-evident that the *total effect* of an act does not necessarily coincide with its total purpose. Especially in cases where there is but a single aim in view, and where in consequence the distinction between leading and incidental motives lapses, effect and purpose necessarily fail to coincide. In such a case none of the incidental effects of the action are included in the motivation of the act  But when these effects have a considerable importance it may easily happen that the main purpose is injured or wholly frustrated by them  Motive and effect are then wholly diverse ; the will strives for something that it does not attain, and attains something for which it does not strive

### (d) The Development of Will. Heterogenetic and Autogenetic Theories.

The distinctions just discussed derive their great importance for the estimation of voluntary actions chiefly from their bearing on the development of the will  Two views have been held as to the solution of this problem, which represent diametrically opposed positions ; we may call the one the *heterogenetic*, the other the *autogenetic* theory of will. The first regards the will as a function originating in consciousness out of other conscious elements, more particularly out of ideas  The second regards it as an original property given together with consciousness. Although we have already laid stress on the impossibility of separating consciousness from its functions, or the latter from one another, so long as we are dealing with direct introspective analysis, yet this does not wholly exclude the supposition that certain aspects of our inner life, which form for us at the present time integral parts of that life, have not always been such ; that elements which our abstraction distinguishes in the developed consciousness were lacking in its original state  But the heterogenetic theory of will is unable to explain the very point upon which it rests, namely, how the will originates from psychical elements of a different nature.  In its attempt to do so it reasons in a circle, assuming what it should explain  Consciousness is supposed to discover that certain movements are adapted to the production of certain results, and accordingly these movements, originally involuntary, gradually come to be performed with the co-operation of the will.  But unless the will were there at the outset, unless the effect of will on movement were already present to consciousness, such an application of involuntary reflex and automatic movements would be impossible, they would be for consciousness as wholly passive as any processes in the external world  Besides, the fact that involuntary, purely mechanical movements are adapted to ends, a fact which this theory looks upon as conditioning the development of purposive, voluntary action, is itself, on the contrary, to be explained by the assumption that such movements develop out of actions which presuppose purpose, hence out of voluntary actions : a sequence of processes that accords with our observations of the lowest forms of animal life, where movements of an unmistakably voluntary character can be traced before any distinctly adaptive reflexes are developed [1]

The autogenetic theory of will also assumes that the complex voluntary activities have been developed  But it supposes that in this development the complex result has proceeded from simple elements of a like nature with the result itself.  This theory dwells especially upon two points, which the heterogenetic view tends more or less completely to overlook.  The first is the fact that every external act of will is the necessary sequence of an *internal* volition, and that in this latter, which, as a change in

---

[1] *Cf. Philosophische Studien*, 1 , pp. 337 ff. , vi , pp. 382 ff.

14          *The Moral Will*          [442-3

consciousness resulting immediately from affective motives, bears the stamp of self-activity, the essential features of volition are involved. In the second place, among those external actions which are accompanied by affective motives, the heterogenetic theory recognises only the more complex instances, where several motives are apparent in consciousness, as, properly speaking, voluntary in character. Really, however, these complex actions are preceded in the natural course of development by simpler forms, where there is no conflict of motives, because the single motive, which is the only one present, immediately determines the action.

Following Leibniz, we shall call that inner activity which bears the stamp of spontaneity *apperception*. That form of external voluntary act, on the other hand, which follows from the direct operation of a single and isolated motive we shall term *impulsive* action. Thus we see that the explanation of voluntary activity given by the ordinary theory of will is incomplete, first, because it overlooks the existence of apperception as an internal voluntary act, and secondly, because it fails to observe that impulsive actions are nothing more nor less than simple voluntary actions. Both points are of great importance in considering the motives, ends and results of will.

### (e) The Forms of Voluntary Activity

Even in the practical judgments which we pass upon the will we are not content with bringing the outward visible effects of will before our bar, as we should have to be, if the voluntary act were purely external in character. Rather we regard the deed as at most a measure of the worth of the inner decision that preceded it. But the latter itself is really a voluntary act, and it maintains this character even when the outward deed is suppressed by some inhibiting

## *Will and Consciousness*

influence. In such cases there may be little or no objective judgment of the act, because the decision of the will, purely internal in character, is hidden from outward observation, but it does not escape subjective judgment. We behold ourselves first and chiefly in the light of our inner will, and so we cannot hide from our self-judgment those inner acts which never become outward deeds, even those which by their very nature are incapable of outward expression If our powers of thought and will did not find themselves constantly controlled by this voice of self, which can never be wholly silenced, the education of the will would lack its most efficient auxiliary. Of course the external effects of the act are not wholly indifferent, even for its subjective estimation It is only in the judgment which we pass upon our own *character* that the volition which has no outward effect is decisive, and even this judgment may be modified favourably or unfavourably, according as other internal volitions or chance external influences contribute to make the transition to the outward act more or less easy. By reason of its effects on the surrounding world, and the helping or hindering influences which our Ego thus exerts on others or on a totality of individuals, the outward manifestation of will must always be of the first importance in moral judgment. Above all, a deeper reason for its importance is to be found in the fact that only when motive and purpose are followed by an external effect can the individual will operate upon a *total* will, and under such circumstances alone can it share to a certain extent in the expressions of this total will. However, even the purely internal activity of the will is not wholly without its effects It brings about continual changes in our inner life, and it is responsible for the permanent influences which certain tendencies of disposition and thought exert upon personal character.

16    *The Moral Will*    [443-4

While internal volitions thus involve all the elements of will, motive, purpose and effect, these elements are not absent even in the case of impulsive actions, which are usually regarded as the very opposite of voluntary; for impulses are nothing but simple, singly determined acts of will. We may call a volition simple where there is but a single motive operating in consciousness, upon which the act unhesitatingly follows  The hungry animal that seizes the food offered to it acts without choice, but not without will. The drowning man, exerting his utmost powers to save himself from the flood, may obey various motives in the choice of means, but most of his movements will be directly governed by that instinct for life which overcomes every other stimulus. The pedestrian, taking a course which he has planned beforehand, starts with a complex act of will, and even in the further execution of his decision various motives may intervene to alter his plans, but for by far the greater part of the time the action once begun follows impulsively upon the single motive which has become the controlling one  Simple and complex acts of will, or, as we may more briefly distinguish them, impulsive and voluntary acts, may thus be blended and combined in all kinds of ways  Only in rare cases does the execution of a complex action belong entirely either to the one class or to the other. Sometimes the process is impulsive at the outset, voluntary movements coming in later in its course. This is the case with most of the expressions of instinct in animals and with similar movements in man, as, for example, the efforts instanced above of a drowning man to save himself. Sometimes, on the other hand, the beginning of the action is voluntary, but later the act becomes transformed into an expression of pure impulse, for instance, the movements of the pedestrian, so long as he follows the direction which he chose at the outset. Under certain conditions it is difficult

## Will and Consciousness

or impossible to distinguish outwardly between the two forms of movement, not only because the mechanical means are the same in both cases, but because the co-ordination of movements is identical. For both kinds of movement involve that congenital mechanism of the central nervous system, whose adaptation to certain physiological purposes is so clearly evident in the reflexes which take place without any conscious accompaniment. This innate mechanism is not, however, unalterable, new purposive combinations of movements may be brought about by the will, and these combinations will thereafter function with mechanical accuracy and without further voluntary control. It is probable, therefore, that the congenital disposition to purposive vital expressions has itself resulted in the general course of development from the after-effects of voluntary actions, especially since our experience can show no other source than subjective purposes for structures that are objectively adapted to ends

This characteristic difference between impulsive and voluntary actions, namely, that in the former case there is only one motive in consciousness, or that if there are several, they act in combination, necessarily implies the absence of the idea of choice from the conception of impulse We express this fact when we say that impulsive actions are univocally determined and voluntary actions equivocally determined [1] An action is univocally determined when its performance was preceded only by actual motives; it is equivocally determined when both actual and potential motives were present. The distinction between main and incidental motives also lapses in the case of impulsive action

---

[1] It is hardly necessary to remark that these expressions must not be interpreted as meaning that in equivocally determined actions the will actually operates in different directions at the same time  In this sense, of course, all actions are univocal  'Equivocally determined' is a short way of saying 'influenced by motives that strive to determine the will in different directions '

# 18 *The Moral Will* [445-6

The latter come into play only when regard is had to incidental or intermediate effects, which are related to the main effect as means to an end But where there is a choice of means, as where there is a choice of ends, the volition is no longer simple. Impulse, on the other hand, follows blindly, without choice of the motive by which it is ruled. It therefore involves none of those elements of moral judgment which in the case of complex acts of will relate to choice, either of means or of ends A purely impulsive action, considered in and for itself, merits neither praise nor blame ; at most, the fact that impulse prevailed under circumstances where we were justified in expecting deliberation and choice, may influence our estimate of the character or mental condition of the agent

Still more important is another characteristic which may distinguish impulsive from voluntary action, though it does not necessarily do so. It is probably always true of the earlier expressions of impulse, and at least frequently true of the later ones, that the motive does not possess the character of a purpose, hence that the action is not preceded by the idea of its effect The child that " seeks the mother's breast "—as the process is usually but inappropriately described—is in reality impelled to movement merely by the feelings which are combined with the sensation of hunger , apart from these accompanying conscious excitants, its movements are precisely like reflexes They seem purposive to the objective observer, just as reflexes do, because they are adapted to the end attained. Such adaptation, moreover, can be nothing but the result of inherited organisation, for the idea which should serve as purpose is first produced by the movement itself. And the whole of experience tells against the supposition that ready-made ideas are innate in consciousness. The case is similar to the primitive expressions of instinct in animals, except that their organisation,

446-7] *Will and Consciousness* 19

being planned for vital ends of a more limited character, is more completely determined at the outset with reference to these ends, so that less remains to be done by individual practice There is no doubt, moreover, that these expressions of impulse without a definitely ideated purpose are not confined to the earliest period of life. We can observe countless such instances among our own movements, actions that cannot be classed as purely mechanical reflexes, because they are preceded by a distinct motive in the shape of feeling. Thus we shift an uncomfortable load because it occasions a feeling of inconvenience, we react against an unpleasant impression by a repelling movement, with no definite intention of attaining an end by such movement The new position that we assume may be more uncomfortable than the old, and very likely the disturbing impression may be quite out of reach of the hand that tries to push it away.[1]

Instances like these of actions which are on the borderland between reflexes and impulses, but which must be reckoned with the latter because of the undoubted presence of psychical motives, manifest the principle of the heterogony of purpose, mentioned above, in its most primitive form. The motive which, when the action was first performed, was a mere feeling, becomes a purpose when the act is repeated If it were not the nature of living beings to produce adaptive effects which are spontaneously revivable in idea, and which, when thus revived, succeed in reproducing feelings and actions having the same results, the development of consciously purposive action, and hence of voluntary action, would be impossible

The subsequent development of purpose is analogous to its origin. As the effect of an act exceeds its purpose, so

---

[1] *Cf* on this point my *Physiologische Psychologie*, 4th ed., ii , pp. 501 ff ; and *Lssays* pp 191 ff.

20          *The Moral Will*          [447-8

new purposes, broader and more comprehensive in character, are formed. The principle of psychical growth manifested in this progressive creation of conscious ends for human action finds its clearest expression in the history of moral ideas[1]

## 2 THE INDIVIDUAL WILL AND THE SOCIAL WILL

### (a) The Ego and Personality

The will is in the first instance given as the activity of a single consciousness, hence as an expression of individual life  As such its development runs parallel with that of self-consciousness, or perhaps it would be more appropriate to say that these two coincide, forming different aspects of a process which is in itself single.  The Ego's self-discrimination is involved in its inner and outer acts of will, and it is in the direct perception of his own activity that the individual discovers himself as a separate personality. While this activity is regularly associated with alterations in the content of consciousness, and, itself relatively unchanged, accompanies every other change of inner state, it appears as that element of inner perception which conditions all combinations on the part of other psychical events  For out of the multitude of actions performed by an individual it is the inner acts, the acts of apperception, that stand out as more original and immediate than the rest; while the outward movements, important though they may be for the earliest stages of self-discrimination, represent merely the consequences of particular kinds of apperceptions.  Hence the final stage of this development consists in the individual's discovery that his own innermost being is pure apperception ; that is, an inner voluntary activity distinct from the rest of conscious content  The Ego feels itself to be the same at

[1] *Cf* Part I , especially chap  ii , pp. 329-30.

448] *The Individual Will and the Social Will* 21

every moment of its life, because it conceives the activity of apperception as perfectly constant, homogeneous in its nature, and coherent in time.

Yet the separation of will from the other elements of inner perception can never be carried out so completely that the relations which always exist between them disappear On the contrary, the greater the intensity with which the will operates as a force independent of external constraint, and manifests itself as the centre of self-consciousness, the more we are led to realise its power over ideas and feelings, and to look upon our inner life as one willed by the Ego Of course, we can never wholly adopt this conception, because, besides the influence of will in inner processes, there is the constraining force of external nature, which is never absent However, in proportion as the will frees itself from these external influences, we approach the realisation of that ideal of personal existence where the whole inner life of man appears as his own creation , where for good or evil he regards himself as the originator of his own thoughts and emotions, and of all the outward consequences that may flow from them Thus the same course of development which led us to consider everything in our inner life that is distinct from the will as foreign to the Ego ends by showing us that the Ego and this inner life are but the more intimately one This unity of feeling, thought and will, in which the will appears as the active power that sustains the other elements, is the individual personality.

As the Ego is the will in its distinction from the rest of conscious content, so personality is the Ego reunited to the manifold of this content and thereby raised to the stage of self-consciousness.

22 *The Moral Will* [449

*(b) The Relation of the Individual to the Whole.*

The single self-conscious personality is continually subjected to a double influence On the one hand, it is always affected by the general conditions of external nature, which sometimes help and sometimes oppose the will. While the independence of the Ego is thus limited by the constraint of natural events, the whole course of the development of will tends to free it from these restrictions The case is quite different with the second influence, which affects the individual will in its inner development as well as in its outward expression. This influence consists in the volition of other and like personalities, which the individual will encounters for the most part in the pursuit of similar ends ; an agreement of purpose which sometimes proves of advantage to the will, and sometimes involves it in conflict with others or even with itself. The whole process assumes a different aspect here on account of the like nature of the forces acting upon each other ; not only because the power of the individual will can bring about its results only when it finds itself in sufficient agreement with the general tendency of other wills, but also and chiefly because the individual will discovers itself to be an element in a total will which supports it in its motives and ends. What seemed from the individual's point of view like a sum of distinct and even conflicting forces now reveals itself to the full self-consciousness of the awakened personality as a more comprehensive unity, within which each individual reflects the motives and purposes that fill the whole. Here we have repeated on a higher plane the same process through which the individual personality itself passed. The Ego began by regarding all the content of consciousness outside of the will as foreign to itself, and ended by reassimilating it in self-consciousness. So the individual

449-50]  *The Individual Will and the Social Will*    23

personality first distinguishes itself from the beings of like nature with itself that surround it, only to reunite with them in a more clearly conscious unity.

The outward signs of this transition from individual to social consciousness, and the corresponding social will, are all those elements of culture and morals which express the common feeling and thought of a society. Speech, religious views, like habits of life and standards of action, point to the existence of a common intellectual possession, which far exceeds in scope anything that the individual can obtain. Political union in such a society, whose members are governed by like ideas, is but the natural result and the self-evident expression of this inner unity. It is a result that can fail to follow or develop under any but the natural conditions, only when external influences operate as a hindrance  Political union, moreover, is that form of the social consciousness which expresses most clearly its character as social will.

None of these influences of morals, of religion, of law and of direct personal intercourse, which are analogous to volition and thought in the individual, could develop if it were not for the fundamental likeness pre-existing between individual wills. Wherever there are men of like dispositions, living under the same natural conditions, they must have ideas and feelings that are identical in content. Nowhere can we find a more striking evidence of this fact than in the earliest of all expressions of a common life, in speech. What seems to one man the most suitable expression for his thought appears equally appropriate to others  Expression and the comprehension of its meaning are one at the outset But along with speech go all the other functions of human intercourse  While speech often serves as the external means for the production of like ideas, its use for this purpose is rendered possible only by the fact that men live in a world of like external impressions and events.

24                    *The Moral Will*                    [450-1

### (c) *Individualism and Universalism.*

The community of human thought and feeling can never have been ignored so completely as to escape a certain degree of recognition when the human race is considered historically. But the origin of this unity and the relation it involves between the individual and the social will remain to be explained. There are two possible theories on this point. According to the first, only the individual will is truly real, it is thus the original factor, while the social will is merely a chance agreement brought about partly by external influences and partly by the free decision of individuals. According to this second theory, the social will is as fundamental and as real as the wills of individuals; it determines the individual will more than it is itself determined thereby. We may term the first theory the individualistic, the second the universalistic theory of will.

At the present time individualism is the ruling tendency in philosophy, in practical life and in the opinions of political theorists. This has not always been the case, and we may anticipate that it will not always remain so The political sentiment of the ancients was grounded on the opposite view, which was that expressed in the works of the greatest political theorists of antiquity, Plato and Aristotle. Not until we reach the philosophy of the Enlightenment, which in its broader sense may be said to include both the empirical and the rationalistic systems of the seventeenth and eighteenth centuries, does individualism take on its present form, that of something very like the incontrovertible religion of public opinion From Bacon to Kant, no thinker could escape it Hobbes' *Leviathan* and Rousseau's *Contrat Social* mark even yet the extreme limits within which the compass needle of political opinions fluctuates, and all the wisdom of the moderate Liberalism

451-2] *The Individual Will and the Social Will* 25

of to-day is essentially contained in Locke's *Letters on Toleration* and Spinoza's *Tractatus Theologico - Politicus*. It would ill become us to put a light estimate upon an age capable of producing such works That was an age for which the individualism inscribed upon their standards by the independent thinkers of all parties was deeply significant and deeply justified For its task was to free men's spirits from the constraint of class prejudices, national limitations and the brutal egoism of the ruling castes This could be done only through an appeal to the feeling for self in each man, which apprised him clearly and emphatically of the original rights of his own personality As opposed to social institutions where countless numbers of men were made use of, for the profit of a few, the theory that the State was made for individuals and not individuals for the State was a blow struck for freedom. The first and essential step towards preparing the way for a higher conception of the social will, a conception that should transcend the narrow humanism of the ancient world, was to establish the moral value of the individual personality.

Wherever they bear on the problem of the relation between the individual and the social will, the social theories of the Enlightenment, which still prevail on our political rostra, are all merely variations of one and the same conception. The truth of this is borne out by the fact that all their spokesmen, Hobbes as well as Locke, Rousseau, or Helvetius, have precisely the same ideas about the origin of the social will and its relation to individuals Of course, they did not go into this question directly, because from the start they recognised no reality save the individual will; but it was indirectly involved in their theories about the origin of speech, religion, morals and law. The individualism of the Enlightenment held all these products of the human spirit to be the outcome of deliberate legislation It believed

26 *The Moral Will* [452-3

either that these institutions, many of which were regarded from another point of view as evils rather than blessings, were the legacy of certain primitive lawgivers, or that the social union originated by an agreement made after taking into consideration the welfare of all individuals The natural outcome of such conceptions is a variety of fictions with regard to the primitive state of society, which assume different forms according to the special tendency of the theory in question, but are all alike in recognising no will other than that of individuals Though the arbitrary and improbable nature of these hypotheses gradually became apparent, it was also perfectly evident that an individualistic ethics could offer no substitute Hume, who expressly terms them a kind of experimental fiction, makes in his own discussion of the origin of justice assumptions that are essentially based on these very fictions[1], and Kant transforms the social contract and the other primitive rights of man into ideas, which, it is true, have no historical existence, but which have to be treated as if they had[2] As a matter of fact, if the individual will alone is real, and if, as a necessary consequence of the first supposition, all our original impulses are egoistic in character, we must either regard those expressions of volitional life which are beyond the power of the single individual as instruments created in a kind of agreement by general consent, or leave the question of their origin in the metaphysical darkness that shrouds the ultimate source of things

But all these fictions must vanish before the simple fact that the isolated individual man whom they presuppose does not exist and undoubtedly never has existed as a fact of experience We know man only as a social being, governed at once by an individual will and by the will of the whole ·

---

[1] *Cf* Part II , chap III , pp 36-77.

[2] *Philosophy of Law*, trans by W Hastie, pp 63, 161.

453-4] *The Individual Will and the Social Will* 27

and there is no evidence to show that the latter had its origin in the former. On the contrary, the relative independence of the individual will is the result of a later evolution As the child becomes conscious of its own will by a gradual process, and slowly develops its own personality out of an environment which at first it scarcely distinguishes from itself, so in the state of nature it is the common feeling, thought and will that dominate Man individualises himself out of a state of social indifference, not, however, to remain separated from the society of which he is a product, but to restore himself to its service with powers more fully developed. To explain egoistic action requires no far-fetched motives or complicated trains of reflection, and they are as little necessary to account for the simplest exercise of care for others or the most primitive expression of a common feeling A man who has fallen into the water and tries to save himself is evidently furnishing an instance of the universal instinct of self-preservation. But for one man to jump into the water to save another requires, it is supposed, the intervention of a complicated series of processes. sympathy to make him realise the other man's sensations, associations that gradually overcome the supreme domination of the self-preserving instinct, even rational reflections on the utility of unselfish actions. Yet observation fails to prove the existence of any of these processes which psychologists and moralists have devised for the support of their theories. One thing it does prove beyond a doubt, namely, that the reaction of the will is equally immediate in the altruistic and in the egoistic act Deliberation and reflection may follow the act, but they do not precede it, and if they should, they would probably tend rather to paralyse than to stimulate the will.

If we mean by sympathy, or fellow-feeling, the mere fact that the emotion produced by the sight of another's sorrow is

## 28 *The Moral Will* [454-5]

itself a painful emotion, corresponding to a certain extent in intensity and quality with the impression that arouses it, no objection need be raised to the terms. But if they signify that the original sorrow and the sympathetic sorrow are qualitatively identical, they state what is evidently false No emotions could be more different than the terror of a drowning man and the determined courage of his rescuer, the hunger and anxiety of the starving workman and the humane kindness of the philanthropist who wishes to help his suffering. If such a similarity between the original emotion and the sympathetic emotion really existed, the latter would be deprived of all the characteristics that fit it to be of use as a practical motive. It is, indeed, a peculiarity of man's nature that the experiences of others are not indifferent to him, but have their influence on his thoughts and feelings, just as his own experiences have. But the individual's environment forms an inalienable part of his conscious life, and gives to every idea its own peculiar feeling-value. It follows that altruistic feelings are as original and primitive as egoistic feelings, but it follows also that they have a specific character which renders idle all attempts to derive them from the latter We cannot make our self-regarding feelings identical with those that relate to our fellow-men, any more than we can, except in dreams and cases of mental derangement, take ourselves to be other people. It is only by recognising this truth that we can understand why the strife between egoistic and altruistic impulses should be one of the most common forms of conflict between motives, and why, moreover, the victory in this conflict should as a matter of experience fall now to the one side and now to the other. If sympathetic feeling were only transferred egoism, no process of association or reflection could explain the defeat of the more primitive and powerful feeling. Psychological individualism leads by in-

**455]** *The Individual Will and the Social Will* 29

herent necessity to ethical egoism. That it usually succeeds in avoiding this issue only proves that here as elsewhere facts are stronger than theories.

### (d) Ethical Atomism and the Psychological Theory of Substance.

The clearest reflection of the ethical views of an age is always to be found in the metaphysical conceptions that embody its thoughts about God, the world and humanity. Metaphysics may free itself from the direct influence of experience, but it will always bear the plain impress of those general assumptions and postulates which the spirit of the age applies to practical life. So we find that the ethical individualism of the last two centuries is most faithfully portrayed in the atomistic conception of the soul maintained by Cartesianism. Psychology has shown the worthlessness of this doctrine, but it will probably continue to survive for some time in the popular metaphysics of persons of culture and eclectic philosophers, as a symptom which, though of little importance for metaphysics, yet furnishes a striking proof of the hold that the ethical ideas of the rationalistic Enlightenment still have upon us. Psychical atomism, with its simple substances whose interaction is purely external and occasional, allows of no spiritual coherence, no universal psychical life, or universal psychical ends, except such as are common to a number of individuals who happen to live together. Such a view is tolerable only if real life is regarded as merely a temporary stage of preparation for a better existence in the future. Even then, the outcome must correspond to the nature of the preparatory stage. As a matter of fact, this ethical egoism goes to the length of regarding the connection of souls as the source of the evil in existence, and extols a condition in which

30    *The Moral Will*    [455-6

its psychical atoms shall be wholly free, that is, wholly isolated, as the state of true blessedness. To be strictly consistent, it ought to demand a separate heaven for each and every soul.

The philosophy of Spinoza represents a powerful reaction, having its source in the deepest religious needs, against this pluralistic conception But even in Spinoza the impulse to secure spiritual liberty to the individual is too deeply rooted He brings two elements into direct combination with no intermediary stages a sense of individual freedom, which feels every kind of political influence that is not absolutely necessary for protection as sheer constraint ; and a consciousness of the unity existing between the individual and the infinite Among the successors of Spinoza it was Leibniz whose vision, in this respect as in others, reached beyond the horizon of his time, and who came nearest to transcending the limitations of individualistic ethics. Such was the significance and tendency of his brilliant reform of metaphysical atomism His principle of pre-established harmony was like a ray of light manifesting the universal psychical Being in the darkness of an age given over to external dualism , an age that reduced all existence to material mechanisms, within which spirits were unwillingly confined as by a spell. Yet Leibniz could not overcome individualism It was eliminated in the doctrine of universal harmony only to be more evident in the absolute simplicity and separateness of the psychical substances. The principle of harmony and the conception of monads are irreconcilable ideas, and the attempt to combine them results in checking the development of the former Hence the philosophy of Leibniz, like many recent revivals of his doctrine, leaves us with the general idea of psychical unities existing in a reciprocal relation that is, so far as they are concerned, purely external, that does not proceed from

## 456-7]  *The Individual Will and the Social Will*  31

the essence of the soul, but is to be understood only in the sense of a law imposed by a foreign power. The social will has no independent existence. It is a law coming to the individual will from without, whether regarded as a moral precept emanating directly from God, or as a principle of external union among simple substances. The intuitionism of Descartes and the English Intellectualists, and the Leibnizian system of harmony, are simply different expressions of the desire to moderate the psychical atomism maintained on theoretical grounds. Such devices, however, only involved their authors in metaphysical contradictions, without really meeting the ethical need.

Herbart must be credited with a resolute and consistent rejection of all notions that were irreconcilable with the conception of monads. He thus gave to psychical atomism the only form in which it is metaphysically tenable. As a result, the whole common psychical life of humanity was a conception foreign to his metaphysics, which was deprived of all relation with ethics. This was its death-sentence, self-imposed. For if metaphysics has any purpose at all, it is surely to solve in a coherent theory of the whole those problems which experience furnishes, but with which experience cannot competently deal. And in what realm of experience can we find more problems, and problems of greater urgency, than in ethics? The services of metaphysics to psychology and natural science may always be replaced by the hypotheses to which these empirical disciplines are guided by their own needs; but the conclusions of ethics cannot be formed without a metaphysical conception of man's psychical life as a whole.

32          *The Moral Will*          [457-8

*(e)  The  Individual  Will  and  the  Social  Will  in  the  Light
of  the  Theory  of  Actuality*

The  truth  at  which  the  doctrine  of  monads  and  other
similar  theories  of  substance  can  arrive  only  by  contradicting
their  own  presuppositions,  is  a  direct  ethical  inference  from
the  theory  that  makes  the  reality  of  the  soul  consist  in  its
actual  psychical  life[1]  As  the  various  psychical  activities  of
thought,  feeling  and  will  are  distinguishable  only  by  a  process  of  abstraction,  and  are  themselves  inseparable  elements
of  conscious  life,  so  the  idea  of  a  soul  distinct  from  the
content  of  consciousness  is  nothing  but  the  empty  concept
of  the  unity  and  constant  coherence  of  psychical  activities,
hypostasised  into  a  real  substance.   As  a  matter  of  fact,
it  is  no  more  an  independent  thing  given  or  postulated  in
any  experience,  than  an  idea,  a  volition,  or  a  feeling  is  an
independent  thing.   We  might  have  pardoned  philosophy
at  the  Platonic  stage  of  the  development  of  abstract  thought
for  substantialising  these  concepts,  as  it  did  those  of  man,
animal  and  the  like.   But  nowadays,  when  we  can  explain
the  origin  of  such  ideas  without  the  assumption  of  conceptual  prototypes,  we  ought  to  give  up  the  process  of
transforming  our  own  thought-products  into  things    In
Plato's  time,  making  spiritual  processes  into  a  kind  of
material  substances  may  have  been  a  good  way  of  insuring
their  independent  reality ,  in  our  time,  it  is  the  best  way
of  destroying  their  independence

If  the  actual  soul  consists  in  nothing  but  conscious
activity,  it  follows  at  once  that  while  this  actual  essence
may  have  its  individual  peculiarities,  its  most  important
determining  influences  transcend  the  limits  of  the  individual
consciousness.   Our  ideas,  with  their  accompanying  feelings ,

---

[1] On  the  relation  between  the  theories  of  substantiality  and  actuality  *cf.*  my
*Logik*, ii , pp. 502 ff , and *System der Philosophie*, 2nd ed , pp  301 ff.

458-9] *The Individual Will and the Social Will* 33

the impulses that govern our movements and insure the fulfilment of our most essential vital needs : these are in their more general features the common property of all our fellow-men, and in their more special characteristics we share them with our neighbours, who are united to us by the ties of birth, speech, customs and historical traditions. It is only by the active exercise of will that the individual personality ever separates itself from the society to which it belongs. Voluntary movement, active apperception and its influence on ideas, are the chief forces that bring about this separation, whose progress accompanies the growth of self-consciousness. Thus on the basis of common psychical activities the individual personality grows to independence, and comes to be the master of a specific range of thought whose individuality, as representing a particular way of appropriating and utilising the common intellectual property of humanity, is almost greater than if it were itself a separate bit of intellectual property. While in the development of self-conscious personality the individual gradually frees himself from the society to which he at first belonged, we find him at a higher stage of self-consciousness returning to it richer in psychical content, because he is now clearly aware of his position in society, and has appropriated through culture and the study of history fields of thought that were originally foreign to him. And the same process which in the individual life results in the production of self-conscious personality is repeated on an infinitely larger scale in the development of the psychical life of humanity. This is shown by the contrast between the theories of life that prevail to-day and those of the preceding centuries. For unless all signs fail, a revolution of opinion is at present going on, in which the extreme individualism of the Enlightenment is giving place to a revival of the universalism of antiquity, supple-

34 *The Moral Will* [459

mented by a better notion of the liberty of human personality, an improvement that we owe to individualism.

It follows that the dividing line between the individual and the social will, and between the broader and narrower aspects of the latter, is not hypothetical, but actual, not extra-conscious, but clearly present to consciousness The will and the ideational content of consciousness are individual, so far as they are peculiar to the individual personality, they belong to a social will, so far as they are common to a society of individuals If the individual soul consists wholly in actual psychical functioning, and not in a separately existent substrate, we are justified in ascribing to the social will a degree of reality not less than that of the individual will. Moreover, the historical continuity between our minds and those of other ages is real just so far as it is represented in consciousness The unity of our life with that of past and future races is real, and not merely apparent, as psychological atomism supposes it to be. Culture and history form a true common life, not a mere chance resultant of innumerable forces whose contact is purely external, and whose ultimate ends are widely diverse.

But in the totality of psychical development all individual wills have not the same importance Here, as elsewhere, the law holds good so much actuality, so much reality The individual will that appropriates the ideas and tendencies which govern the whole, and brings them to self-conscious operation in its own activity, does more than merely fulfil the social will It gains the power to stamp society with its own characteristic and individual features Hence a theory like Hegel's historical philosophy, which regards the social will as the sole objective ethical force, and holds that the function of the individual will is merely an unconscious partaking in and fulfilment of the social will, is an exceedingly partial view of the truth. Such a theory is a complete

## 459-60] *The Individual Will and the Social Will* 35

antithesis to the equally one-sided individualism of the preceding centuries. Yet we find, in accordance with the well-known rule that extremes meet, an occasional development of the most advanced individualism within the Hegelian school itself.[1]

At first the individual consciousness simply draws on the stock of ideas furnished to it from without and shared by it with surrounding society. Gradually, however, it begins to work these ideas over after its own independent fashion. It develops impulses which, though already foreshadowed in the tendency of the social will, were there too diffused to operate as actual forces. Here that power of energetic and self-conscious concentration on a definite end, which is characteristic of the individual will, comes into play. The social will lacks this power, until such ends are indicated to it by individuals who epitomise the tendencies of their age and environment. Hence the enormous importance of leading minds. The social consciousness reflects itself after some fashion or other in the mind of every individual partaker in it; but these reflections are in most cases partial and dimmed by prejudice. Prejudices are accepted habits of thought, ideas of a bygone age, which were, for the most part, adequate to the needs of their own time, but which, when applied to the problems of the present, lead to illusion. Memory is indeed that mental power which we oftenest exercise. Through its aid we see the present in the light of the past, and the future in the light of the present. But the leading minds of an age are those who are more clearly conscious than others of the impelling forces of public opinion, who concentrate these forces in

---

[1] Ludwig Feuerbach, and more especially Max Stirner, in his book, *Der Einzige und sein Eigenthum*, are instances; as also Ferdinand Lassalle, with his efforts to combine, after a sufficiently curious fashion, Hegel's historical philosophy and the extreme individualism of a Rousseau as expressed in the French Revolution.

# 36 *The Moral Will* [460-1

their own personality, and thus gain the power to determine or vary their direction, so far as such a power can operate within the limits of the tendencies of universal will

The scope within which the individual will holds sway may be wider or narrower according to the power that will exerts, and the favourable or unfavourable conditions under which it has developed. In like manner the social will is related to the individual will, not as something single and unanalysable, but as a series of simple volitional forces Each little society, distinguished from the background of universal humanity by reason of certain ideas and endeavours that are common to its members, represents a social will, which has all the characteristics of an independent reality, in that it operates as a self-active force both on the individuals comprising it and on the regions of life above it Thus the individual is simply the last member of a series whose ascending order is lost in infinity. For those impulses which are the common possession of humanity are in their turn influenced by historical conditions, whose ultimate grounds escape our investigation. Hence religion postulates, to complete this infinite regressus, the divine will as the last and highest unity out of which develop all the stages of the finite realisation of will

By reason of this graded series of stages in the development of will, the significance of the notion of leading minds varies in intension and in extension The family, the community, professional associations, the school, societies for the promotion of culture, the State,—all these departments of life are based on a reciprocal relation between the individual and the social will. In this relation the majority of individual wills represent the passive and receptive element ; the real force that occasions every alteration and transformation being exerted by the leading minds. The original, creative intellectual power is thus always the in-

461-2] *The Individual Will and the Social Will* 37

dividual will. True, the tremendous influence that we always experience from the society where we have our origin and our life proceeds from social forces that can never be reduced to a mere sum of isolated will-elements. But every new impulse in development points to an individual cause. It is an important characteristic of all intellectual life that the individual does not remain individual, but becomes universal. The individual will resolves itself into the universal will, and again in turn produces out of the latter individual minds of creative power.

Here, again, we have an idea which results directly from a consideration of the world-process finding its outcome in a religious conception. Religion associates the idea of God with that of a guiding spirit whose personal volition is the ultimate ground of all psychical development. Of this development the empirical world-process gives us only the fragmentary outline, which is not easy to decipher when seen in details. In the idea of a transcendent deity religious thought thus combines the two elements of will which are for ever separated in the phenomenal world. For to the religious consciousness God is the creative world-will, which means that He is at once individual and social will.

### 3. THE FREEDOM OF THE WILL.

#### (a) General Characteristics of Freedom.

Freedom is the capacity of any being to be determined in its action by a reflective choice between different motives. Absence of freedom may be either external or internal; in the former case it consists in the constraint which external forces exert on motives; in the latter case it means absence of reflection, where motives are insufficiently developed, either because they are temporarily inhibited in the agent's

38            *The Moral Will*            [462-3

consciousness, or because his mind is permanently deficient in a normal capacity for motivation.

The mere existence of psychical activities as inner motives is thus an insufficient criterion of freedom. The dreamer and the madman are not free, though they follow motives of which they are conscious. In like manner no purely impulsive action is free, the single determining motive has a force of absolute constraint, because no other motives exist which could produce a different action. To be free, an action must be voluntary Even this, however, is not enough, an insane person may balance motives one against another, and proceed with thoughtful circumspection, yet we do not call his decisions free. Our criterion of free action is not choice merely, but free choice; and we call choice free when it takes place with reflective self-consciousness What distinguishes the latter from simple self-consciousness is the fact that it involves a consciousness of one's own personality together with all those characteristics which result from the past development of the will. To reflect concerning oneself means to be conscious of one's personality as determined by previous volitional development; and to act with reflection is to act with a consciousness of the significance which the motives and purposes of the action have for the character of the agent. The man who dreams or is insane may act not only voluntarily but self-consciously, since he is conscious of his own Ego. He cannot, however, act with reflection, for either he has lost the power of reflecting on his personality as conditioned by his previous mental history, or his personality has been altered by disturbing influences

### (b) The Causality of Will.

It is evident, from our definition of free action, that such action involves psychical causality. Freedom does not consist in the absence of efficient causes, but in the absence of causes whose nature is such that they suppress psychical causality, wholly or in part. Moreover, the causality of will resembles other forms of the causal relation in leading to an infinite series. Hence we do not mitigate the error of converting the true antithesis between freedom and constraint into the false one between freedom and causality when we follow Kant's theory of the intelligible character, and, while referring the voluntary act itself to psychical causality, ascribe the latter to an uncaused essence of personality. This conception, which merely puts the interruption of causality one step further back, does not commend itself, even to our practical judgment, any more than the other view, according to which the breaking of the causal chain comes with the act. Whenever we judge, we take into consideration the agent's whole previous history just as much as the motives that immediately determined him. Nor can appeal be made in this controversy to the consciousness of freedom ; it tells us that we act without constraint, but never that we act without cause, or that the motives which determine us are independent of our natural dispositions and the circumstances of our lives.

Thus we see that the whole controversy about the causality of will would be practically unthinkable if both sides were not influenced by a misunderstanding that makes them take constraint and causality for equivalent terms. This misunderstanding consists in the substitution of mechanical for psychical causality. It is a fact of great moment for modern theories of will that Kant, whose influence is still strongest on this question, wholly ignored the fundamental

40          *The Moral Will*          [464

difference between psychical and naturalistic causation, using, as he did, mechanical causality synonymously with causality at large. Now the concept of matter which governs natural philosophy gives to the notion of cause as applied to nature a peculiar character that is foreign to its more universal logical significance. For the principle of constancy, intimately connected with the idea of matter, involves certain laws which govern all cases of natural causality, and may really be regarded as corollaries of the law of causation in this realm. For example, theie are the laws of conservation, in accordance with which the principle of the constancy of matter is manifested in the processes of nature; and, most important of all, there is the principle of the equivalence of cause and effect.

Now the notion of material substance, which is an aid to our knowledge of natural processes, has no meaning whatever when we come to consider the activities of knowledge and will. But if we insist on transferring the concepts of energy and force into the psychical realm, all the empirical facts of individual psychical development teach us that the fundamental law here is the direct opposite of the principle of equivalence. It is the law of increasing psychical energy, and it means, in its application to the will, that while the effects of voluntary acts are always determined by definite psychical causes, they are not already contained in such causes. We really assume this position whenever we pass judgment on the consequences of volition, a fact that is especially evident when we are dealing with the higher order of intellectual creations. No one would hesitate to explain a poetical work by referring to the conditions under which the poet lives, thinks, and has developed. On the other hand, no one would defend the absurd supposition that the final result of intellectual activity in such a case is the quantitative equivalent of these conditions; as, for example, the effect produced by a falling ball is equivalent to the work done in raising it.

It follows that while we can get a tolerably sufficient causal explanation for events in the psychical realm when we argue backwards, *i.e.* with reference to that portion of the causal series already traversed, we can never argue forwards. Under favourable conditions we can predict natural events with certainty. But in the case of psychical events the most we can do is to indicate the general direction, not the specific form, of the result. There is a psychical history of the past, but no sure prophecy of the future; and so far every attempt at a historical philosophy that has presumed to foretell coming events has gone astray. Laplace's fiction of a world-formula is inapplicable to psychical processes not only because it is shattered by the incalculable complexity of events, but because it is itself in contradiction with the laws of psychical processes.

### (c) Indeterminism and Determinism.

The ordinary view confuses this impossibility of foreseeing events with a denial of their causation. Because no one can foresee the form that psychical causality will take in a given case, it supposes such causality to be non-existent; and since vulgar determinism and vulgar indeterminism are alike in their erroneous substitution of naturalistic for psychical causality, it is not surprising that they should be more nearly alike than they realise in their outcome. For ordinary determinism, assuming the whole burden of proving the existence of an unbroken chain of natural causation, makes the more remote causes of volition to consist in physical brain processes, which, by reason of their dependence on the general course of nature, are completely determined. Now only the last of these processes is accompanied by con-

42 *The Moral Will* [465-6

scious activity introspectively perceived : motor excitation and volitional impulse coincide. The train of psychological causation is followed no further, and from this point of view every act of will is *causa sui* Thus the physiological determinist is a psychological indeterminist On the other hand, ordinary indeterminism, in its efforts to do justice to the claims of natural causality, is generally quite willing to allow with Kant that there are two ways of regarding the external act of will · as a physical process subject to the sway of natural causality , and as an internal volition, free from such causality, or determined only by the intelligible character, which is not affected by the category of cause. Where is the difference, aside from the fact that the one party lays stress on the physiological, the other on the psychological aspect of the process ? Really, it seems quite superfluous for these opponents to get angry with each other ; they might clasp hands in token of reconciliation. They are perfectly agreed in their mistaken limitation of the concept of cause to its naturalistic sense, and in their ignoring of the psychological causation of will Hence they come to the same conclusion . they give up trying to find a scientific explanation. For the fanciful suppositions maintained by physiological determinism, concerning a mechanics of brain molecules ultimately deducible from the general course of nature, can hardly be taken seriously in lieu of such an explanation. Instead of following the easy path of psychological investigation, these theorists rest satisfied with referring to an imaginary science of the future, whose very nature precludes the possibility of its ever becoming actual For we are mistaken if we suppose that the idea of infinity is involved only in discussions about the ultimate bounds of space, time and causality in the universe. It comes into play whenever the course of nature produces an event that embodies in concrete form conditions whose separate investigation would necessitate insight into the whole endless process of nature. To attempt to regard the mechanics of the human brain after the fashion of a simple astronomical problem is thus an undertaking that has about as much prospect of success as a plan to determine the total weight of all the bodies in the world, or the centre of gravity of the universe. It is the more fantastic to abandon psychological investigation in order to lose oneself in the infinities of natural causality, because in so doing one forsakes for an illusory hope one's best chance of getting at the conditions of organic life. There is no doubt that impulsive and voluntary actions, which are directly influenced by definite psychical motives, are of the greatest importance in the development of the various forms of life.[1]

But here a metaphysical difficulty arises, which must be discussed in order to dispose of all obscurities on the subject. If physical and psychical causality differ so essentially, how shall we explain, not only the parallelism of the two in all the sensational activities of mind, but their apparent interference? Physical causality seems to interfere with psychical throughout our ideational life, with its dependence on external impressions; psychical with physical causality in voluntary acts, and in all the temporary or permanent changes which they bring about in the outer world. It is evident that the practical philosophy of life will always hold to the dualistic view; and that even science, to avoid prolixity, must occasionally use the terms of everyday life, as the astronomer speaks of sunrise with no intention of being false to the Copernican system. But since the banishment of ordinary dualism from metaphysics is far from being as final as that of the Ptolemaic theory from astronomy, it becomes necessary to explain briefly what metaphysical significance is to be attached to the words ' reciprocal action,'

---

[1] *Cf.* on this point my *Logik*, ii., pp. 449, 471.

# 44 *The Moral Will* [467-8]

as they have been or will be applied to the relation between the physical and the psychical realms [1]

### (d) *Psychical and Mechanical Causality.*

External nature is a constituent part of our consciousness. We are impelled by motives that belong to our immediate inner experience, first to separate out *ideas* from the total content of psychical life, and then to distinguish these as objects and images of objects Finally, our idea of the external world as a whole is that of the sum total of objects It therefore belongs to our inner experience just as much as any single object does, and has no reality apart from that experience. For all the elements that condition the separation between inner and outer experience are themselves nothing but psychical acts,—facts of our consciousness. When I represent to myself an object, I have merely made a distinction in my own consciousness, the external object does not cease to be an immediate inner experience, and the idea of its externality is itself one of my ideas. In like manner we must include in our psychical experience all processes by which objects are worked over in conceptual thought, as it accompanies even the simple representation of the object, is further involved in expressing the results of our common experience concerning the coherence of things, or finally manifests itself in the concepts of science

Into our experience, as thus constituted, scientific thought introduces an important new element when it seeks to satisfy

---

[1] It has been my frequent and unfortunate experience to have my expressions misunderstood, in the sense above indicated, by philosophers and physiologists, despite my express declarations in decisive passages (*e g Physiol. Psych.*, 4th ed., ii , pp. 636 ff ; *Logik*, 1 , p 486 I will therefore state once for all that I do not believe in the Cartesian *influxus physicus*, and that whenever I speak of the effect of psychical activities on the body or *vice versâ*, the terms are to be understood in the sense which I shall proceed to explain.

the demand of our reason for unity by the logical postulate that all experience may be included in a single self-consistent whole It is evident that the influence of this postulate will be most marked on those facts which lend themselves to it with the greatest readiness, and we have already seen that such a class of facts is constituted by the ideas that we call objects of the external world  The constancy of these objects and the regularity of their relations to each other have long since given rise to certain systems of concepts which prove that in some departments of nature the postulate of a self-consistent unity, formed in accordance with thought laws, is undoubtedly realisable, and that in still other fields there is at least a possibility of fulfilling it  In consequence, our experience of the constancy of objects has crystallised into the notion of matter as an absolutely permanent substrate of phenomena.  It is a concept purely hypothetical in character, but it has proved very useful in the establishment of further principles ; and it is, in particular, the foundation of all those laws of constancy referred to above as giving to natural causality its peculiar features  Now if we remember that the principle of causality is merely the application of this logical postulate of a self-consistent unity to any kind of empirical content, that is, to all possible phenomena of consciousness, it will become evident that the laws of constancy must originate not from the nature of causality itself, but from the special conditions of one particular realm of experience.  In the case of all other psychical activities, where there is no such reference to permanent objects, we must indeed postulate a causal relation, since otherwise we cannot think at all , but we shall have no occasion for any of those special principles which are derived from a hypothetical material substance.

The notion of a permanent substance, appertaining to those ideas which we call objects, involves the further supposition

# 46 *The Moral Will* [469-70

that the series of natural causes and effects is sufficient to itself All the reasons for assuming the existence of matter may be reduced to one, namely, the necessity of regarding it as the universal substrate of all natural causality and of referring all natural processes to the objective interaction of its parts Evidently the whole theory would be shattered if we were to suppose the existence of other substrata besides matter, with the power to interfere with natural causality Either such substrata are material,—which leaves us where we started, or they are not material,—in which case our concept of matter is illusory, since it is not really the universal substrate of natural causality Besides this dilemma for natural philosophy, a deeper and purely metaphysical contradiction is involved. Matter is a hypothetical conception which we ourselves, impelled on the one hand by the relative constancy of objects, and on the other by the logical demands of thought, have manufactured. To suppose that this hypothetical substrate which we have constructed for certain of our ideas can exert any influence on our other ideas or on our thought in general, or that psychical activities as such could ever operate upon it, is perfectly absurd. It is a supposition that could arise only as a result of first transforming a product of conceptual thought into a being independent of thought, and then, to complete the absurdity, regarding mental activity itself as an existence of like nature with its own product A notion of this sort necessarily involves all the contradictions that were ever ranged side by side in human thought The soul is supposed to be immaterial, and yet to influence and be influenced by matter as if it were material. It is in its own nature persistent, and yet in all the phenomena which are its sole manifestation to us, it shows the utmost variability. It is simple, and yet possesses an infinitely manifold content This self-contradictory conception of an immaterial matter,

470]            *The Freedom of the Will*            47

a substance lacking in permanence, an infinitely divisible atom, can be regarded only as a metaphysical superfluity, which perplexes rather than facilitates our understanding of psychical life.

Our own body is among the ideas that we call objects. It is that object which, by reason of the regular correspondence between its changes and those of other objects, we regard as the substrate of all our ideas. This view, also, is merely a causal construction of our thought, very early in its origin, though developed in full detail only under the influence of science. Like other material objects, our body is affected by other bodies, and affects them in turn. Some of these changes which take place in our bodies we think of as material processes accompanying our ideas; others as processes which run parallel to our volitional activities. But all of them must, of course, be subjected to the laws of the constancy of matter and energy, since these laws are essential to the notion of a permanent substrate for material things. And so we are led of necessity to suppose a parallelism, extending throughout the whole objective region of our consciousness, between ideas and the corresponding movements that take place in the hypothetical substrate of ideas, matter. According to this view, objects become our ideas when our body takes part in the interactions of this substrate. The parallelism is not, however, as Spinoza supposed, a parallelism between two infinite realities independent of each other. There is but one reality in question; and this, when we regard it as it is immediately given to us, appears under the form of ideas; when we consider it in the light of its conceptual transformation, is a series of movements in matter. But the objects of the external world form only a part of our psychical life. Their intellectual relations, like the emotional reactions of consciousness, cannot be classed as objects. Hence it is merely the outward sensational part

## 48 *The Moral Will* [470-1

of psychical life that finds its substrate in particular material processes. And thus we see that for such processes, which we conceive under a twofold aspect, immediately as sensations and mediately as material processes, we must have a twofold causality. As representations, the sensational elements of consciousness share in its psychological causality, as material movements, they belong to the causality of external nature The two forms of causality bear the same relation to each other as their corresponding substrates. Psychical causality is the immediate form, given directly as that of motives and purposes in thought, it involves no hypothesis beyond the immediate fact as it exists in thought Mechanical causality is the mediate form : while it originates through the content of certain ideas immediately given, these are merely the occasions for the application of conceptual constructions whose basis is wholly hypothetical, dependent on the postulate of a self-consistent unity among all ideas relating to objects.

It is a self-evident consequence alike of the extraordinarily contracted horizon of our experience and of the limited powers of our intellect that we should be unable to get more than a very narrow conception both of internal and of external causality, whether our effort is to comprehend the former immediately or to trace out the latter with the aid of hypotheses bearing on the exact analysis of experience Nevertheless, the logical character of the concept of cause requires us to postulate both the complete causal determination of all psychical acts, and the impenetrable coherence of all natural processes under the rule of mechanical causality. These postulates are regulative ideas, they warn us to trace back every event as far as possible within its own peculiar form of causality, and never to admit the hypothesis of an uncaused event But since both causal series extend to infinity, the ideas in question do not suggest the slightest

471-2]            *The Freedom of the Will*            49

prospect of an actual fulfilment of their postulates. Human thought, however far it may reach, must always remain in the realm of the finite, infinitely removed from its ultimate goal.

While these two ideas both indicate an infinite regressus, they refer to infinities of different orders. Mechanical causality, associated with a permanent material substance, is, if we assume an universe finite in extent or a sufficiently isolated portion of an infinite universe, a causal series that is indeed inexhaustible by actual measurement, but not, strictly speaking, infinite. In this realm the world-formula of Laplace, though a fiction, is yet indicative of the direction in which the exact investigation of nature proceeds. Psychical causality, on the other hand, is an inexhaustible process, ever bringing forth new psychical products. Even supposing that the sum of ideas possible to the finite human mind, inclosed within definite bounds of time and space, were in any way limited, yet the sum of intellectual processes for which these ideas might furnish the sensuous material would remain infinite. And granting complete knowledge of the previous course of events in the world, that principle of increasing energy which we can trace in all processes of psychical development would render for ever impossible every prophecy regarding future creations. Applied to the mental realm, Laplace's world-formula is not an unattainable ideal, but a false analogy. The fact that the infinity of mechanical causality is of a lower order than that of psychical causality is evidence that the two series are not independent, parallel in their course while entirely disparate in character ; but that the mechanism of nature is really only a part of the whole complex of psychical causality. It consists of a series of concepts connecting, in accordance with the general principle of reason and consequence, all those ideas which we term objects. The idea of the external world, together with all the conceptions relating to it, is contained in the whole

50 *The Moral Will* [472-3

causal complex of our psychical processes. It is a product of our thought, developed under the special conditions that govern objective ideas

No error on the part of the makers of scientific systems is more widely diffused than that which treats the regulative ideas requiring that rational thought shall proceed to infinity within each causal series, in accordance with the special principles of that series, as constitutive principles of our knowledge This error appears in an intellectualistic and in a materialistic form. Of the two, the former has the more warrant, for the regulative idea from which it starts really does take in the whole content of our knowledge, the external world included But intellectualism claims the power of extending to infinity the limited range of psychical causality that is accessible to the individual mind Consequently everything is regarded *sub specie individualitalis*, and we often find some special form of psychical causality, like that of logical reasoning or of the motivation of will, made to cover the whole world of ideas Still more untenable is the position of materialism For it makes the idea of a causal connection between objects, an idea that originates in the needs of rational thought and hence is based on psychical causality, equivalent to causality at large Such a theory, even if we grant the possibility of transforming the regulative idea of the universal mechanical coherence of nature into a concept whose whole content is fully known, would eliminate psychical life altogether, or at most, if the series of psychical phenomena is supposed to be given together with the parallel series of material brain processes, would transform it into a mere phantasmagoria, wholly lacking in the coherence that is produced by thought The only remaining alternative is to regard the notion of an all-embracing psychical causality, which includes our concepts relating to the external world, as an ultimate regulative

473-4] *The Freedom of the Will* 51

idea. Two postulates for use in empirical investigations result from this idea The first is that all psychical processes, so far as possible, should be brought under the laws of psychical causality as immediately given to us The second is that the whole system of our ideas of the external world should be governed by the laws of a specific kind of causality originating from logical principles, and therefore psychical in character, but based on the relation of these principles to an absolutely permanent substrate, which can undergo no change save that of position in our intuitional space. Mechanical causality is thus a subordinate form of psychical causality. But in the case of all empirical relations, where psychical processes may be regarded from an external as well as an internal point of view, these processes may either be assigned to the complex of psychical events by virtue of their immediate characteristics, or may be ranked within the causal nexus of mechanical processes by virtue of their external sensible aspect It is evident that convenience will indicate now the physiological and now the psychological view to be preferable. Thus psychology will sometimes have to refer to a physiological explanation, hence to one whose nature is ultimately mechanical; while physiology may occasionally have recourse to psychological theories For instance, it is possible to make use of the physiological conditions of brain mechanics when we are discussing the ordinary association of ideas, and while it is true that they do not give us a complete explanation of the process, they make it somewhat easier to understand[1] In like manner certain physiological facts show traces of psychological causation, while if we attempt to explain them mechanically we have no available means at our disposal, save the regulative idea that all physical effects do ultimately result from mechanical conditions. ˙ Thus the objective adaptation of

[1] *Cf* my *Grundzuge d. physiol. Psych* , 4th ed., ii , p. 473.

## 52 *The Moral Will* [474-5]

organic nature may be partly accounted for by supposing, what can be directly observed in animals, that the development of organic forms is influenced by the voluntary acts of living beings, whereas our power of explaining by mechanical causality most of these forms, especially those which occur among the higher animals, will probably be always very limited [1]

Turning now, in the light of the principles discussed, to the consideration of volitions, we need have no hesitation as to which kind of empirical causality we should use So far as volitions involve material processes, nerve excitations and muscular contractions, we must of course postulate a place for them in the complex of mechanical causality. But it is only as a regulative idea that the postulate of mechanical causality functions here, for as soon as we go beyond the most immediate conditions of the external act, the mechanical causality of bodily movements is lost in an infinite regressus that takes in the whole history of living beings. Even if it were possible to follow out this regressus, we should get nothing but a sum of mechanical processes, which would furnish no means of determining whether an action were voluntary or involuntary, preceded by various motives or by one only, etc In a word, the only part of the causal conditions of will open to our investigation would be the part that has to do with those ideas accompanying the voluntary act which refer to a permanent objective substrate. When we are dealing with volitions, then psychological causality is the only kind involved, for it is the kind that makes the will truly will. Now, like all processes of subsumption under conditions, whether they relate to internal or to external causes, psychological causality leads to an infinite series The will, however, comes under those forms of individual psychical

---

[1] *Cf.* on this point *Logik*, i , p 580, ii , pp 439 ff , and *System d. Philosophie*, 2nd ed., pp 492 ff

475-6]          *The Freedom of the Will*          53

causality whose course we can trace to a fairly adequate extent  Not only are its immediate causes given under the guise
of motives, but we can explain the origin of these motives
and their various degrees of efficacy from the earlier conditions of individual development, and even in some measure
from the conditions of universal psychical development.
Thus the point of view from which we shall regard the will
is that of determinism  Not determinism in the mistaken
sense of applying the naturalistic concept of cause to the
will and undertaking to predict the action from its conditions,
but in the sense of maintaining the absolute sway of psychical
causality and explaining events that have actually occurred
by referring them to their causes  Without a psychological
determinism of this sort there can be no psychology, no
science of mind whatever  To reject it is to come into
conflict with that law of our reason which requires us to seek
the conditions for all that is conditioned, and to regard them
when found as in turn conditioned.

But even if indeterminism could be harmonised with the
requirements of psychology and logic, it would be objectionable on ethical and religious grounds  As a matter of fact,
only the cold-blooded egoism of an age for which the moral
order was a convenient arrangement for the benefit of the
individual, and religion a guide-post to his future happiness,
could really maintain that the salvation of morality and
religion depended on absolutely freeing the individual will
from causality

It is said that men may be known by the fruits of their
actions.  On the other hand, much light is thrown on the
true nature of a theory, at least of a philosophical theory,
by the character of its partisans.  Two philosophical schools
have helped to build up the indeterminism that prevails at
present in popular metaphysics  the scholastic nominalism
of the fourteenth and fifteenth, and the theological utili-

54 *The Moral Will* [476

tarianism of the seventeenth and eighteenth centuries In opposition to the doctrine of predestination championed by Augustine and Luther from motives of a profoundly religious nature, the Nominalists stood for absolute indeterminism They applied this notion to God as well as to man, and thus regarded the sanctity of the moral law as residing not in its own nature, but in its origin from the divine command ; a position which offered a convenient excuse for placing certain outward forms that happened to suit the purpose of the Church on an equality with the moral law. The practice of granting indulgences was a sufficient indication of the moral value of this system The theological utilitarianism of the succeeding centuries was less extreme , but the barren rationalism of its theology and the gross egoism of its ethics were well adapted to drive the profounder thinkers of the time into freethought or mysticism The Kantian ethics has a moral earnestness about it that makes it far superior to this vulgar indeterminism, with its poverty of thought. Kant, however, was still under the spell of the naturalistic conception of cause. Recognising that this notion was inapplicable to the realm of morals, he distinguished reason, as the faculty of seeking conditions for the conditioned, from the understanding as applied to causes ; though the latter is really only a mode of exercising the former faculty. He thus reached the wholly untenable position that human beings are to be regarded under a twofold aspect : that while their actions, which belong to the phenomenal world, are subject to natural causality, as intelligible characters they are perfectly free with reference to the same actions This union of contradictions, which was entrenched behind the antithesis of the phenomenal and intelligible worlds, found its appropriate climax in the remarkable doctrine that the intelligible itself becomes phenomenal in the will.

The distinguishing mark of moral responsibility is the

476-7] *The Freedom of the Will* 55

causality of character    A man's action is free in the moral sense when it results wholly from inner causality, which is conditioned partly by his original disposition and partly by the way in which his character has developed    If his act is not determined by the inner causality of his whole psychical history, rather than by the motive of the moment, he is not free, but the plaything of whatever impulses are excited by the motives that chance to be in consciousness at the time. Really, the opposite of freedom and responsibility is not inner determination, but the so-called *liberum arbitrium*. For indeterminism itself acknowledges that actions cannot take place without a motive    Hence, unless the causality of character be the deciding influence, we are left to absolute chance , that is, to the guidance of whatever motive happens to be uppermost in the mind    And we are to believe that the moral order, as it is phenomenally revealed to humanity, is made up of such accidental impulses.    That such a view should be regarded as not only moral but religious is an error possible only to an age abandoned to ethical egoism and religious indifferentism, or completely misled by theoretical prejudices    An hekastotheism of this sort, where every individual looks upon himself as a god, has precisely the same claim to be called a religion that egoism has to be called a system of ethics

### (e) The Causality of Character.

It is certainly a curious fact that discussions on the subject of causality should wax fiercest with regard to the very phenomenon that furnishes the most conclusive instance of psychical causality, a phenomenon whose series of causal conditions lies open to our investigation with a completeness found elsewhere only in the simplest cases of natural causality.    Moreover, it is characteristic of the will that our

56 *The Moral Will* [477-8]

insight into the series of conditions is most complete in the case of complex rather than of simple volitions. When we have to do with a simple impulse we cannot go behind the motive immediately present to consciousness, the more remote causes are lost in the obscurity of individual temperament. But the conditions of a voluntary act, which takes place with forethought and deliberation, may under some circumstances be traced back into the agent's earliest history ; sometimes, indeed, we can get at the remoter influences of inherited family or racial traits The fact that so many conditions, more or less clearly traceable, co-operate to produce the voluntary act occasions the necessity of comprehending in a single concept the total disposition of the individual as it exists at a given moment, the product of all previous causes, and an influence encountered by each new motive that enters the field. Such a concept is that of character. What we understand by character is thus the total result of past psychical causality, itself forming part of the cause of each new effect. In accordance with this view we may divide the causes of every self-conscious volition into two groups. transitory causes, given under the form of definite and actual motives, and permanent causes, the totality of which is represented by the causality of character. Indeterminism itself has not infrequently recognised such a distinction, and has thought to reconcile itself with the doctrine of the causality of will by holding that the character itself, and not the single volition which proceeds from the character under the influence of motives, is *causa sui*. This view, of course, brings us back to Kant's theory of the intelligible character. Unfortunately the latter concept has about as much connection with that of the empirical character, which is what we are dealing with here, as the thing in itself has with the objects of the external world The two bear the same name, but they have nothing else in common The intelligible character is uncaused ; the empirical character is the effect of a sum of causal conditions, and itself forms part of the cause of every action. As the conditions that determine character become more constant, and crystallise into the fixed moral tendencies of the individual's disposition, we are able not only to deduce actions from character after the fact, but to predict from our knowledge of a man's character the way in which he will react to given motives. Thus we see that in this highest form psychical causality approaches the invariable regularity of the mechanism of nature.

Such a degree of constancy, of course, belongs only to the fully developed character, which is no longer subject to important changes. Strictly speaking, indeed, absolute regularity of character is a mere ideal, to which reality can never correspond. This ideal constitutes the intelligible character in its true sense ; it is the regulative idea in accordance with which we pass judgment on the wills of others and form our own wills. The empirical character, on the other hand, is involved in the ceaseless flux of psychical development. Its germ lies hid in the earliest tendencies of the individual consciousness, an inheritance from our ancestors, unfolding in the individual life, and destined to be transferred, enriched with new tendencies, to future generations. Its development is at first brought about by external influences, by education, and the other experiences of life. We soon find, however, that the most important factor in the process is the exercise of will. Every act of will leaves behind it a permanent disposition to similar acts. Thus the individual tendencies of the will are formed; and the less the results of the exercise of will are interfered with by sources of variation in special cases, the more fixed and definite is the stamp which they leave on the character. In this way, while external education begins the process of character-building, self-education completes it.

58 *The Moral Will* [479-80

But the individual will is contained in a social will. And this social will, again, comprises various gradations, dependent on the spread of common ideas and endeavours It follows that the tendencies of the individual will are subordinate to those tendencies of a collective will which go to make up the character of human societies and organisations. In its narrowest form, that of family and racial types, the social character finds clearest expression at the lower stages of human culture. The manifold interactions involved in a higher grade of social development tend to obscure these simple manifestations of the social character. They are represented less in the character itself than in its earliest tendencies, which express the influence of the most primitive of all social ties, that of birth. On the other hand, the existence of a common history, the spread of a common speech, and the intellectual life which is thus rendered possible, all contribute to the growing importance of the national character. Here the individual consciousness feels the sway of tendencies reaching far beyond the sphere of its personal relations. It shares in the creation of a social will, and the latter, in turn, is an important factor in the development of the collective mind of humanity Thus there comes into being the social character of humanity as a whole, a creation of will whose earliest stages, even, are not to be traced among the original conditions of human society. It is, throughout, the product of historical life and intellectual culture. As such it has already found expression, at least among civilised nations, in many common tendencies based on like intellectual and moral ideas. We often hear it said that the savage has no character save that of his race and tribe, that he lacks individual characteristics ; and the state-ment is doubtless true to a certain extent. But we are wrong if we suppose it to imply that the process of character-development exhausts itself in individualising Along with

480-1]                    *Conscience*                    59

the ultimate and undeniable decline of the immediate influence of family and race there goes a process of opposite nature, which consists in the formation of a broader national character, and in the final development of a character typical of humanity at large.   Here, in the absence of all disturbing influences arising from conflicts between individuals and between nations, we finally reach the expression of those tendencies of will which have permanent value for humanity as such, apart from the special conditions of time and space.

### 4. CONSCIENCE.

### (a) *The Various Conceptions of Conscience.*

Freedom, in the sense of the determination of will by the inner forces of character, is the source of those distinguishing features which make our self-judgments so different from the judgments we pass on matters independent of ourselves. Self-judgment is based on a law essentially voluntary in character, whose content we can vary not only in thought, but in reality.   And for this reason it is directed not only towards the outward effects of our actions, but also and chiefly towards their causes, the motives that determine them and the character that displays susceptibility to those motives. But the psychological process whose logical outcome is self-judgment is not originally a process of judgment.   Before it has developed into such a process, it occurs in the form of ideas, endowed with a strong affective tone, which are immediately associated with the emotions of approbation and disapprobation.   When these emotions conflict, we may have tendencies to opposite self-judgments simultaneously present. All these states of mind, so far as they find self-conscious expression in a judgment made by the agent on his own motives and character, are included under the term conscience.

## 60 *The Moral Will* [481-2]

Evidently the word stands for a concept whose meaning is far from being well-defined. It is not even restricted, in the first instance, to the moral realm, but is applied wherever there is a possibility of self-judgment with its antecedent stages Thus we speak of a logical, æsthetical, political conscience, and the like,—notions which do not necessarily have anything in common with conscience in the moral sense Still more important is the fact that there is only one name for the process in all its stages, from the primitive emotion that accompanies one's own acts to the developed self-judgment. This lack of definiteness has left its trace on ethical theories. Some of them, like those of many theological moralists of modern times, make the essence of conscience to consist in feeling or impulse ; others, with Kant, in a process of internal judgment; while still others, adopting the theory of scholasticism and the school of Wolff, go so far as to call it the conclusion of a syllogism, for which the moral law supplies the major premise and the concrete act the minor premise. All of these theories, save the artificial notion of the 'syllogismus practicus,' which is another instance of a doctrine that mistakes subsequent reflection on the object for the object itself, may be said to be true in some cases and false in others,—a natural result of the psychological ambiguity of the concept. The single act of conscience may be a feeling, an emotion, an impulse or a judgment ; and as for conscience in the sense of a faculty distinct from the particular acts of the human mind, there is no such thing. The concept in its broad sense is merely a generalisation from all these particular facts, whose nature varies greatly and whose only bond of union is their relation to the motives and character of the individual Ego.

There is another idea which is more unfortunate in its influence than the ambiguity residing in the concept of conscience, or even than the notion of a specific psychical

482] *Conscience* 61

force, which is sometimes associated with the term    It is a kind of mythological idea that is involved in the conception of conscience. The expressions *Gewissen, conscientia, syneidesis* refer directly to a *knowing with* someone.[1]   We have the process of knowing with, *conscire*, opposed to that of knowing, *scire*, as if it were the activity of a second self   The expression, 'the voice of conscience,' often used in ethical works even at the present time, originates in this same set of mythological ideas.  The emotion and process of judgment that accompany our consciousness of our own motives and tendencies are supposed to be not our own psychical acts, but the effects of a foreign power, which exerts a mysterious influence on our consciousness   There are always in existence some philosophical tendencies to which this mythological conception is welcome , and so we find it constantly reappearing, with little variation from its original form, on the field of ethical theory   If the latter regards the moral law as the direct command of God, it naturally transforms 'the voice of conscience' into the voice of God.   In reality the original significance of the term conscience, as a knowing with, was a knowing with God   For with the idea that the gods can see the deeds of men there was early associated the belief that they can look into the human heart   Here, as so often, we find thought moving in a circle.   Man first objectifies his own feelings, and then uses the objects thus produced to explain those very feelings.

But even where conscience is no longer regarded in this mythological fashion as an activity foreign to the Ego, the attempt is made to separate it absolutely from the motives

---

[1] GASS, *Die Lehre vom Gewissen* (p 14), considers it a distinctive feature of the German language that its *Gewissen* means a direct knowing, and not a knowing with.   But the prefix *Ge* is fundamentally identical in meaning with *con*, and there is no doubt that the word *Gewissen* itself, which originated, of course, rather in the literature of the learned than in the speech of the people, is a direct translation of the Latin *conscientia*

# 62 *The Moral Will* [482-3]

and inclinations that determine the act. We find moralists supposing the existence of an immediate sense of duty, derived, it may be, after the Kantian manner, from the intelligible character; and this sense of duty assumes the rôle of a categorical imperative with reference to all other motives, supplying the standard whereby these motives and the empirical character are tested This view may be looked upon as a philosophical reconstruction of the mythological theory of conscience, and it is in its turn objectionable, because it involves two assumptions, of which the one conflicts with moral experience and the other with the psychological nature of man Historical experience gives us no warrant for supposing that duty is always the same, and that conscience is therefore exempt from the changes of time. True, it furnishes us with a series of facts which go to show that men are gradually developing a certain degree of final unanimity in their views on moral subjects But we may be equally certain that agreement in such matters will ultimately result only after a long course of development Conscience functions at every stage of this evolution. its phenomenal forms are many and varied, and only gradually does the firm ground of common convictions emerge from the shifting contents of commands that have no real moral significance. The philosophical theory that makes 'the voice of conscience' say the same thing under all circumstances is but a revival of that old inversion of the truth which is poetically expressed in the myth of the Golden Age The only way in which intuitionism can reconcile itself with the actual variability of conscience is by doing the utmost violence to the facts. A sufficient argument against it is furnished by the single circumstance that there have existed whole nations and ages where murder from motives that we should consider wholly reprehensible was looked upon not as criminal, but as highly praiseworthy. Supposing that conscience did furnish us with an absolutely invariable law, it might indeed be occasionally obscured by egoistic impulses; but what becomes of our supposition, if we find such a law wholly lacking in a primitive state of moral cultivation? A franker recognition of the facts is to be found in the religious conception that God and the devil are struggling for the possession of the human heart. Despite its fantastic and mythological form, this theory, expecting as it does the final triumph of the good, does take account of the law of development that governs all moral life. On the other hand, that philosophy which transforms the voice of God into an unalterable categorical imperative of duty, and assigns the equally invariable sensuous impulses to the devil, sacrifices in so doing the most precious content of the moral life, namely, the possibility of development in moral ideas. Finally, can there be any doubt as to which is the greater, and hence the more truly moral theory,—the one that raises morality above the intellectual life of mankind, and makes it a law for ever foreign in its stern unchangeableness to that life, or the belief that morality shares in the endless development of mind, a process traceable throughout man's psychical life, of which morality forms an inalienable part?

Further, the theory that conscience is something opposed and foreign to the other activities of mind violates not only objective, but subjective experience, our whole knowledge of man's nature. We know no such thing as a voluntary act without feelings and impulses, for these are not processes different in kind from will, but elements of voluntary activity itself and separable from it only by abstraction. Hence it is impossible for a man to be determined in his action or even in his judgments on action by the pure command of duty, with no accompanying affective motives. Such a view would make the will, as well as conscience, an abstract intellectual process, of a sort that can have no

64 *The Moral Will* [484-5

real existence, and that certainly could not co-operate with real motives to produce actions As the will has real existence only when combined with affectively toned ideas, so conscience cannot be separated from the motives of the will · it must be based solely on the relations of different motives to one another There is, however, a characteristic peculiar to the realm of moral action, which is immediately involved in the fundamental nature of morality, and which is shared only by those other departments of thought where the conception of a norm or standard has been developed, thus giving rise to the broader sense of the term conscience, mentioned above. This characteristic is the development of imperative motives.

### (b) The Origin of Imperative Motives.

All motives are impulsive in character Each one of them, acting alone, would be an irresistible impulse; in combination they form impulsive forces, which react upon one another, and determine the will in such a way that it follows the predominant motives. Imperative motives are likewise impulsive, but they have a further property. They are associated with the idea that they must be given the preference over all purely impulsive motives. Of course, imperative motives in turn may conflict with each other, under such circumstances there takes place in conscience the process that we call a conflict of duties. But the simpler and normal function of conscience is to accompany the struggle between impulsive and imperative motives with peculiar emotions, which tend to strengthen the imperative motives, and often render them victorious in cases where their feeling-value would be too weak to make them prevail These emotions, which must precede or at least accompany the act in order to produce their effect, are generally termed

485-6] *Conscience* 65

prescriptions or promptings of conscience while the operations of conscience after the act are distinguished as the judgments of conscience. The function of conscience is essentially different in the latter case, because the emotions produced result not from the conflict among motives, but from their relation to the consequences of the act. All these aspects of conscience, however, follow directly from the existence of imperative motives. Hence the real problem of conscience does not relate to them, but may be expressed in the question : How is the development of imperative motives possible ?

Intuitionism sets out with the assumption that the imperatives of duty are not motives at all. They are supposed to consist rather in dictates of a purely intellectual character, which are yet capable of influencing the impulsive motives Such a psychological impossibility as this would hardly have been propounded had it not been for two reasons. First, a purely autonomous origin for these imperatives was believed to be impossible. And secondly, the intuitionists had in mind such objective principles regarding the content of moral action as are to be found in the precepts of religion and law They thus arrived at the odd compromise of maintaining that the imperatives are objective norms, which yet reach the consciousness of the agent through immediate subjective experience. The following proposition is still adduced as the final word in this discussion : Principles that are unconditionally valid cannot be derived from empirical motives, which are always conditioned

Now in addition to the fact, already discussed, that moral ideas are variable, the possibility of a conflict between duties proves that unconditional truth exists at no stage of moral development There is no moral law so sacred that it may not in special cases have to yield to the superior sacredness of the more general functions of morality. Where duties

F

# 66 *The Moral Will* [486

thus conflict our choice cannot be determined by any *a priori* principle residing in ourselves It must be governed by that wider conception of the moral life and its problems which is to be gained through one's previous intellectual development and on the basis of a ripe moral experience Again, nothing could be more unfounded than the supposition that any special contrivance is needed to impress men's minds with the necessity and universality of certain principles. What principle is there, from the dawn of science on, that has not at some time been regarded as unconditionally necessary? And how trivial have the grounds later appeared, upon which assertions, sometimes of the most arbitrary character, have been declared to be apodictically true! As a matter of fact, the moral imperatives would be in hard case if their certainty had no better basis But if we recognise that the causes which produce human convictions are not always of the highest order, we need not be surprised to learn that the same thing is true of some imperative motives. Nor need we be perplexed even by the fact that for the immense majority of mankind these lower motives are of the first importance. The worth of morality is not endangered because the grounds of its realisation in special cases do not always correspond in elevation to the moral ideas. On the contrary, it is one of the most wonderful things about moral development that it unites so many conditions of subordinate value in the accomplishment of high results. This is but another expression of that principle of the heterogony of ends which governs all moral evolution. If, then, we undertake to enumerate the conditions that transform impulsive into imperative motives, we may group them under four heads external constraint, internal constraint, permanent satisfaction, and the conception of an ideal moral life, together with the emotions and impulses accompanying such a conception.

### (c) The Imperatives of Constraint.

The lowest of these motives is that of external constraint. It operates in the form of punishments for immoral actions, and of the social disadvantages which such actions involve. Even under favourable circumstances it can produce only the lowest grade of morality, that of propriety of behaviour and conformity to law,—a mere outward appearance, which may exist without any real morality behind it, but has yet a certain value, since it avoids what is morally offensive. We say of a person who is influenced by external constraint to refrain from direct violation of the moral law, that he has a good reputation. He represents the lowest grade of moral character, whose sole virtue is the negative one of avoiding immoral actions.

The second imperative motive, that of internal constraint, is usually combined with the first, and leads us a step further. It consists in all those influences which are exerted by the example of others and the practices and habits of our own will, as they are conditioned by education and example. On account of its importance for the moral order, this kind of constraint is usually spoken of as the essentially moral constraint; but we must not take this expression to mean that the constraint itself is moral. It is the same kind of constraint that we speak of in many cases where we are dealing with matters that have no moral significance,—for instance, when we talk about the social duties that a man owes to his position, and the like. Internal constraint is called moral not because it is itself moral, but because along with various kinds of reference to others it involves some of a moral nature. Thus its first function is to strengthen the negative effects of external constraint. It is, however, notably superior to the latter, in that it implies a tendency towards positive morality.

# 68 *The Moral Will* [487-8]

Beneficence, efforts to secure the public good, fidelity to professional and family duties, may be developed by the mere influence of example and habit, as well as by the desire to emulate others in so high a degree that the apparent virtue resulting cannot be distinguished from real virtue in the ordinary walks of life We may predicate of the character that acts under all conditions from the imperative motive of internal constraint the quality of respectability, and the term, when extended from special cases to the whole conduct of life, means something far beyond mere decorum of behaviour.

### (d) The Imperatives of Freedom.

Constraint in its two forms can do no more than produce the outward symptoms of morality, or at best a feeling of repugnance, the product of habit, towards what is immoral A morality with no better basis than this will always suffer wreck when the decisive test comes, and it is one of the saddest experiences of human life to see decent and respectable characters driven by what seems mere accident from their previous course of life, and to be obliged to acknowledge that but for this evil chance they would probably have finished their lives with honour When a character withstands such dangers as these, its power of resistance is never derived from the imperative motives of constraint alone. Other motives are demanded ; and these, since they are wholly independent of external influences, and have their source in the agent's own consciousness, we shall call the imperatives of freedom

The first of them is the motive of permanent satisfaction. We find the element of permanence emphasised by Socrates, who, here as elsewhere, is simply the interpreter of a sentiment widely diffused among the profounder thinkers on moral questions.[1]  The problem as to the origin of this distinction he did not, of course, investigate, and hence he represents that stage of moral development which is but one remove above the influences of constraint.  The fact that certain actions do give more lasting satisfaction than others is recognised as an imperative motive for their preference, but the why of this preference is not discussed.  And since its grounds do not form part of the immediate content of conscience, we must ourselves postpone consideration of them until we come to our general investigation of the motives of morality.  Here we are concerned only with their result, namely, that in general the actions that give permanent satisfaction are unselfish actions.  The imperative of free preference and the imperatives of constraint are in agreement here; hence they tend to intensify one another, especially since resistance to the motives of constraint increases the unpleasant feelings that interfere with satisfaction.  This is why constraint is so important as an educational means to the production of free morality.  The character that has the latter developed into the instinctive form, where the right thing is done without inquiry into its grounds, may be called righteous.  The righteous man, doing right for its own sake, withstands temptations to which the man whose only thought is to preserve his outward respectability falls an easy victim.  Since, however, he takes no account of the ultimate end of his action, he is easily led to waver between conflicting duties and to follow chance impulses, which may result in a victory for the less worthy cause.

And so the processes of conscience find their completion in the last of the imperative motives, that of a moral ideal of life.  Here one supreme life-purpose is the guide of each and every action.  This supreme purpose becomes a motive for the individual consciousness, when the individual com-

[1] *Cf.* Part. II., chap. i., pp. 5, 6.

70 *The Moral Will* [489-90

prehends the universal ends of moral development under his own temporal and spatial conditions, and looks upon them as the ends of his own personal life. Thus the ideal as individual, as determining the tendencies of the individual existence, necessarily assumes whatever special form the ideal of universal humanity takes on, with reference to definite limits of time and the external circumstances of life, and to the particular sphere of operation that belongs to the individual moral personality. For the ideal of the whole is not something completed, something given once for all; it is always in process of becoming, and never finished The consciousness of every age comprehends it in certain ends, motives and laws The true value of these last, however, consists not in their absolute, but in their relative permanence, in the fact that they really share in the general process of development, whose coherence is demonstrated by the steadily increasing perfection of moral ideas. It is not until this final stage is reached, when ideal motives rule, that we get clearly conscious morality Conscience now regards the motives of constraint as morally indifferent · at a crisis it may even decide to disregard them altogether, recognising that there are turning-points in moral development where that which has hitherto been right and moral becomes the very opposite The instinctive performance of right actions has now given place to a righteousness enlightened by knowledge of the moral end, and reference to this end serves to decide all conflicts between duties.

Evidently, this final form of the moral character is oftener to be met with in imperfect approximations than in anything like ideal perfection Such approximations are what we call noble characters. Like everything that approaches even remotely to perfection in a personal form, they are rare exceptions, arising out of the dead level of respectability and integrity which goes to make up common morality

They are the true intellectual aristocracy, towering far above those morally mediocre natures to whom the term is often falsely applied, and whose only distinction is an unusual degree of mental cultivation. But supreme in this aristocracy of morals, as the sun among the planets, shines the ideal character, the moral genius, infinitely rarer than any other form that genius takes, and brought forth by the spirit of history perhaps once in hundreds or thousands of years. While the great sum of moral forces works for the present, or at most for the immediate future, the ideal character seems to embody the whole spirit of humanity. It comprehends the entire moral development of the past and radiates its influence into the remotest distances of the future.

The highest artistic, scientific and political gifts are not met with every day; and it is doubtless a matter of equal necessity that the ideal character should be the rarest of all endowments, hence to be regarded as the very manifestation of God on earth. A society where the majority are careful to maintain a good reputation, and where a considerable number, especially of the more important citizens, aim at propriety of sentiment and behaviour, may claim to have reached a normal degree of morality, if it possesses even one or two really upright characters. It will make no remarkable advance in moral culture and all that moral culture involves; but neither will it fall behind. If, on the other hand, the masses are disposed to care nothing for reputation, if even the most influential men think more of their own profit than of the respect to be enjoyed as the reward of correct behaviour, such a society cannot be saved from moral degradation by any ordinary degree of righteousness. The situation demands that men of truly noble character shall set themselves to the task of bettering affairs. Finally, in those decisive periods when some great change in the conditions of human life, extending beyond the boundaries of

# 72    *The Moral Will*    [491-2

a single nation, has brought about a moral crisis affecting the whole history of the world and demanding a revolution in moral ideas and theories, then the historical process awaits completion by the power of an ideal character, an ethical genius, whose influence can awaken slumbering impulses to life.

It accords with the laws of psychical development that such periods should produce such men  For it is not in the desert of the commonplace that greatness takes its root  We must have conditions such that a need felt in the universal consciousness shall become an impelling force in the mind of some individual, which in turn exerts a powerful reaction upon the whole.  Such phenomena seem like miracles to the common mass of men, who can see only the effects and not the silent creative forces of mind.  But miracles of the same sort can be traced in every process of intellectual development.  Everywhere the individual is impelled by the spirit of the whole, in which he partakes with all his thoughts, feelings and volitions  But in the leading minds of an age—and the creative moral genius is a leading mind of the highest order —the entire process of past development is comprehended, and new paths are marked out for the universal mind

### (e) The Religious Form of Moral Imperatives.

It is probable that the influence of these four imperative motives, the motives of external and internal constraint, of permanent satisfaction and of the moral ideal, has been felt since the very beginnings of the moral life.  Rarely, however, and only at the later stages of moral evolution, have they assumed that universal form which the present discussion, abstracting from particular phenomena, has been obliged to give them  In the case of the moral motives, as of other moral ideas, the religious form is the earliest.  Thus

492] *Conscience* 73

the imperative of external constraint first appears exclusively as a religious command, and the way in which the political authority comes to share in the exercise of constraint is simply by the gradual transfer to its charge of the means by which this command is enforced. Similarly internal constraint first makes itself felt in the relationships of religious society; it is only by a gradual process that the influence of custom is freed from religious elements. The highest form that the imperative of permanent satisfaction can assume depends on the prospect of eternal punishment and reward. And the moral ideal, too, has its religious embodiment; indeed, the religious conception is peculiarly effective here, for it represents to each individual a personal prototype of the moral conduct of life. In all these ways, religion fulfils its function as the great educative force to morality. Yet we must not forget that it can perform this function only because it is not, what dogmatism even at the present day supposes it to be, something distinct from human nature; but the very concrete sensuous embodiment of the moral ideal itself. That which man early feels to be the content of his moral consciousness, his imagination represents as a world objective and yet permanently related to himself. If, then, we subtract from religious ideas the form with which imagination clothes them, we find their true content to be the imperatives of conscience.[1] But it is in the last of these imperatives, which regards the moral ideal as an endless task, that we find embodied the idea whence religion derives its real value, a value that is unchanged amid every variation in its presentative form, and makes religion superior to all the lower mythological embodiments of moral postulates. This idea is that of a moral task which is unending, and therefore essentially transcendental.

Of the four imperatives of conscience, the last is the only

[1] *Cf.* Part I., chap. ii., pp. 95, 96.

# 74 *The Moral Will* [492-3

one that involves real knowledge about the true motives and ends of the moral life. But any attempt to give it final expression would be contrary to the proper nature of the moral ideal If moral ideas develop, the science of morals cannot stand still. The best that we can do is to express these ideas as adequately as possible from the point of view of a given age and a given stage of historical development. There is all the more reason why we should eliminate from our formulas all that does not bear the stamp of permanence, everything that holds good only from a particular standpoint. This character is especially marked in the case of the distinction commonly made by ethics between goods, virtues and duties In the first place, the notion of goods is specifically eudæmonistic in its origin, hence, even if we abstract from its eudæmonism, it is always liable to misuse. The concept of virtue, referring as it does to the whole conduct of personal life, is too remote from the motives of particular actions, while the idea of duty, finally, obscures the objective and universal significance of moral laws behind their subjective and individual applications. Hence in what follows we shall substitute the expression 'moral ends' for 'goods,' 'moral motives' for 'virtues,' and 'moral norms' for 'duties.'

493-4]

## CHAPTER II.

### MORAL ENDS.

#### I. THE PRINCIPAL FORMS OF MORAL ENDS.

WHEN he begins to speculate about himself, man becomes conscious of his own being as that of an individual personality which is also part of a social community, and realises that in union with this community he forms a factor, however insignificant, in the immeasurable universe of the spirit of humanity. It follows that the ends sought by the individual will may be individual, or social, or pertaining to humanity at large. Moreover, the narrower of these ends may be accompanied by incidental results whose influence reaches into wider spheres. In particular, it is impossible to study individual ends without taking account of their remoter consequences to society and humanity.

Two ways are open for the methodical treatment of this problem. First, we may try to get a general conception of morality, and to determine the various moral ends by analysing it. This is the method ordinarily used in modern ethics: so much so, in fact, that one lays oneself open to the charge of proceeding without any guiding principle if one neglects to follow it. The method which first lays down a principle and then brings the detailed facts under it is a legacy to modern moralists from Christian ethics, which could get its principle directly from its religious postulates.

# 76 *Moral Ends* [494-5

Secular moral philosophy abandoned the religious postulates, but held to the method originally in vogue. Even empiricism was no exception in this respect; when, for example, it asserted the principle of self-love or general utility, it did not do so on the basis of a systematic induction It first determined its conception of morality in accordance with the principle chosen, and then tried to show that deductions from this conception really corresponded with the requisites for a happy or a moral state of society Thus for facts, which are the true test of a conception of morality, it substituted dubious hypotheses and deductions, whose experimental confirmation was impossible.

The second method of ethical research, therefore, starts with our empirical moral judgments. On the basis of these judgments it first tries to get at the various moral ends, and then to reach a general ethical principle through study of the ends. This is the method that Socrates pursued in ancient ethics, whose superiority to modern ethics, so far as freedom from prejudice goes, we must allow, and it is the method that Aristotle perfected in a form which was definitive for ancient theories of life Nowadays we think Socrates childishly naive in beginning his search for an ethical principle by trying to find out what all men thought on the subject. Yet we shall never obtain a higher test of truth than that of universal consent. What every normal consciousness, under conditions of sufficient enlightenment, recognises as self-evident, we call certain Logical and mathematical axioms have no better foundation for their evidence. Science, however, should not rest content with this factual evidence, but should trace out its remoter sources. However, it would be an inverted order of proceedings to seek for sources before one had ascertained the course of the streams flowing from them ; and so the first problem in the investigation of moral ends is to answer the question ·

495-6]                    *Individual Ends*                    77

What ends are universally recognised by our judgment as moral? If we meet with contradictions in answering this question, then we shall be justified in abandoning the method which we have followed, and seeking for something outside of the conflicting moral judgments that will settle the difficulty We shall find, though, that here as elsewhere theories are more contradictory than facts With all the diversity among the ethical views of philosophers, there is little variation, even during long periods of time, in men's judgments as to what ends shall be called moral, and within a given stage of moral development these judgments are hardly less constant than those which deal with logical relations.

## 2. INDIVIDUAL ENDS

It is usual to state that the first end which a man seeks in his own behalf should be that of self-preservation Based directly on those sensuous impulses which serve to maintain individual life, this is looked upon as the lowest of moral ends Generally speaking, it would seem to have moral value only when it is a means to some further end The individual is required to preserve his own life in order to act for social and humanitarian ends, or for other individual ends There are two of these individual ends which are to be indirectly reached through self-preservation, namely, self-satisfaction and self-perfection But while self-preservation is merely a means to certain other ends, these two, on the other hand, must always be results that accompany other objects directly sought. Hence they must always be pursued indirectly We may be satisfied *by* something and perfected *in* something; and the direct object of our action will be in both cases the something that we conceive to be the means of attaining happiness and perfection. Further, we may be satisfied or rendered happy by those of our actions which relate to ourselves, or by those which find their object in reference to other men, and have thus a social or broadly human tendency. These latter fall outside the sphere of individual ends; while the former can be nothing but individual feelings of pleasure, to which, again, we can allow no moral value The case is similar with the end of self-perfection, so much exploited by the moralists of the German Enlightenment In the last analysis it must relate to the perfection of functions that aim either at individual or at universal ends, and such functions would be considered moral only in the latter case The way in which individual ends eliminate themselves so far as moral value is concerned may be represented in the following scheme —

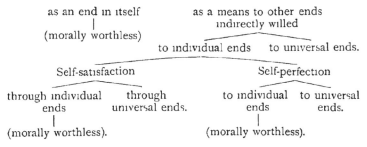

Self-preservation for universal, not for merely individual ends, satisfaction through universal, not through merely individual ends of action, the development and perfection of capacities to serve, not individual, but universal ends: such is the principle that should govern our moral judgment of individual ends. According to this principle the individual end can be moral only when it is the immediate, but not the ultimate object; in other words, the agent's own personality as such is never the true object of morality.

## 3 SOCIAL ENDS

If the true object of the moral will cannot be our own Ego, we are confronted with this alternative either it is some other Ego, the individual personality of our neighbour, or it is society as such in its various divisions of state, community and family. Now, if my own Ego is not an ultimate moral end, it is not easy to see why any other Ego should be The preservation and happiness of an individual, the development of his capacities, are in and for themselves precisely equal in value, whether the individual in question is myself or someone else. Nay, my own Ego is, if anything, the more important, because the means of furthering its happiness and development are more fully in my power. Nor does the multiplication of individuals much alter the state of affairs. You cannot get a real quantity by putting zeros together. If an individual feeling of pleasure has no moral value, then neither has the pleasure of many or all individuals Utilitarianism is thus only extended egoism It makes an ultimate end out of what can be only a proximate end or a means to further ends. Considered as means, the furtherance of one's own welfare and of that of others have both of them a relative moral value, to be measured by the relation of the means to the true moral end. This explains why we believe it better to work for our neighbour's advantage than for our own, and why, when the two conflict, we recognise the former course as the only moral one. The reason ordinarily alleged for this, namely, that nature has already disposed us to look after ourselves, while unselfish action usually results only after a victory over egoistic motives, is hardly the final one If unselfish as well as selfish impulses were not implanted in the human heart by nature, they could never develop, and the furtherance of one's own being, understood in a higher sense than that of the mere satis-

# 80 *Moral Ends* [498

faction of sensuous impulses, undoubtedly means more self-denial and renunciation than, for instance, the ordinary exercise of sympathy, which is attended with a minimum of sacrifice  The final ground for the preference of altruistic actions is rather to be sought in two reasons, the one objective and the other subjective, which mutually support each other  The objective reason is the fact that an altruistic tendency on the part of actions makes possible a more extended functioning of the moral will, and thus serves the common ends of society and humanity at large.  The subjective reason, which is perhaps the more important, is that every unselfish action serves as a test of character, by which we can measure the general worth of the individual personality.  The man who comes to the aid of a suffering fellow-being is possibly doing very little for the general welfare, but the particular action shows that he subordinates his own interest to objective ends  And it is just this symptomatic value of an action, rather than its external result, that determines our judgment of its moral goodness.  The poor man who shares his scanty stock of bread with an unfortunate brother has done more than the millionaire who assures him an ample competence

If the individual Ego, whether my own or that of another, can never be the ultimate end of morality, there remain two social ends as the true objects of the moral will,—public welfare and universal progress.  These two correspond to self-satisfaction and self-perfection in the case of the individual  Like these, they are so intimately connected that public welfare without universal progress has no permanence, while progress, in turn, consists wholly in the furtherance of general welfare.  Thus the second merely adds to the first the element of progressiveness  While the enhancement of public welfare stops at the attainment of a given end, universal progress extends its efforts beyond this end to further aims in a similar direction

498-9] *Social Ends* 81

Now when we use these expressions, what do we mean by the terms 'public' and 'universal'? Does public welfare consist in the sum of the welfare of all individuals, or of as many individuals as possible,—in a 'maximum of happiness'? Is universal progress, in like manner, the progress of as many individuals as possible? Evidently, an affirmative answer to these questions would make the notions of general welfare and progress eliminate their own moral value, just as we found the notions of individual welfare and progress doing. The more extended the happiness that an action produces, the more the act reveals a conscious striving to subordinate the individual to the social will, the higher do we rank it in our moral scale. But why we should do so is a mystery, except on the supposition that the happiness of no matter how many individuals is not the ultimate end, but only a means to the attainment of remoter and wider ends Our way of regarding social facts is in accord with this view As we pass from narrower to more comprehensive spheres of society, the acts of the universal will, embodied in those individual volitions which are directed towaids universal ends, take account of matters that transcend the limits of the individual. And by-and-by we find it impossible to explain them as expressions of care for the well-being of any sum of individuals Nearest to the narrow limits of individual existence stands the family We all wish to ensure the future welfare of our children and grandchildren, but we are not much concerned about the fate of our posterity in remoter centuries The foresight of the community extends somewhat further; it would show want of conscience if it took account only of the living or their immediate successors in its care for public affairs. But it is the eye of the State that sees farthest into the future. The State alone has the right to expect great sacrifices from the present in behalf of a more distant time to come. Hence it is only right that whenever

G

## 82    *Moral Ends*    [499-500

the profit of the present generation is subordinated for the benefit of future generations, the responsibility should be assumed, not by any individual, or even, in many cases, by the community, but by the State.

And these facts are in harmony with our feelings about the future. If we could be absolutely assured of the misery of a descendant living two centuries hence, we should probably not be much disturbed It would trouble us more to believe that the State and nation to which we belong were to perish in a few generations. The prospect would have to be postponed for several centuries at least before our knowledge that all the works of time must be destroyed would make it tolerable. But there is one idea that would be for ever intolerable, though its realisation were thought of as thousands of years distant : it is the thought that humanity, with all its intellectual and moral toil, may vanish without leaving a trace, and that not even a memory of it may endure in any mind This is why, when we come to the limits of individual existence, we look beyond, and rejoice in the hope of a future for the great social communities to which we belong and with which we labour for more lasting moral ends. And when, gazing far into the future, we see these communities disappearing, we live in the confidence that the moral end of humanity, in which all that is individual is absorbed, will never vanish. This confidence is born of faith, not of knowledge ; but of a faith based on dialectical analysis of the concept of a moral end, which shows that every given end is only proximate, not ultimate,—is thus, finally, a means to the attainment of an imperishable goal.

The ultimate reason, then, for this continual postponement of the moral end is to be found in the transitoriness of individual existence The individual, however happy and perfect, is but a drop in the sea of life What can his happiness and pain signify to the world ? The nothingness of individual existence was forcibly realised by Christian ethics, which, in its promises of eternal blessedness, developed the opposite idea of a happiness infinite in value and duration. But that fruition which religious hope seeks in the infinite alone may be found in real life. True, real life offers it only in finite and inadequate approximations ; but on the other hand, these forms lack the egoistic limitations that affect the religious conception. And nothing but the fact that this life of ours does offer such fruition ensures to it the imperishable character of its ultimate moral end

So long as we hold to the individualistic and pessimistic conception of finite existence, the Indian solution of the world-riddle is perhaps the most direct : eternal oblivion and annihilation are the surest deliverance from the pain of existence. But just because the sphere of individual volitions never can furnish the supplement to the finitude and limitations of actual life, we must seek it, not in the form of subjective feelings of pleasure, which as such can have no universal significance, but in the form of objective intellectual values  These originate in the common intellectual life of humanity, and react to elevate the individual life , not by resolving themselves into an objectively worthless sum of individual happinesses, but by producing new objective values of richer content through the creative force of the individual psychical life. We need but refer to the realm of historical criticism to assure ourselves that this way of estimating social ends is the only admissible, because the only real way By what standard do we form moral judgments on men and nations which belong to a long-vanished past, and in whose case we may therefore most reasonably expect that transitory and apparent ends will have given place to permanent and real ones ?  Not by the happiness which they themselves enjoyed, nor by the happiness they gave to their contemporaries ; but solely by what they have done for the total development of humanity in all subsequent ages.

# 84          *Moral Ends*          [501-2

### 4 THE ENDS OF HUMANITY.

A study of the loftiest examples of morality inevitably leads us to the conclusion that in order to rise to the highest forms of moral action, the individual must not work merely for his fellow-citizens and contemporaries. Still less must he labour for himself alone  Here, as elsewhere, the principle holds that when we are seeking to explain a conception, the instances we select should be as pregnant as possible To attempt to define the essence of the moral character from the phenomena of average goodness is just like trying to discover the universal laws of mechanics from the most complicated meteorological processes. Now the life and actions of a Moses, a Socrates, or a Christ were for all ages : the traces of their moral influence will last as long as human history. True, this influence was at first felt only in limited circles, and many of their actions aimed directly at the immediate present. But the direct purpose of their greatest deeds transcended the limitations of the present ; and even those actions which were determined by proximate conditions have indirectly, as integral parts of an ideal character, a significance extending far beyond their immediate aim.             ·

While it is granted only to a very few favoured mortals directly to seek and attain the ends of universal humanity, yet all, even the lowest, may do so indirectly in various ways. Here, too, we find the principle of the heterogony of ends and the law of the inexhaustibility of the creative power in mind running through the whole process  The mission that any nation has to perform in the world's history is the function of the innumerable individual forces which go to make up the various departments of that nation's social life and political organisation: it is thus in the end the

## The Ends of Humanity

function of individual wills. The least as well as the greatest may say in the words of the Earth-Spirit—

> "'Tis thus at the roaring loom of Time I ply,
> And weave the living garment of Deity"

However restricted the immediate ends of an individual's action, they always transcend their immediate object, and lose themselves at last in the immeasurable stream of the intellectual development of humanity.

What are, then, those broadly human ends which are the final outcome of all more limited moral endeavours? Do they consist in universal happiness, embracing all the temporal and spatial conditions of human existence? Or in universal progress, which seeks to increase the happiness of mankind beyond every given limit? Evidently, to answer either question in the affirmative would be to make our moral good consist in individual sensations of pleasure, which we have already seen cannot be moral ends, at least not ultimate ends. And so we find that our ultimate ends can be nothing but the production of psychical creations, a process in which the individual consciousness bears its part, yet whose final object is not the individual himself, but the universal spirit of humanity. Happiness is a secondary result brought about in the subjective consciousness by these psychical products; it is also a motive operating on the will Thus it may be regarded as an indispensable means to the attainment of moral ends, but never as the moral end itself. Kant's position, that the good must be done without inclination, while the ultimate end of morality is eternal happiness, completely reverses the functions of means and end. Man can seek the good only because doing so makes him happy; yet the good itself is not happiness, but an objective psychical product, which becomes a good in the ordinary sense of a pleasure - producing force solely through its reflections in the individual consciousness.

## 86 *Moral Ends* [503-4

If the humanitarian ends of morality thus fall within the scope of the universal teleological activity of mind, whose essential natue consists in its creative functions, then when we investigate them we must remember that in all intellectual life our study is restricted to the stages of development already attained. We can never predict what the future will bring forth from the present, except in so far as we may speculate concerning the immediate outcome of processes already begun. But the moral ends attained at any given period consist in the total intellectual culture of that period The very possibility of talking about the ends of humanity nowadays is due to a relatively new state of affairs to the fact, namely, that the universal spirit of mankind has reached such a degree of self-consciousness as to produce the idea of humanity in the sense of a collective intellectual life, functioning in the processes and results of history. Along with this idea there has developed a conviction that the universal psychical products of human society are those moral objects attainable by us But since such objects, like human action itself, have their origin in will, and since for that very reason the innermost essence of morality consists in ceaseless, never-resting effort, no single stage of moral development once attained can be regarded as a permanent end The past has ceased to be an object of moral effort ; the present will cease to be so when another moment has passed. Thus the ultimate end of moral endeavour is ideal , it can never be realised Yet, as the sphere of moral action widens, we must come nearer to those limits beyond which, outside of our possible experience, the real and the ideal meet. The concepts of ethics cannot represent the ideal as attainable , that remains for religion, which supplements the sensuous world with supersensuous postulates expressed in symbolic form

The religious form of the moral ideal emphasises one

## The Ends of Humanity

factor, which affects all departments of the moral end, but which is likely to produce a mistaken conception of the problem of morality where, as is always the case in practical ethics, the end falls within the immediate radius of human activity. Enlightened religious feeling realises that outwardly religious actions, consisting in an unreflective obedience to religious precepts or in a mere cult, are in themselves of no value, that their whole worth lies in the disposition for which they stand, hence in the motives that produce them Now since practical morality does, as a matter of fact, have a value over and above its symptomatic significance, in that even when it proceeds from impure motives it may bring about certain moral results, we tend to fancy that the moral character of an action resides wholly in the moral ends as above described. If this error is avoided, the opposite one is apt to arise. We may doubt whether these ends are moral at all, under the impression that an end can be moral only if it is moral under all circumstances. Such a view means a confusion between the morality of an end and that of an act or disposition. For dispositions and actions to be moral, both motive and end must be moral The motive, on the other hand, may be moral when the resulting action is not, this is the case when for any reason, *e g.* an error in judgment, the end striven for is not a moral end. Or, again, the end may be moral and the act to which it leads morally indifferent, this may happen when the end is sought for indifferent or impure motives. It is evident that the necessity of having motive and end coincide if the act is to be moral will be more stringent in the case of the ends of humanity than in that of individual and social ends, for the nature of moral development requires that the latter should reach ever outward into wider spheres of life, and so it is *a priori* clear that no given individual or social end is ultimate and final. The case is different with humanitarian

# 88 *Moral Ends* [505-6

ends. Beyond these there is nothing for which man can strive. And for this reason the objective end of all moral effort, which as such must be directed towards outward results, must lie wholly in the products of the creative power of mind. The fact that this end cannot be exactly defined, that it transcends every goal once attained and points to a remoter and higher goal, is expressed by religion in the doctrine that the ultimate end of moral endeavour is supersensuous; though religion, too, acknowledges that the end has moral worth only when it determines the motives and ends of daily conduct. It is but an imperfect, and at bottom an immoral form of the religious conception of a supersensuous end for morality that, as in the case of the religious application of the retribution idea and its philosophical reflection in theological utilitarianism, finds both motive and end in the happiness of another life

As individual ends refer back to social ends, and social ends to the ends of humanity as a whole, so these last demand in their turn to be supplemented. There is no higher realm in which they can be included, but the indispensable ethical complement of the humanitarian end is the motive. The highest ends of humanity are not moral unless the motives that lead to them belong to the series of moral motives which we shall consider later. There are two important corollaries from this postulate of harmony between end and motive First, we must at the outset exclude from the realm of moral ends all those cases where such harmony is impossible, for the reason that the end is incompatible with moral motives Thus even within those spheres of activity to which humanitarian ends belong, as, for instance, art, science and universal culture, there exist ends that are not only morally indifferent, but even immoral Secondly, when the end aimed at is moral, we must distinguish between an estimate of the result of the action and an estimate of

506]          *The Ends of Humanity*          89

the action itself   The former depends on internal and external conditions, part of which have nothing whatever to do with the moral character of the agent's personality.   But the moral action as such depends on the moral disposition alone ; and the quiet fulfilment of duty in the modest round of daily tasks may show a higher morality than any achievements, however outwardly brilliant, that spring from impure motives.   There is certainly great injustice in the fact that we are so ready to judge the agent by the consequences of his action.   But the compensation demanded by moral sentiment is not lacking : it is furnished by the satisfaction that we all feel when we are faithfully trying to do our duty in our own sphere of life.   The joys of a good conscience, far excelling all other sources of happiness, are so great that the really moral man is entirely satisfied with the position assigned him by Fate : he would not change places with anyone.   And the fact that even in the humblest walks of life this feeling of satisfaction with self may atone for outward differences in position and worldly goods is, perhaps, as convincing proof as could be found of the principle that, in the infinite sum of forces that combine to perform the great tasks of humanity, the moral worth of each individual is measured, not by results depending on chance conditions, but by the moral energy manifested in the purity of his disposition, and the power of moral motives to overcome all resistance   In the totality of the moral world there must be diverse gifts and diverse stations   Few can labour at the higher tasks of humanity, and perhaps for centuries there will be only an occasional individual who can work directly for its supreme ends   But indirect co-operation, involving an infinite number of gradations, is quite as necessary to the attainment of these ends,—a fact that represents the reverse and external aspect of that inner law of compensation which we have just discussed   True, the state of humanity has

90                    *Moral Ends*                    [507

never been such as to give free play to this law of compensation, the law of the supplementing of end by motive We find, on the contrary, that the general principle of moral development, which makes the end a thing ever striven for but never fully attained, must be extended to the forces of the moral life itself   The harmonious co-operation of these forces remains an ideal, to which the individual may gradually approximate in his internal and external moral endeavours , while society works towards it by bringing about a state of affairs where every individual may co-operate in the moral task

And so we see that the ultimate end of human morality is the moral ideal, and that its immediate end is the progressive perfection of humanity.   All narrower fields of human effort, where the aim is individual and social perfection, are finally included in this last and highest realm. Perfection is but a fictitious concept if it is understood in the eudæmonistic and utilitarian sense of a mere increase in the happiness to be attained through sensuous and intellectual sources.   Such a theory makes happiness the real and ultimate end.   The idea of perfection has no independent significance unless we realise that the ultimate moral end is ideal, to be reached only in approximation This means that happiness has little ethical importance . it is not an end in itself, but a by-product of moral effort, though, at the same time, an aid to morality.   Since the moral ideal belongs to the realm of the infinite, our only way of defining it is to characterise it indirectly in two ways. In the first place, we may define it positively as meaning the development of all the psychical forces of mankind in their individual, social and humanitarian functions, a development that progresses beyond every stage once attained and proceeds to infinity   Secondly, we may define it negatively by saying that it involves a progressive diminution of all

507-8] *Immoral Ends* 91

the influences tending to check this development. Such influences have their source in acts of will that, considered from the point of view of the moral end, may be generally designated as counter to that end. And since these volitions are an important factor in the totality of moral evolution, we must study them more closely.

### 5 IMMORAL ENDS.

The influences that work against the moral end spring from two sources moral weakness and moral wickedness. The former results from weakness of will, the latter from a perversion of will The former leads to negative opposition, neglect of the good , the latter to positive opposition, production of evil The man who, because he is afraid of danger or discomfort to himself, lets a fellow-being perish when he might save him, is morally weak The man who plots the destruction of a person who stands in his way is morally wicked Of course, there are many and various degrees to both these forms of immorality. The most frequent and excusable form of moral weakness is when a man fails to devote his whole intellectual energy to the development of his own moral capacities ; the worst form is when he is too indolent to obey the direct social and humanitarian requirements of the social will Weakness is here closely allied to wickedness, and in its further consequences often leads to wickedness

There are two kinds of moral judgment corresponding to these two kinds of immorality non-approval and disapproval. In both cases judgment is determined by the conflict between the action in question and the four imperative motives of conscience. And here, again, we find the motives of constraint ranking lowest in the scale. Yet in ordinary life they are almost the only guides of our

92 *Moral Ends* [508-9

judgment, and their fitness to perform this function is proportioned to the degree in which law and custom satisfy the requirements indicated by the two imperatives of freedom as the external conditions of social life Here, again, the result transcends the immediate aim All we need ask of the vast majority of men is that they shall regulate their conduct by law and custom , and where the demands of practical life leave no room for the investigation of the deeper springs of morality, law and custom prove their value as a code of ready-made precepts embodying the whole moral development of the past, and constituting it an effective force. It is only in the decisive situations of life, or in cases where a conflict of duties makes an appeal to the guidance of imperatives of constraint untrustworthy, that the choice of ends must be influenced by the thought of permanent satisfaction, or, if this too fails, by the moral ideal. Fortunately such situations are rare ; and since ethical development is essentially an affair of the social will, it is sufficient if the leading spirits who direct the social will have the higher imperatives in mind. They can so order the customs and laws of a society as to guide all individual effort towards the more perfect moral ends

Yet even the ordinary individual is not· wholly devoid of guidance by the imperatives of freedom in his moral life. He encounters them in the form of certain religious ideas about the supersensuous world, which are in their turn closely associated with the imperatives of constraint. For instance, religion expresses in its own peculiar way the real ground of our condemnation of immoral ends, when it declares that the sinner has forfeited eternal happiness. The objective result of sin is made into a subjective result the sinner has denied the objective moral ideal, and so he is forbidden the attainment even of a subjective ideal. For

509] *Immoral Ends* 93

as the moral action, reaching out in its consequence to infinity, finds its ultimate goal in the moral ideal, so the immoral action has its final outcome in the annihilation of that ideal. And this is the fundamental reason for the unconditional primacy of the social will over individual wills, which is manifested in all law, but especially in penal law. The mere habit of constraint may suffice to keep the individual from moral error ; but it can never justify the existence of constraint itself.

[510

# CHAPTER III

## MORAL MOTIVES

### I. THE PRINCIPAL FORMS OF MORAL MOTIVES

OWING to the nature of the will, it is the affective elements of consciousness that are chiefly influential in the causation of action  Desire or aversion must always accompany will , and feelings of pleasure or pain are always associated with these impulses  Hence there is no such thing as a special class of affective motives, different from other motives : human action does not result sometimes from feeling, directly, and sometimes from reflection, but always from feeling.  These feelings, however, are in some cases associated with particular perceptions,—this is what we ordinarily mean by affective motives , or, again, they may result from a more or less complicated train of ideas relating to the immediate or remoter empirical ends of the action , or, finally, they may spring from a conception of the ultimate ideal end of moral endeavour, given to direct experience only in remote approximations.  We shall call such conceptions of the ideal end, Ideas , that power of the human mind which reaches out beyond empirical limits and creates ideas, we may term Reason

We shall thus have to distinguish motives of perception, motives of the understanding, and motives of reason  It need hardly be said that these terms do not refer to distinct faculties of the mind  According to the view adopted here,

94

510–11] *The Principal Forms of Moral Motives* 95

the ideas of reason originate in the sphere of voluntary activity just as the assumptions of the infinity of space, time and causality do in the philosophy of external nature. These assumptions, too, may be called ideas of reason. Like the ultimate ends of volition, they are never really given in experience But just as we find it impossible to think of space with limits, of time standing still, and of the series of causal conditions having a beginning, so the final end of will is an ultimate postulate never to be actualised in experience.

### 2 MOTIVES OF PERCEPTION

Immediate perception is always the first guide of our will. But perceptions soon come to be associated with ideas of the imagination, which connect the phenomena given in intuition with past and probable future events All these ideas, taken together, operate as motives of perception. Thus the sight of a man in mortal peril usually arouses in our minds a dim idea of the events that led up to the situation, and a very lively idea of what will happen next; and this train of ideas, operating as a whole, produces emotions that may become strong motives to determine our action.

Self-feeling and sympathetic feeling are the two fundamental forms of feeling that regularly function in this way as moral motives The first of these is directly involved in self-consciousness and in the idea of one's own personality that grows up along with self-consciousness. But in the course of moral development many different sets of ideas have become embodied in the notion of self And so motives of perception are produced, having the power to hold their own even against complicated external impressions, and to determine the will in a direction adapted

# 96 *Moral Motives* [511-12

to the situation of the moment. Thus we may have simple reactions of self-consciousness which are yet so admirably adapted to the moral end that no amount of reflection could have improved them Indeed, it may often happen that when deliberation intervenes, it falsifies the surer instinct of the original impulse. For reflection can draw only on the stock of individual experience that is nearest in point of time, while in instinct we have the co-operation of an immeasurable series of impulses belonging to the past Practice and the growing fixity of character give increasing certainty to the direct operation of self-feeling Thus the chief characteristic of moral maturity is the power to do right without deliberation ; at least wherever the decision is not complicated by a conflict of duties To be faithful to professional obligations, to keep one's word, to speak the truth, —these are instincts that function as immediate reactions of self-feeling in everyone who is morally sound, though they may not always be able to withstand the opposition of other motives As the character develops, there is an increasing stock of motives which formerly had their source in the understanding, but which are now incorporated into self-consciousness as impulses of perception. And the appropriate action follows upon the perception of a given situation with ever-increasing certainty. Hence it is evident, not only that the law requiring us to do right without inclination, *i.e.* without a motive, is easier to state than to obey, but that the real mark of a mature character is its power to fulfil the moral law from pure inclination, without stopping to deliberate

Sympathetic feeling supplements self-feeling And it is the fact that the latter cannot get on without the former which has given rise to mistaken attempts at a derivation of sympathy from self-feeling, through reflection or through an associative transference. The major premise here, which

512-13]                *Motives of Perception*                97

makes sympathy develop later than self-feeling, is uncon-
firmed by experience. The individual consciousness finds
itself included in a social consciousness, and the individual
will in a social will, with which its most vital instincts are
shared , thus sympathetic feeling and self-feeling are equally
original  For along with the development of self-consciousness goes that of the consciousness of objects distinguished
from the self. The Ego cannot exist without objects, any
more than objects can exist without an apperceiving Ego
But objects are not perceived as indifferent things : the
nearest and most important objects appear to be beings
of like nature with the Ego, sharing its thoughts and feelings.
Sympathetic feeling and self-feeling are thus affective modes
that develop side by side, just as self-consciousness and
objective consciousness are modes of thought simultaneously
evolved  And hence all motives springing from sympathy
involve the existence of a real social will. They do not
relate to all objects whatever, but to those which we recognise as beings like ourselves , hence as self-conscious personalities with similar tendencies of will.

Thus the sole object of sympathy is man, or, as we say
in order to indicate the closeness of the relationship, our
fellow-man. The lower animals we regard as fellow-creatures,
a term which expresses our recognition of the fact that our
fellowship with them has its sole basis in the ultimate ground
of all things,—creation  Hence, while we may feel emotions
in some measure akin to sympathy with reference to animals,
the fundamental source of true sympathy, namely, the inner
unity of our will with theirs, is lacking. Thus, it is evident
that this kind of transferred sympathy can extend no further
than we have reason to suppose the existence of conscious
elements like our own  It is limited to sensations and
feelings , and even within these limits it is only the kind
of sympathy that voluntarily condescends to its objects, not

H

98 *Moral Motives* [513-14

the kind that is based on a feeling of likeness and equality. We may suffer in sympathy with the sufferings of an animal, but the nobler feeling of sympathetic joy is impossible where animals are concerned, subjectively as well as objectively it is the exclusive privilege of man. We may note, also, that the relation of animals to us is like ours to them in this respect, although for opposite reasons. An animal whose higher instincts have been developed by intercourse with man may rise to the point of sympathy with human suffering, but it can never share in human joy,—at least not with feelings of pure and disinterested sympathy This highest of all the motives of perception is for ever beyond the reach of the lower animals, and man can feel it only for his fellow-men It is another proof that animals are in a pre-moral stage of development, this fact that the highest of them can feel, even for their own kind, no other sympathetic emotion save sympathetic suffering, and that only occasionally. True, they enjoy certain pleasures in common, but each individual is occupied with its own subjective satisfaction They are unacquainted with that sympathetic joy which is derived from the pleasure of others

The development of sympathetic feeling is precisely like that of its kindred sentiment, self-feeling. Here, too, we find motives of the understanding and the reason gradually crystallising into pure motives of perception. On the other hand, these impulses, even in their most primitive forms, contain the germs of the higher motives. In particular, sympathetic feeling is the immediate precursor of the social instincts. These originate directly from sympathetic feeling, as soon as the social will begins to express itself in impulses that transcend purely individual feeling. And as this result generally involves a logical sequence of ideas, it presupposes the transition from motives of perception to motives of the understanding.

### 3. MOTIVES OF THE UNDERSTANDING

When deliberation intervenes between the impelling ideas and the decision to act, we have motives of the understanding. Here it is not the immediate, but a remoter end that determines the action, and the exciting cause is to be found in the feelings accompanying this end, which is the result of reflection The motive of volition is thus an idea of the end, though it can operate only through the medium of the feelings indissolubly united with it.

The ends which reflection presents to the will fall into two great classes. On the one hand, we have those ends which are directed towards the furtherance of our own welfare , on the other, those which serve the purposes of our fellow-men or the community at large The two forms of feeling corresponding to these two classes of ideated ends are the self-regarding and the social-regarding impulses. They are complexer forms of self-feeling and sympathetic feeling, but they differ from the affective elements of the motives of perception by reason of the different value that moral judgment ascribes to them. While self-feeling and sympathetic feeling have an equal warrant, so that it is the endeavour of the moral character to make them balance, the self-regarding impulses are recognised as being less worthy than the social-regarding impulses ; and when the two conflict the latter are unconditionally preferred.

There are two reasons, the one subjective and the other objective, for this difference. On the one hand, a proper regard for self is an essential requirement of the moral character , but it is not a product of reflection : it is the direct reaction of self-consciousness upon external impressions On the other hand, sympathy, being equally direct in its operations, relates to the individual moral subject alone, while the social-regarding impulses refer to a whole, which

100                    *Moral Motives*                    [515

is a higher ethical end, not only because it includes many individuals, but because it produces more lasting results in the way of moral development   But knowledge of universal ends presupposes reflection about the nature of this whole and its relation to individuals   Hence it is through the understanding alone that the social will becomes self-consciously active in individual wills   When immediate perception gives rise to such a functioning of the social will, it is because, as character develops, motives of the understanding have become transformed into motives of perception.   Further, the self-regarding impulses, as we shall understand them, are, while distinctly inferior, by no means immoral.   For we must wholly reject the base significance which the term 'self-regard' has come to have, as a result of the original inferiority of the sentiment and the tendency of language to exaggerate distinctions once established Considered in its true nature, self-regarding activity includes not merely the furthering of one's happiness—which is for ethics only a means or a side-issue, never an end in itself— but first and chiefly one's own intellectual development and moral perfection   In this higher sense self-regard is not only natural, but moral , for it is the necessary means to the building up of a character that shall serve the higher moral ends.   There is certainly no virtue in the unselfishness of the lazy and the ignorant   The higher form of self-regard is immoral only when it claims precedence over the self-regarding impulses.   Hence we have in the unconditional supremacy of the social-regarding impulses an instance of the dialectic of moral ends, whereby the individual end always resolves itself into some social end which it serves, thus becoming, finally, merely a means in the service of universal ends

It is the more important to establish the primacy of the social-regarding impulses with reference to the motives of the understanding, because it is just here that the conflict between the interests of the Ego and those of his fellow-men wages most fiercely. The motives of perception antedate this conflict · natural instinct follows the immediate impulses of self-feeling and sympathy In the event of a clash between these two impulses, the preponderant force of some one motive would soon decide matters, and not infrequently the happy agreement of natural disposition with natural conditions makes the intenser motive decide in a way that satisfies our moral sense. On the other hand, the motives of reason are beyond the sphere of the conflict between egoism and altruism. In their case it is not the immediate or the more remote, but the ultimate ends of morality that are transformed into impulses ; and hence, while doubt and error may arise regarding the means to be chosen, there can be no dispute about the ends to be preferred. The motives of the understanding are thus the only field for a conflict of interests Egoism, continually suppressed by the moral superiority of the social-regarding impulses, is always renewing the struggle At times it seems wholly victorious, and then the balancing of individual interests is the only force that restrains the otherwise unbounded power of selfishness. Hence we can easily see why an exclusive consideration of the ethics of the understanding should have given rise to the theory, so often maintained in the history of ethics, that the social-regarding impulses themselves are a mere limitation, invented by egoism, of the self-regarding activities. If the partisans of this view had contented themselves with showing that egoism is not, as it seems at first sight to be, in sheer opposition to the common welfare, but that it often serves universal ends when it seems to be directed solely towards the individual, no objection could be brought against their position. The fact that an intelligent selfishness often results

102                    *Moral Motives*                    [516-17

in public benefits, a fact which our own age, with its astonishing development of competition, has perhaps made more apparent than it has ever been before, is but another instance of that principle of the heterogony of ends, which holds good throughout the moral realm.

But effects like these, so different from their causes, would cease to be produced if they could not be brought about independently, by means of causes really adequate to them Experience shows that this kind of heteronomous production of good may suffice to preserve a balance of forces once established, or to sustain impulses that tend directly towards the public welfare But shocking examples of the fate of moral progress, where egoism alone rules, are to be found in the phenomena of the moral downfall of whole races, as history occasionally presents them. Where faithfulness to professional duties, trustworthiness in social intercourse, self-sacrifice for the State, have once reached the minimum that will just about meet the demands of individual welfare, then the community is doomed to inevitable ruin. Of course, such an outcome will wreck the happiness of the individual. But where egoism rules supreme, what do the living care for future generations? '*Après nous le déluge,*' they will say, until the flood sweeps them away with the words on their lips.

Yet it cannot be denied that self-interest occupies a leading position among motives of the understanding, at least when we consider that the interests of the community are, broadly speaking, ensured through their association with individual interests But this very fact, again, represents a powerful impulsive force operating within the sphere of conduct governed by the understanding, and constantly opposing self-interest The official who serves the State perhaps does his duty in the first instance merely because he finds it to his own advantage. The worker in industrial arts who benefits the public by a technical application of some useful dis-

517-18]   *Motives of the Understanding*   103

covery may have an eye, first of all, to his own personal
interest. But ultimately neither of them can ignore the
wider results of his activity. And so the universal end
attained becomes one of the motives to action   Later, under
the influence of practice, it may even become the ruling
motive

The production of social-regarding impulses is greatly
helped by the co-operation of the lower and higher kinds
of motive, those of perception and reason. It is a fact of
special importance that the impulses of self-feeling and
sympathetic feeling, which accompany direct perception,
already involve a certain balance between the egoistic and
altruistic tendencies in man's original disposition, so that
if self-interest has too much to say in the reflective delibera-
tions of the understanding, it is checked by natural feelings
involving no reflection at all.

Yet however useful this kind of instinctive check may be
for individual development, the motives of the understanding
offer stronger incentives to unselfish action than those of immediate perception, because they are directed towards wider
ends   For while motives of perception can determine only
the conduct of individual life and the personal intercourse of
individuals, the motives of the understanding are the source
of all those voluntary actions through which society gains
an organisation based on the relation of reciprocal rights and
duties   In such an organised social life, based on reflection,
the collective will, whose only form of expression in individual intercourse is impulsive in character, functions with
a clearer self-consciousness   Yet it may conceivably happen
that the chief end present to consciousness in this process
of reflection is the liberty of the individual will, while the
social ends lying beyond and trenching on the domain of
reason are willed instinctively, rather than definitely sought.
We see this very clearly in the fact that social practice

104 *Moral Motives* [518-19]

usually approaches more closely to the ideal than juristic theory does, guided as the latter is almost wholly by a balancing of individual interests. Theory bases political and social institutions mainly on their utility to individuals But the sacrifices of which the individual is capable for social and political ends, which are even demanded of him, can neither be explained nor justified on the ground of individual utility Such faithfulness to duty as is shown by the official who sacrifices the security of his private existence for the public good, or by the soldier who gives his life for his country, could never be reached by starting from the point of view of individual interests, were it not for the fact that behind the understanding with its motives there is the idea of reason, telling us that the immediate material and intellectual ends of society serve as means to an ideal end of absolute value, before which the importance of the individual existence utterly vanishes.

### 4. MOTIVES OF REASON.

We shall include under the head of rational motives of moral action all those which proceed from the thought of the ideal destiny of man. The nature of this thought is such that it can be realised only approximately in consciousness. It is a kind of prophecy, extending not only beyond every given limit, but beyond every thinkable limit, and can no more be pictured completely than the representation of infinite time or infinite space. This is just what makes it an idea and not a true representation All that can be immediately represented in consciousness is the direction in which the moral life at a given moment must tend, if it is to approach the ideal destiny And this, in turn, can be done only when the tendency is already present in the motives of perception and understanding, hence all that is

## 519-20] *Motives of Reason* 105

needed to raise them to the level of motives of reason is an insight into their deeper nature

Now we have already seen that all the impulses of perception are based on the reciprocal relation of self-feeling and sympathetic feeling, the latter being regarded not as transferred, but as extended self-feeling. That is to say, it is the feeling of the immediate unity between individual wills and a social will extending beyond all definite limits, in a spatial infinity that comprehends all beings of a like order of consciousness, and a temporal infinity that includes all the future conscious states of these beings. For every act, though it takes place in the present, is directed towards the future, and hence enters into the infinite causal series of future developments of will. All motives of perception thus come under this twofold infinity, however little the agent himself may be conscious of the fact. And just here a distinctive feature of feeling comes into play. Feeling never exists without a representation. But since it expresses rather the effect of the representation on consciousness than its direct objective significance, certain relations may have their influence on feeling that far transcend the immediate content of the representation, and that can be studied only by a process of deliberation which investigates the ultimate causality of motives. The man who risks his life to save a strange child from the flames may see at the moment of action nothing but the immediate impression, absorbing his whole consciousness. The content of this impression bears no relation whatever to the emotion that urges him to action This substitution of one's own personality for that of a stranger is thinkable only as the product of a feeling of the direct unity between oneself and another, a feeling that at the critical moment forces one to save that other's life as if it were one's own But the thought of the unity of two beings, almost wholly feeling at this stage, is but a single random link in an infinite chain of

106                    *Moral Motives*                    [520

unifying relations which binds the individual Ego to the whole psychical being of humanity. Only on this supposition can we understand the emotion of happiness that accompanies such actions  To derive it from our sensibility to honour, gain, return services, etc., neither explains it nor accords with actual observation, though one cannot deny that selfish components sometimes enter into the enormous complexity of human motives.

The like may be said of the motives of the understanding It seems *a priori* inconceivable that a mere balancing of interests should account for the unconditional preference given to the social-regarding impulses in our estimation of moral value  For the maxim that a man serves his own interest best by furthering the common good is of doubtful truth as a general formula, and almost wholly useless as a motive.  At least it can serve as a motive only after subordination of the individual to the social will has occurred, and brought about results that form the empirical basis for the maxim.  Again, we find the consciousness of direct unity with the social will giving rise to that feeling of happiness which accompanies activity for the common welfare, and which is strengthened on the one hand by the emotions involved in the conquering of self-interest, and on the other hand by the external results of unselfish action, among which respectability and social influence play a certain part even at this stage of moral progress

Motives of perception and understanding are thus indirectly, by virtue of the anticipations of feeling, rational motives to a certain degree.  But they develop into true motives of reason only when the direct continuity of all individual actions with the infinity of the moral world, and the perception that the individual will corresponds to the idea of this continuity, come into clear consciousness as the determining grounds of action.

Of course, these complex rational motives must be again transformed into feelings before they can become effective Since, however, such feelings spring neither from direct perception nor from reflection about ends that are immediately and empirically attainable, but from the general assumption of ideal ends, we may distinguish them as ideal feelings. Traces of them are to be found in the earlier stages of moral development They are there associated with the religious conception of an ideal world contrasted with the actual world. In the first stages of religion the ideal is regarded as given, gradually it comes to be thought of as something posited, something that must always be sought, but can never be attained in sensuous experience When religion has reached its final stage as an expression of the deepest moral sense, it transfers, not indeed the ideal itself, but the ceaseless effort after the ideal, from the future life to this life. It makes that effort the immediate motive to action, the central force of every empirical act. With this conception, the religious consciousness associates the postulate that an adequate object must exist, corresponding to the longing after an ideal Ethics does not deny this postulate, but it bridges the chasm that separates empirical morality and the supersensuous ideal in the ordinary mind by regarding empirical morality as itself the gradual realisation of the ideal In truth, the only sufficient ground for faith in the moral ideal lies in the fact that we can set no limits to the process of moral and intellectual development; or, what comes to the same thing, that we cannot conceive its complete annihilation This, however, is a basis that is absolutely secure We cannot ground our faith in the moral ideal on the hypothesis of any supernatural revelation, or even on our demands for compensatory justice On the one hand, the revelation hypothesis holds good subjectively only, not universally; its validity is lost as soon as subjective faith in the

108 *Moral Motives* [521-22

revealed testimony is lost. And on the other hand, to demand justice is to regard the ideal from a point of view that is not only narrow and empirical, but wholly egoistic Thus regarded, it must necessarily cease to be a moral ideal in the true sense

## 5 IMMORAL MOTIVES.

### (a) The General Conditions of Immoral Volition.

If the moral life is the infinite and never-ending realisation of an ideal life, how are we to understand the existence of immorality? How shall we explain the efficacy of motives irreconcilably opposed to the moral instincts and continually offering obstacles to the development of morality? Is not the existence of evil, even if it is psychologically conceivable, a moral and metaphysical contradiction of that fundamental belief in a world-order which, to our minds, essentially implies the thought of this order as moral?

As a matter of fact, there are two positions in ethical theory from which no satisfactory interpretation of immorality, consistent with its phenomenal manifestations in experience, can be reached. One of these positions is that of extreme individualism in its two forms, egoism and utilitarianism, the other is that of extreme universalism The perplexity of both these theories, when confronted with the problem of evil, is evidence against them For egoism, to set aside one's own interest is always an act of resignation, wherein the individual will does violence to those natural impulses which, as the sole forces governing it, are essentially justifiable When such an act is demanded by society and its organisations, the demand is a mere exertion of brute force against the individual will, justified only by its conduciveness to the majority of egoistic interests Even in its motives crime is merely a case of faulty adaptation to ends, it is not real guilt, for which the social will not only can in justice but ought to exact atonement from the sinner. Utilitarianism, like egoism, makes the immorality of bad motives to consist wholly in their inutility It differs from egoism because it has a more comprehensive moral end, the welfare of the whole Hence it regards immorality as a striving after individual welfare exclusively, and morality as being essentially an endeavour to promote the general welfare, which last resolves itself into the welfare of all or of a majority of individuals Thus the distinction between the moral and the immoral becomes purely quantitative, and it may be doubted whether the effect of the more extensive scope of actions for the general welfare is not cancelled by the greater intensive force of egoistic actions Finally, extreme universalism considers all individual motives as relatively indifferent factors. Where they oppose the social will they may be left out of account altogether. Thus immorality becomes a mere negation of morality, a nullity that has no place in the infinite process of the moral spirit

Hence both these extreme positions fail to do justice to that profound antithesis which pervades all the motives of human action. It is easy to see why this should be so, for according to the one view only the individual will is real, and according to the other, only the social will If either of these alternatives were true, then as a matter of fact, since the ultimate spring of immorality is egoism, the distinction between good and evil would either be reduced to a matter of quantity, by reason of the individual character of all moral ends, or become a mere appearance, by reason of the nothingness of the individual,—an illusion that vanishes as soon as things are regarded in their true nature But the individual and the social will are equally real. The latter may surpass the former in moral worth and in comprehensiveness, but not in reality, for if we do away with the indi-

110                    *Moral Motives*                    [523-24

viduals, the whole necessarily disappears. On the other hand, it is equally evident that there is no such thing as an isolated consciousness; man's whole psychical existence is bound up in the society to which he belongs and with which he takes his place in the immeasurable chain of universal moral development. From this point of view we can understand at once both the unconditioned primacy of the social will over the individual will, and the significance of a conflict between the two. The will is moral as regards its results, so long as its action conforms to the social will; as regards its character or disposition, so long as the motives that determine it coincide with the ends of the social will. Motives that relate to ends which are indifferent to the social will are morally indifferent. That disposition or tendency is immoral, on the other hand, which represents a revolt of the individual against the social will    Hence the ultimate source of immorality is always egoism. All other motives opposed to the social will, such as hatred, revenge, carelessness, or indifference to the general interests, are finally reducible to egoism.

Since, however, the social will is not a single all-embracing reality, but is divided into various gradations, evidently the authority which the motives governing a given social will have over individual wills is relative rather than absolute. The social will of a community may be diverted for a longer or a shorter period from its permanent ends. This is regularly the case when the self-seeking of individuals has taken possession of the collective will. in such circumstances the strife between the individual and society often means only a conflict between weaker and stronger egoism   The same conflict occurs in another form when a narrower social will opposes a more comprehensive one; when, for example, the interest of a single family enters the lists against that of the State, or when the temporary advantage of a people is

524-25]    *Immoral Motives*    111

opposed to its permanent interest. Here we have simply the battle of egoism waged on a higher plane. The broader and more lasting ends must always be given precedence in such cases. But critical situations of this kind may involve a sharp conflict of duties in the individual consciousness The ordinary fulfilment of duty may even become an immoral act, and resistance to the existing legal order a duty. Of course, it is only characters of great moral energy and insight, where the more universal social will has attained clear consciousness, that are called on to settle such conflicts. For the development of ordinary characters the performance of ordinary duties must suffice But the fact that society, like the individual, is subject to perversions of will, that states may transgress and err as individuals do, does not ultimately interfere with the permanence of moral laws For this permanence does not mean that morality is always the same, nor yet that all products of the social will, as they are brought forth in historical development, are equally real, and therefore, considered in the light of the age in which they appear, equally moral. This second view, that of the extreme historical school in philosophy, confuses the relative with the absolute social will. The latter is an idea of the reason, by which we must always suffer ourselves to be guided, but which loses all its significance if it is supposed to be realised in any single historical product, even the most sublime.

Of course, the spirit of history is always in the right. But races are transitory, like individuals, they are subject in the same way to passions, prejudices and weaknesses. The eternity of moral laws consists in eternal becoming, and this process, again, cannot be thought of save as involving continual resistance and conflicts, growing out of the strife between wills. If morality is essentially a development of will, it is for that reason necessarily associated with the

112 *Moral Motives* [525-6

actual conditions arising from the relation of the individual to the social will, and of the various forms of the latter to one another. As in the egoism of individual life, so in that of historical life, the source of immorality is sometimes a subordination of the social will to individual interests, and sometimes the preference of a narrower to a more comprehensive form of the social will The conflict of good and evil is just this strife between wills. Since the empirical social will is finite and liable to error, the ultimate solution of this conflict is to be found only in an idea of reason, which makes the infinite series of will-forms terminate in a supreme will, phenomenally manifest in the individual consciousness as the imperative of the moral ideal, in the State and in society as the Spirit of History, and in the religious conception of the world as the Divine Will

*(b) Individual Forms of Immorality.*

The ordinary form of immorality, and that which is of most importance practically, is individual immorality, which springs from a revolt of the individual against the social will. Since the various forms of the latter operate as the imperatives of conscience in the individual consciousness, this kind of revolt is not merely external, but internal as well, a violation of the individual's own moral character. It must be so, because the individual will is itself a part of the social will that it opposes The four imperatives of conscience thus represent different forms of the social will, and the significance of resistance to these imperatives is correspondingly different

The imperative of external constraint answers to the legal community represented by the will of the State. Resistance to this imperative leads to the worst form of immorality, namely, violation of the external legal order, crime. The imperative of internal or moral constraint is the product of the will of civilised humanity, hence of a social will that

# Immoral Motives

526-7]                                                        113

transcends the limits of particular legal communities, though as a community of morals or customs it is restricted within certain bounds determined by similarity in degrees of culture and in the conditions of life. Resistance to this second form of the social will results in immoral action. Crime, too, is always an offence against the imperative of internal constraint, an immoral action ; but not every immoral act is a crime. There are innumerable courses of life that run counter to the broadly human requirements of morality without conflicting in any way with the legal order.

Offence against the two imperatives of constraint constitutes the notion of moral wickedness, or the positive form of immorality. On the other hand, actions that are opposed merely to the imperatives of freedom, that of permanent satisfaction and that of the ideal life, spring from moral weakness alone. We judge them less severely in proportion to the degree of moral force that it would take to obey these imperatives in a given case.

Moral evil, considered with reference to individuals, is thus restricted to two forms, illegality and immorality. The outward difference between the two consists in the fact that the former is ordinarily liable to direct punishment, while the only public penalty for immoral action is general condemnation of the agent's character, and the social consequences of such condemnation,—a penalty known to be very uncertain in its operation. This difference is based, not only on the circumstance that the social will of humanity, against which merely moral wrong is directed, has no executive, but also and chiefly on the fact that crime involves an objective danger to the community which immorality does not involve to the same degree. Moreover, since immorality is manifest less in single clearly definable actions than in the whole conduct of life, it is impossible to subsume it under any definite moral system ; and when we find such a subsumption,

I

as in primitive stages of culture where morals and law are as yet insufficiently distinguished, it involves the most serious disadvantages to individual freedom and hence to moral development

Despite this difference in form, the distinction between illegality and immorality may be almost wholly disregarded in the study of immoral motives. Considered from the point of view of motive, the chief difference between the criminal and the immoral person lies in the outward opportunities which have influenced them as causes. There are positions in life where it would be hard to become a criminal, and there are, unfortunately, others where it would be almost impossible to avoid becoming one The immorality that is clever enough to keep itself carefully within the limits of what is legally allowable is especially at home in what is called 'good society,' which might sometimes be more appropriately termed bad society. crime dwells oftenest with need and misery Hence the most important condition that affects the origin of moral evil is social position This is the chief factor in producing, or at least in facilitating the production of the two classes of motives that, independently or in conjunction, are the main sources of moral evil One of these two classes is pleasure-seeking, the other is envy. They are degenerate forms of self-feeling and sympathetic feeling. In the search for pleasure we have self-feeling transformed into self-seeking, which makes its sole and ultimate end its own enjoyment. So long as it can keep within certain limits, it may surround itself with the appearance of morality, but the moment it becomes a ruling passion it loses this capacity. The spirit of prudence and calculation, hitherto a modifying influence on the turbulence of desires, is now itself taken into the service of passion The reckless use of others for one's own ends is the sole motive of action.

While pleasure-seeking generally results from situations

527-8]                    *Immoral Motives*                    115

in life that offer sufficient or too abundant means of satisfaction, envy springs from the soil of want. The fact that other people enjoy pleasures denied to himself arouses in the envious man a grudge against fate, and this sentiment passes all too readily into hatred of the fortunate individual in whom he sees his hostile fate embodied. So long as a man feels an inclination to work and a real pleasure in his calling, as incentives to activity, such a disposition will never develop in him   But where laziness and absence of occupation are associated as negative conditions with the stimulus of self-seeking, sympathy becomes nothing higher than a sense of one's own lack of the happiness that others enjoy. Pleasure-seeking and envy, joined to carelessness and want of occupation, will thus inevitably lead to moral degeneracy

It were vain to look to any principles other than those involving a fundamental reform of social conditions for an improvement of this state of affairs. The social problem is not a question of justice, as it is thought to be by those social parties which are themselves infected with the egoistic motives of their adherents. Justice distributes according to desert. But how many of the people who demand an improvement in their situations, and for whom such an improvement is urgently needed, can claim really to deserve it?  "Treat every man as he deserves, and who is safe from blows?"  Yet the social problem is essentially an ethical problem   No unprejudiced person can shut his eyes to the fact that the relations of property and labour, as modern civilisation has established them, are in the highest degree adapted to increase the power and extend the influence of immoral motives. The state of society to-day tends to produce two social classes, which combine the conditions of immorality under their two opposed aspects  a class with material possessions and without employment, the end of whose existence is pleasure ; and a class devoid alike of

116                    *Moral Motives*                    [528-9

possessions and of employment, which exhausts itself in the struggle for forbidden enjoyments. What is the use of educational reforms while these social wrongs continue? Nothing short of a new system of law, which should reform society itself, could gradually effect a change. There is no slight foundation for the conviction that such a reform must come, in the fact that our present state of society is the product of two factors which fail to harmonise a theory of law whose source is partly to be found in outgrown social relations, and a mass of new elements of culture which only violence can force into the old conceptual schemes

### (c) *The Connection of Immoral Motives.*

Nearly all the motives of the will tend to multiply themselves. But none have this characteristic more strongly marked than immoral motives. It is not only that crime "is ever bringing forth crime anew," because habit blunts the conscience, and the fact that enjoyments are forbidden heightens the desire for them, making them assume new and often unnatural forms. Even before it leads to action, or while it is producing action, the motive which was at first predominant tends to associate with itself other motives, whose influence works in the same direction, and which not infrequently heighten the immorality of the act. This process is the more tragic because it is usually helped on by the promptings of conscience. For conscience is a monitor of doubtful effect. It may check action at the critical moment, and in such a case it generally settles the conflict of motives for a long time to come, and often in a way that is decisive for the agent's whole future life. But what happens perhaps oftener is that the motives opposed by conscience are but the more powerfully reinforced by auxiliary motives which were at first entirely ignored. Thus it may come about that the original motive of a criminal act is not the one that finally decides it; the agent may be himself deceived as to the motive that impelled him to action. This reinforcement of one motive by others not only makes the immoral tendency more nearly irresistible, it almost always increases the gravity of the action. An attempt on the life of another, undertaken from self-interest, is transformed into a murder committed in a spirit of cruel hatred Thus hatred and anger, in particular, are comparatively rare as the primary motives to crime,—rarer than they might seem to be from the criminal's own statements and opinion,—but they seldom fail to be among the immediate motives, especially where the offence is one against the person. Even in the case of an assassin whose purpose is robbery and who attacks an unknown victim in the street, these passions are always present ; a violent onslaught would be almost impossible without them. The fact that the man he assaults is in possession of something that he himself wants, and the self-defence to which the victim is forced, arouse a mixture of hatred and wrath, which often enough leaves its trace in the way the deed is performed.

While this complication of motives is of the highest interest to practical psychology, its significance for ethics is relatively less Ethically, the essential consideration is the fact that however various the motives to immorality may be in individual cases, the fundamental and ruling motive is always that immoderate egoism which leads to a revolt of the individual against the social will Immorality, in the narrower sense, is a mode of life directed wholly towards the satisfaction of selfish impulses, while crime is an individual act tending to annul the ends of the social will for the sake of satisfying individual impulses.

118                    *Moral Motives*                    [530-1

### (d) Theories of Punishment.

The notion of punishment is intimately connected with that of crime  Punishment is always an act of the social will; hence, more especially, of the will of the State, since it is the State that as a rule expresses and fulfils the will of the legal community  The judge and the executive officer are merely the organs of this social will.  In other cases also, outside of the realm of law, punishment has the same general character : the father who punishes his child embodies the social will of the family, and the teacher represents in his punishments the social will of the educational community.  There is no such thing as punishment inflicted by an individual will.  This is just what constitutes the complete antithesis between punishment and the action punished, which usually proceeds from the will of an individual.  The moment that punishment loses this character, and, whether in public life or, as frequently enough happens, in the family or the school, assumes a form that shows it to be a mere arbitrary act of the individual will, it ceases to be punishment, and becomes revenge or ill-treatment. These facts should be kept in mind as carefully as the fundamental motive of crime, if we are to avoid wrong views of the nature of punishment.

The most frequent form of error is where the acts of the social will are regarded from the same point of view as the conflict between individual wills  Punishment then becomes retribution.  This is closely akin to revenge, and hence is often wholly identified with it,—always wrongly.  Revenge meets the injury received with any kind of injury whatsoever in return ; retribution measures the deed and its retaliatory deed against each other, requiting good for good and evil for evil ; so that in both cases the amount of good or evil returned corresponds to the merit or demerit of the act.

531]                    *Immoral Motives*                    119

Hence the most perfect form of retributive punishment is the *jus talionis*, to which, as a matter of fact, it was reduced by the older theories of punishment, as well as by Kant, following their example   But how can the *jus talionis* be applied to actions like fraud, perjury, or treason to one's country?   And would not the penal power of the State itself become immoral, if it undertook to punish the cruelty of murder with an equal cruelty?

Retribution is the principle of private life   There it governs all our intercourse with others.   Hence, so long as punishment is regarded from the point of view of individual rights, which is always the case in the older theories of law, the notion of retribution, and, so far as it is practicable, the *jus talionis* itself, are the sole ruling principles.   At this stage of development punishment is still a mere reaction of one individual will against another, as is shown by the fact that it leaves the very worst forms of evil to be dealt with by the avenging will of an individual or his kinsmen   The case is different where the social will is the conscious representative of the general conception of law.   It stands so high that it cannot inflict evil on the individual merely in order to square accounts with him for the evil he has done.   Such a position simply transfers the standpoint of the individual will to the social will   Since punishment is and should be an evil, it continues to involve the element of retribution which at first constituted its whole nature, but this element does not exhaust the content of the notion.   Retribution and punishment are conceptual spheres that overlap partially but not completely.   Punishment ceases to be identical with retribution in proportion as it ceases to be an act of private revenge, and becomes an act of public authority.   Hence the barbarous conclusions to which the retributive theory leads, especially in its older forms, are to be rejected, not for the criminal's sake, but because hatred and revenge are emotions

120                    *Moral Motives*                    [531-2

which should have no influence on the social will  The
single fact that it is, or at least ought to be, dispassionate,
constitutes the immense superiority of public legislation
The postulate maintained by philosophy and religion both,
that judgments about right and wrong should never be
disturbed by emotion, must remain a mere ideal for the
individual will.  But the social will can fulfil it approximately,
if not completely.

The retributive theory makes punishment an end in itself
If the act is atoned for, the balance which it originally
disturbed is restored , any further results are at least outside
the sphere of punishment as such.   In this respect the theory
agrees perfectly with a second conception, otherwise quite
dissimilar,—the theory of security.  This is based on the
view expressed in Spinoza's phrase, "Security is the virtue
of a State, but freedom is a private virtue."  While the
retributive theory makes individual emotion the vehicle of
punishment, here, on the contrary, it is held to be essential
that the State should confront wrongdoing in a wholly
dispassionate spirit ; hence judging it, one might say, not
by its moral significance, but merely with reference to the
degree in which the criminal endangers public safety
Security is to be ensured by punishments involving restraint
on personal liberty , such punishments being sufficient, according to some theorists, for the majority of cases, and
according to others, for all.   Thus it is requisite that the
punishment should last until the danger is in all probability
removed.   Evidently the result of this theory would be to
mete out punishment, not according to the gravity of the
offence, but according to the likelihood of future offences
of a similar kind.   The wife murderer, who has once for
all attained his end by his action, the official who has
embezzled funds and whose removal from office has destroyed
his chance for further peculations, might be allowed to go

## Immoral Motives

at liberty, while, on the other hand, tramps and petty rascals, of whom the judge can confidently prophesy that they will steal and beg again at the next opportunity, would have to be locked up for life. It is evident that a theory so absolutely inconsistent with our moral sentiment and with the general notion of punishment must lead to error. But it seems to me that this inconsistency makes it impossible for us to predicate of the theory of security even that partial truth which belongs to the retributive theory. Punishment does not undertake to serve the end of security at all: it leaves that to the police and to the private vigilance of each individual If it were the task of penal justice to render innocuous all those subjects who tended to become dangerous by reason of inclination to crime, habitual carelessness, propensity to drink, mental derangement and the like, then the population of a country might be divided into two classes, the one sitting under lock and key and the other keeping guard.

Conscious of this weakness in its position, the protective theory usually seeks further support by associating itself with another conception of punishment, which may also exist independently,—the theory, namely, of reformation. What distinguishes this view favourably from the two preceding is the fact that it makes punishment a means to the attainment of a further end, and not an end in itself The school of Krause, which made an especial point of the reformatory theory in its propaganda, requires that punishment be executed with direct reference to this end. It aims to bring the offender to a consciousness of the immorality of his life by teaching and moral exhortation Of course there is nothing to be said against such efforts, so long as they are combined with punishment. But if the whole conception of punishment is exhausted in them, it ceases altogether to be punishment, that is, an evil, and thereby loses a large

122 *Moral Motives* [533-4

portion of the moral effect that it is intended to produce. When the reformatory and protective theories are combined, the next step is to make the degree of reformation attained the standard of our judgments as to whether further restraints on the criminal's freedom are necessary or superfluous If one of the objects of punishment, reformation, is reached, the other, the security of society, follows as a matter of course. If the most dangerous of assassins has given convincing proof that he will lead a good life from now on, why should we hesitate to release him? How such proof can be obtained is another question. Requiring prison officials to take a course in criminal psychology would hardly meet the difficulty. As a matter of fact, the greatest connoisseur of human nature in the world could not predict with any degree of probability whether the promises of good behaviour, made in all good faith by the culprit in prison, would really be kept under the wholly different circumstances of freedom. Moreover, since it is a well-known fact that honest repentance is oftener found among great than among petty criminals, the absurd result of this proposition, even if it were practicable, would probably be the liberation of assassins and poisoners after a brief period of custody, and the maintenance of beggars and footpads all their lives in prison at the expense of society.

Finally, the deterrent theory of punishment accords with the reformatory theory in regarding punishment as a means rather than an end, however differently it may conceive the essential nature of punishment It agrees with the protective theory in maintaining that punishment exists not for the sake of the criminal, but for that of society The murderer is executed, the thief imprisoned, to set an example Aside from the fact, proved by statistics, that this result is not, as a rule, attained, since crimes tend rather to increase than to diminish in number and cruelty in proportion to the cruelty and publicity of executions, it is essentially absurd to attempt to influence by punishment a third person rather than the individual punished   The basis of this conception is apparently failure to discriminate between the existence of the legal order in general and the special cases of its application.   The fact that the State has penal power is, indeed, not to be underestimated in its importance for public morality   It is the most forcible means of making the individual realise that his will is subject to a social will, and this consciousness is a prerequisite to the efficacy of all the special moral motives   But such a realisation on the individual's part is quite independent of the manner in which the penal power is administered   It deters from crime, not because the latter as a particular act is met by a particular punishment, but because crime contravenes the conduct of life that is publicly sanctioned and operates in the individual conscience as the imperatives of constraint   When conscience has once been silenced the fear of punishment is powerless. Moreover, in accordance with the universal tendency of human nature to believe what it desires, almost every criminal beguiles himself into disregard of this consideration by confidently hoping to escape discovery.

### (e)   The Essential Nature of Punishment.

All these theories, some of them partial and one-sided, some of them wholly untenable, suffer from the same defect. They do not seek to derive their conception of punishment directly from the essential nature of crime, but instead introduce secondary or wholly irrelevant considerations   Crime is a revolt of the individual will against the social will, hence punishment is the natural reaction of the latter against this revolt.   It is a reaction that as such has a specific nature, and, while it is related to other conceptions like retribution and reformation, must not be identified with them   An

# 124 *Moral Motives* [535-6

individual may inflict retribution on other individuals: the individual will may work for its own reformation, or a single free personality for that of another. But punishment pre-supposes the subordination of the person punished to the power that punishes In the legal community of to-day, — and this constitutes its great advantage, an advantage not too dearly bought by the extreme individualism of the preceding centuries,—one individual will can never be subordinated to another. When it seems to be, the superior will really em-bodies an universal will Personal supremacy is exercised only by a master over his slave, or, at all events, over his villein, though even in the latter case the relationship is so far connected with the common family property that the dependence ceases to be purely personal Our modern view of law rejects the idea of subordinating one individual will to another, which involves a transference of the concep-tion of property into the sphere of free personality, as opposed to the fundamental notion involved in the concept of law. Hence it makes punishment exclusively the function of the social will Punishment may be inflicted by the father as the representative of the family, or by the teacher in the name of the educational community , the officer may punish the soldier and the civil official his subordinate in virtue of the authority assigned them by public law But as an individual personality I cannot punish anyone for the ill-treatment I have received , I can only revenge myself and retaliate The person who retaliates must be prepared for further retaliation on his victim's part , thus the ven-detta, which was a kind of retaliation of one individual on another representing an earlier stage of development than punishment in the true sense of the word, often resulted in a conflict long drawn out Punishment puts an end once for all to such conflicts · it is impossible to retaliate against the will that punishes And this is evidence enough that those who identify punishment and retaliation have, to say the least, failed to reach an adequate definition of punishment [1]

To express the general object of punishment, as a reaction of the social will upon the individual wills subordinated to it and in revolt against it, we may say that its significance is essentially disciplinary This expression implies more definitely than the word punishment itself the supremacy of the will that punishes. Discipline, however, involves two ideas closely akin to it even in language, namely, chastisement and education The object of punishment is to chastise, to inflict an evil on the rebellious subject, and thereby to bring his wrongdoing clearly before his mind. And its object is, further, to educate ; when there is any prospect of success, to produce a permanent alteration in the faulty will, and thereby to avoid similar wrongdoing in the future

Besides these ends, which relate chiefly to the individual punished, a broader purpose is involved in punishment. It must set at rest the general sentiment of law, which has been disturbed and rendered uneasy by the outrage committed. There must always be preserved a lively consciousness of the fact that crime is an evil which recoils upon the criminal himself Thus punishment gains the added significance of expiation It expiates crime, that is, it conciliates the disturbed consciousness of law. As expiation, however, it differs qualitatively from the expiated crime · the criminal is not punished because of the injuries he may

---

[1] The word punishment, however, is occasionally used in senses that do not coincide with the conception here discussed ; for instance, when we speak of 'the punishment of social convention.' But the jurists themselves recognise that this is merely a matter of laxity in usage The punishments of convention are obligations incurred by contract They are established beforehand with the agreement of those who eventually have to undergo them. Hence they lack one of the essential elements of punishment, namely, constraint

# 126 *Moral Motives* [536-7

have inflicted upon an individual. The case of crime is unlike that of private offences, for which the State, whose function here is simply that of the dispenser of universal justice, and which as such is the arbiter between conflicting individual wills, allows the individual to atone   Crime is a violation of public right, and the individual on whom it is committed is merely its accidental object   Thus private offences are atoned for by making good the injury received the *jus talionis* holds here so far as it can be applied   Crime, as an offence committed against the social will, can be expiated by nothing in any measure corresponding to its own nature, for the objects of crime and punishment are wholly different: the one is the violated social will, the other the offending individual will.   They agree only in their general nature as manifestations of will.   For this reason punishment cannot be made qualitatively like crime , but it may and must correspond to it in quantity.   The heavier the guilt, the heavier must be the punishment   This is the point where the ideas of punishment and of retribution agree   But even quantitatively the relation of crime and penalty must fall short of that absolute proportion which the retributive theory in its stricter interpretation postulates   In particular, there must always be a maximum and minimum of punishment, beyond which it cannot follow the various gradations of wrongdoing which may still be possible.[1] However, in any case, punishment has from the start a distinctive feature which the idea of retribution lacks.   In punishment, namely, the will that inflicts retribution is superior to that which suffers retribution, and, as the social

---

[1] Thus, when the adherents of the retributive theory object to the death penalty on the ground that it allows of no further gradations, the argument affects the retributive theory itself in its extreme form rather than the death penalty ; for the same thing is true of every maximal penalty, for instance, lifelong imprisonment.   The retributive theory would lead to the qualified death penalties of the older systems of deterrent punishment

## 537-8] *Immoral Motives* 127

will, is qualitatively different from it. For this reason punishment is not retribution at all : it is chastisement.

But punishment aims to influence not only the individual punished, but the general consciousness of right. This has been disturbed by the transgression, and it will be set at rest when it sees that the transgressing will has expiated its wrongdoing through the suffering it undergoes in turn. Again, while the idea of expiation corresponds in part to that of retribution, the two are not wholly identical For when we consider expiation in its essential nature, we find that it has both an active and a passive significance The individual may expiate a wrong action by voluntarily undergoing some evil which expresses his own inner wish that the wrong had not been done Or he may perform involuntary expiation, when the social will to which he is subordinated inflicts an evil on him, to make him feel that his wrongdoing was itself an evil, and repent of it as such. Now punishment is primarily this second kind of expiation, imposed on the guilty subject and passively received by him. But it may become active expiation, if the penalty inflicted arouses the consciousness of guilt with sufficient intensity to make the culprit regard the punishment he gets as deserved, or even welcome. Anyone who has sought out in the solitude of their cells those guilty of the graver crimes must acknowledge that while such cases are not the most frequent, they occur often enough to represent one object which punishment must always have in view. This is the only way in which it can become a means of discipline, in the sense of chastising in order to educate. One of its objects, and not the least important, must always be that which, according to the reformatory theory, is its exclusive end. But to attain this end we must not follow the extreme partisans of the reformatory theory, and confuse punishment indiscriminately with any of the other means

128                    *Moral Motives*                    [538-9

of education, such as instruction or information. Instruction as such is usually inapplicable to the cases where punishment is needed as an educative influence this is true even of education in the family, and it is still more true where the penal power of the State is concerned. Its reformatory effect on the criminal must always be regarded as merely one object among others to be attained by punishment; and if this object fails to be reached, by reason of the trifling nature of the offence or the incorrigible character of the offender, the punishment does not thereby become purposeless However true it may be that excessive cruelty in punishment is objectionable, even with reference to its subjective end, we must not overlook the fact that punishment as such exerts its reformatory influence only when it is felt as a merited expiation of wrongdoing, that is, as an evil Other humane efforts in the direction of instruction and moral exhortation may be combined with it, but they have nothing to do with punishment itself.

Punishment thus combines in its essence three elements, to which it owes its distinctive character the elements of chastisement, of expiation and of educational influence. The first of these is wholly involuntary; chastisement forces the individual will to bend to that social will against which it has revolted Expiation is also in the first instance involuntary, it is a kind of satisfaction which the culprit must render, against his will, to the general consciousness of right. It may, however, become voluntary where the offender regards the penalty inflicted on him as a suitable atonement for his action, and one that he himself desires to make. Where this is the case, the third end of punishment, its educational effect, is attained. This, finally, is wholly voluntary, it can never be brought about by constraint, but solely by a change in the inner disposition of the offender.

The conceptions of punishment prevalent in different ages

have not always involved all three of these elements, and this fact partly explains the variations to which its meaning is still subject The earliest of the three essential elements is that of chastisement · this is the direct outcome of the idea of revenge, transformed by a growing consciousness of the significance of the social will as the power that punishes The element of objective expiation comes next, then that of subjective expiation and of educational influence

K

[539-40

# CHAPTER IV.

## THE MORAL NORMS

### I THE GENFRAL SIGNIFICANCF AND CLASSIFICATION OF MORAL NORMS.

#### (a) Fundamental and Derivative Norms.

THE conception of a norm may be understood in a narrower and in a wider sense  In the latter instance, where it includes laws, rules and axioms, as well as norms in the stricter significance of the term, it means any principle which we make a postulate with reference to a given realm of facts  In its narrower sense, on the other hand, which is also its original sense, a norm is a precept of will.  It designates which one of various possible kinds of action ought to be preferred.  Now there are two sorts of voluntary activity which may be subjected to norms of this nature : theoretical activity, the activity of thought, and practical or moral activity.  Accordingly logic and ethics are the true normative sciences, and of these it is to ethics that the concept of a norm belongs in its original form, namely, that of a pure rule of will, which opposes an 'ought' to an 'is'[1]

If we take the conception of a norm in this general ethical significance, it further becomes necessary to distinguish fundamental and derivative norms ; the former being moral requirements that cannot be derived from any more general principles, and the latter such special precepts as result from the application of the fundamental norms to particular cases

[1] *Cf.* on this point the Introduction, pp. 7 ff

## 540-1] *General Significance and Classification* 131

under particular conditions. Hence the fundamental norm is an ethical axiom It has the same universality and necessity as an axiom Particular moral laws, on the other hand, are derivative norms. And just as all the theorems in a mathematical discipline refer back to axioms, so every special moral law owes its attestation to its agreement with the universal and fundamental norms of ethics.

It would be a mistake to conclude from this that the fundamental moral norms originated earlier in time than the special moral precepts Such an assertion would be as far wrong as the statement that those abstract theoretical principles which we call axioms were known before their particular applications Men used the logical laws of thought thousands of years before Aristotle propounded the principle of contradiction Acquaintance with special numerical formulas and geometrical principles was current long before anyone tried to demonstrate the axiomatic presuppositions on which they were based, and possibly we have not yet found the most rational formulation for all these presuppositions. It need not surprise us, then, that while in practical life the truth of certain moral precepts has long been agreed upon, an unsettled conflict should still be waging on the question of the correct formulation of the universal norms. The fact is that precepts like those of the Mosaic Decalogue cannot be called fundamental moral norms, in the sense in which we use the term, any more than the principle that $2 \times 2 = 4$ can be termed an axiom But if our fundamental norms are to be, not special moral precepts, but principles each one of which comprehends a whole class of precepts as particular instances, then the conflict of opinion on the general problems of ethics will inevitably betray itself in their formulation. In particular, their mode of statement will be affected by differences of opinion with regard to the nature of moral ends and motives; for it is the peculiar characteristic of the broadest

132                    *The Moral Norms*                    [541-2

moral principles that they do not tell us what the nature
of our acts must be, but rather what motives ought to guide
our conduct   An essential mark of the transition from the
concrete formulation of moral precepts to the more general
formulation of fundamental norms is the fact that while the
former usually leaves motives and ends wholly out of account,
their consideration is indispensable to the latter.  The Mosaic
precepts are a classic example of concrete laws   Evidently
where one stops short to a certain extent at the outer aspect
of actions, as the Mosaic commands do, one cannot reach
any fundamental principles   Thus the reference of actions
back to their motives and ends, in the investigation of ethical
norms, may be considered analogous to the reduction of
arithmetical operations and geometrical constructions already
performed to the elements of the number and space concepts,
in the discovery of mathematical axioms

### (b) Positive and Negative Norms.

Besides the considerations just discussed, which are the
general conditions under which all fundamental principles
must be established, a peculiar condition affects the investigation of moral norms.  The particular moral precepts from
which the norms are gradually derived through abstraction
are in their original formulation for the most part negative
rather than positive   for instance, " Thou shalt not kill ",
" Thou shalt not commit adultery", " Thou shalt not steal,"
etc.   The commands to keep the Sabbath holy and to
honour one's father and mother are the only real commands
in the whole Mosaic Decalogue , all the others are prohibitions   The immediate reason for this negative character
of moral precepts is to be found in their direct relation to
the human will   For they differ from all rules of a purely
theoretical nature in that their fulfilment is entrusted to a
power having free choice   Hence cautions against deviation

542-3] *General Significance and Classification* 133

from the norms are an immediate and practical necessity. It is only in logic, itself an ethics of thought, that a similar phenomenon appears; and logic displays it to a more limited extent Logic, like ethics, may formulate its precepts negatively, prohibiting combinations of ideas that are logically wrong And we find the original tendency to the prohibitive form showing itself in the noteworthy fact that even its earliest axiomatic formula, the law of contradiction, is a negative principle. Modern systems of logic are, of course, correct in making this principle subsequent to that of identity, which it presupposes

But the class of negative norms is much more important for ethics than for logic. And it is impossible not to see that the deeper reason for this lies in the fact that deviations from the norm assume far greater importance in the moral realm A logical error may mislead an individual or even a number of individuals for a longer or a shorter time, but as soon as the error is once discovered its effects are remedied On the other hand, an offence against moral laws leaves behind it far more serious results, often of such a nature that they can never be made good. It injures not only the person who commits it, but others, and in many cases the whole society to which the wrongdoer belongs The effort of the human mind after knowledge gets little help from the kind of thinking that is satisfied with avoiding logical errors, and for this reason we prefer the bold thinker who would rather err than' give up the search for truth to the too cautious sceptic who seeks to avoid the danger of mistake by a convenient ignorance In the moral realm, on the other hand, we think a good deal has been gained, if the graver errors have been shunned Here, too, the error once committed can hardly ever be remedied, as it can in the logical realm when it is once known to be an error, and the opposite tendency, the fatal impetus with which

134                    *The Moral Norms*                    [543

the wrong act leads to new transgressions and strengthens the inclination towards them, is in like measure increased

Moreover, the above considerations explain the important fact that those moral precepts which aim at the prevention of serious injuries to the moral life are made the special charge of the political community, and hence come to form an important element in the system of public law. Again, we can see why prohibitive injunctions should play a prominent part among particular legal norms, and why whole departments of law, criminal law especially, should consist, to-day as in the age of the Mosaic Decalogue, almost entirely of negative norms

Yet it would be rash to conclude that, because certain norms are given to us in a negative form, they have no positive significance    The fact of the case is rather that, just as the logical principle of contradiction is only the negative aspect of the law of identity, so, in ethics, to every positive norm there corresponds a negative norm, and *vice versâ*   The proclamation, " Thou shalt not kill," stands side by side with the injunction, " Thou shalt respect and guard thy neighbour's life."   Cases occur when choice between the positive and the negative form cannot be determined by any calculation, and hence may vary almost at will.   When a decided preference is given to the one or the other, it is because of the influence naturally exerted by the ultimate object of the norm upon its formulation.   In particular, the example just given illustrates the fact that morality and law divide between them, after a fashion, the two parallel norms   the positive norm belongs especially to the province of morality and the negative norm to that of law.   The reason for this is to be found in the character of the legal order as above indicated   True, law does not furnish us with a comprehensive summary of the contents of moral maxims, but it is the most powerful protective influence for the maintenance

543-4]  *General Significance and Classification*  135

and advancement of the moral life. Because it has this nature, its norms are always prohibitive, especially in those departments whose direct object is the protection of morals. The task of expressing the positive ends to be protected is assigned not to legal norms, but to certain moral norms. Even in such cases, however, the distinction is absolute only in the realm of law  Morality, including as it does the positive complement to every given negative norm in the sphere of law, does not thereby exclude the negative norms  Every prohibition decreed by law in the interests of the moral life is at the same time a moral prohibition. When a moral norm sets up a certain end as the object of endeavour, it *ipso facto* prohibits all acts tending to nullify or endanger that end. The moral norm always demands more than the legal norm does, and necessarily includes the fulfilment of the latter.

This brings us to another fact of importance with regard to the nature of ethical norms. As we have already seen, negative norms in the realm of law are sometimes found among the ultimate and first principles of the legal system. In criminal law, particularly, the few norms that can be expressed positively are all secondary, and most of them are auxiliary in their character. The exact opposite is true in the ethical realm  Here the negative character of a norm may be at once taken as a sign of its derivative nature, while the fundamental norms, which cannot be reduced to more primary principles, are always positive.

This difference between morality and law, again, is a necessary consequence of the fact that the ultimate ends of morality are positive, aiming at the production of new results, internal and external ; while the immediate function of law, by reason of its nature as a measure for the protection of certain goods and their defence against the dangers that threaten them, must be, at least in very many

# 136 *The Moral Norms* [544-5

cases, the establishment of norms to regulate the prevention of wrongdoing. The form of these norms, therefore, will be prohibitive or negative, in accordance with the prohibitive character of their end. Now the authority of negatives must always be relative rather than absolute. Hence the fact that law includes negative norms, which are irreducible to any more ultimate positive principles within the sphere of law itself, is merely an indication that such ultimate principles are to be found in another department, one which lies at the very foundation of the whole meaning of the legal order. And this department is that of morality.

The above distinction definitely fixes the relation of law to morality It indicates that fundamental norms, in the true sense of the term, belong to morality alone, not to law Where the latter aims at the realisation of moral ends, which is undoubtedly the case in by far the greater and most valuable part of its functions, legal norms may always be referred back to moral norms. But where law prescribes things that are morally indifferent, as we must allow that it does in certain particulars, then it is impossible to suppose the existence of fundamental norms moralising such particulars. We are dealing with arbitrary stipulations, somewhat like the conventions necessary in the exact sciences to bring about an understanding of the meaning of concepts, or to obtain the standards of measurement required for comparison of observations Where such prescriptions, in themselves external and indifferent, are essential to the furtherance of the moral ends of the community, as, for instance, in the case of certain delays in civil proceedings and the time limitations put on rights, the moral end they serve is only an indirect one. It is not the nature of the regulations in question, but the fact of their existence, that is in a certain sense deducible from the fundamental social norms of the moral life

545-6] *General Significance and Classification* 137

### (c) The Conflict of Norms.

That there is no legal norm without an exception is a well-known truth, and one confirmed by universal experience It may be applied to all the special moral precepts in whose fulfilment the sum of practical morality consists. The legal prescription, "Thou shalt not kill," yields to the call of a higher duty in the mind of the soldier on the battlefield or the officer charged with the execution of the death penalty. The moral law that requires us to respect our neighbour ceases to apply with reference to those who have lost by their disposition and conduct all claim to respect. The old moot question, whether it is ever necessary to lie, is answered affirmatively a thousand times in the practice of life, under the constraining influence of situations that offer us the alternative of sacrificing the more important to the less important moral precept, or *vice versâ* Although this fact, of course, does not justify us in putting mere convenience before truth.

No doubt such exceptions are rarer when we are dealing with norms of a more general character Yet the principle that norms are rules with exceptions holds good, within certain limits, even for the fundamental norms, unless one is satisfied with putting an empty formula in their place, instead of making them express, as they should do, the sum of the tendencies of the moral life. But the fundamental norms show clearly what is occasionally apparent in the more special moral precepts, namely, that the only ground which can justify such exceptions is a conflict between different norms This conflict, since it must always be decided in behalf of the more urgent and important norm, demands the infraction of the norm of less urgency and importance

The chief question that now confronts us is this How can

138        *The Moral Norms*        [546-7

such a system of laws with exceptions exist, unless the system itself is full of contradictions at the outset? While one may grant that subordinate moral precepts, dealing with the concrete conditions of life, are subject to the fluctuations of these conditions, no such variability can affect the fundamental norms of ethics. And it is an important test of the trustworthiness of moral principles that they shall form a whole wherein there are no contradictions Thus, as a matter of fact, we require that the ultimate presuppositions of all theoretical disciplines shall be internally coherent, this is especially the case with logic, the theoretical and normative science nearest akin to ethics.

However, these scruples may be met by the statement that we are not dealing with a contradiction between the fundamental principles themselves, but merely with the question of their applicability to special cases A moral fact may present certain features that would lead one to class it under a certain norm ; but further characteristics may render such a subsumption a mistake, and another and higher norm may take the place of the first. We are really as fully justified in holding that such instances are only apparent exceptions to the norm as we are in the case of those exceptions to natural laws which so often result from their crossing with other natural laws.[1]

But this kind of interpretation does not do away with an essential difference that undoubtedly exists between the two cases. Where a fundamental principle of logic or a law of nature is inapplicable, it is yet impossible that anything should result which is entirely opposed to the principle in question But this is just what happens in the case of a conflict of norms Hence we must recognise at the outset, as a characteristic feature of moral norms, that one of them

---

[1] *Cf.* my essay, *Ueber den Begriff des Gesetzes, etc.. Philosophische Studien,* iii , pp. 201 ff.

547-8] *General Significance and Classification* 139

may involve subordination and sometimes even disregard of another. This brings us to a further characteristic that is, as a matter of fact, peculiar to the moral realm, and is based on the relation existing between the various spheres of the moral life Not only is that relation one between different values, but it involves a difference in the content of ends For while there is harmony and agreement among the various departments of life so far as the ultimate end is concerned, divergence is possible with reference to transitory ends, and the will is confronted with a choice between ends of different values, the one agreeing and the other conflicting with a given class of norms Consequently an action no longer becomes moral by virtue of its conformity to any moral law, but only by its conformity to that law which belongs to the higher order of values.

But an important question arises here as to which of the two conflicting norms shall be regarded as the higher and worthier. Is the question to be decided in each case on its own merits, or is there a general principle that *a priori* removes the choice from the sphere of individual estimation ? Clearly, if the former is the true state of affairs, it means that ethics must abandon general principles If there are such principles, then the question of precedence among moral laws cannot possibly be left to the mere instinct of the practical conduct of life,—or at least only in the sense in which we usually trust natural tact and acquired habit to choose what subsequent reflection approves as proper in the given case

Now, as a matter of fact, the hierarchy of moral ends has already provided us with a principle that decides the values of different ends and settles the question of precedence in the event of their mutual conflict The hierarchy of moral ends we found to be that social ends were to be preferred to individual ends, and the ends of humanity to those of a

140 *The Moral Norms* [548-9

society Accordingly, the rule by which every conflict between norms is to be decided reads as follows:

'When norms of different orders contradict each other, that one is to be preferred which serves the larger end social ends come before individual ends, and humanitarian ends before social ends.'

If, however, we take the notions 'social' and 'humanitarian,' the latter especially, in that wider sense in which the history of manners and customs uses them, we shall misunderstand this rule, and arrive at conclusions that are in flat contradiction to its real meaning. The difference between custom and morality is nowhere more evident than just here.[1] Custom prepares the way for morality. It is replete with moral ideas, but they are for the most part undeveloped, or expressed in a form that merely gives a symbolic hint of their deeper moral purpose. In particular, the immediate objects even of the social and humanitarian ends prescribed by custom are often nothing but individual ends. the humanitarian idea behind them is indicated only by the way in which they are sought It is thus that the forms of social courtesy express respect for one's fellow-men, and beneficence shows a spirit of self-sacrifice for the sake of one's neighbour, irrespective of family and political ties Thus all forms of custom, even those which, like beneficence, are really moral in their nature, are mere hints of the fundamental social and humanitarian norms, not direct applications of them. When they do, in addition, correspond to certain moral norms, the latter always belong to a lower order of ends For instance, beneficence does reflect the idea of humanity, the duty of sacrificing the individual to mankind at large; but the beneficent act itself is an act of individual morality merely, having an individual for its object Hence, it must yield precedence to other and higher duties of a social or truly

[1] *Cf* above, Part I , chap iii , pp. 156-7 , 281-2.

549-50] *General Significance and Classification* 141

humanitarian character,—even, under some circumstances, to individual duties of superior worth Such men as St Nepomuk, who, the legend tells us, stole leather from the rich to make shoes for the poor, or the millionaire, a type occasionally met with even in our modern society, who founds orphanages and hospitals with the money he has made by fraud and treachery; are not obeying the law of the primacy of the wider norm On the contrary, they are sinning against the higher social law in order to satisfy the claims of a lower individual duty Thus we see that the rule giving precedence to the more comprehensive duty is not applicable to such individual actions, where certain indirect and reflex influences of the universal moral ends are manifested, but solely to the realisation of these ends themselves.

If we follow this principle, there can be no doubt that even the practical judgment, when confronted with a conflict of duties, will accept the hierarchy above defined as unconditionally decisive. In particular, we can trace in our whole system of law the increasing influence of the idea that social duties should take precedence of individual duties, and that among the various classes of the former, duties to the political community stand first Further than this, of course, the gradation of values as sanctioned by positive law does not go. It is left to the freedom of private judgment to balance social against humanitarian ends, but history finally gives its sanction, in these most difficult instances of moral choice, by recognising that actions which run counter to existing law and to the social morality that law protects are justified by reason of the higher ends which they accomplish.

There is a second point wherein the above principle may be questioned. It is not essentially necessary that the conflicting duties should belong to different orders of ends Under certain conditions a conflict may occur between ends of the same order. This is especially true of the

142 *The Moral Norms* [550

various social duties. For instance, the duty of an official to obey his superiors may conflict with the general duty of a citizen to exercise his franchise according to his best judgment, or to dissent from others in legislative assemblies, and the duty of a judge to decide according to law may conflict with the duty of exercising justice

While our principle is not directly applicable to such cases, it may yet be indirectly applied through the medium of the scale of values that it suggests. In general, those norms are to be preferred which express the more comprehensive duty, or whose effects reach into the wider field of duty  Thus the duties imposed on the individual by membership in societies and unions for the protection of special interests are inferior to his duties as a member of the community, and the latter are inferior to his duties as a citizen of the State  Where different legal prescriptions conflict, the more important one should decide the action, and the more important one is always that which protects the broader and more comprehensive right.

It need hardly be added that principles, such as those which we have been working out, regarding the preference of certain norms over others, can never do more than indicate the general direction in which we are to look for a solution of the conflict of duties in particular cases, and that they do not supersede special investigation of the conditions preceding each individual choice of duties  It is only by such investigation that a right application of the general maxims is ensured.  Free choice between different courses of action must always be a necessary element in the moral life.  The advantage of getting at fundamental moral principles is not that it does away with free choice, but that it guards it from the influence of accidental and varying impulse.

## (d) The Relation of Moral Norms to the Concepts of Duty and Virtue.

The task of discovering the fundamental norms or principles which contain in themselves all possible laws is not exactly facilitated by the practical tendency that belongs to ethics by reason of the nature of its subject-matter. The practical character of ethics is responsible for the fact that the propensity, usually peculiar to an earlier stage of reflection, towards substituting concrete applications for real principles, has lasted longer than would otherwise have been the case. It is significant in this connection, that no distinction, even in name, has commonly been made between subordinate and fundamental principles, both being termed indiscriminately "moral laws" The earliest attempts at investigation go so far as to disregard the imperative form of moral norms They simply include the various tendencies of the moral will under certain general concepts which are derived by abstraction from particular facts, and which, in consequence, are usually lacking either in definiteness or in the requisite logical connection with each other,—the latter being the especial defect of the concepts in their original form

There are two classes of concepts that have been successively used in the history of ethics as substitutes for norms in the proper sense of the word, namely, virtues and duties. They may be treated as conceptual embodiments of the facts of morality regarded from different points of view; though foreign elements are not wholly excluded. For example, the virtue-concepts treat the facts of morality from the point of view of motives, while the duty-concepts regard them from the standpoint of ends. It is thus evident that both classes of concepts will be dependent in great measure on the opportunities furnished by experience for the formation of ideas about the motives and ends of conduct. We

# 144 *The Moral Norms* [551-2

can see that it is one's view of the moral personality that determines the nature of the virtue-concepts; behind the ideas of courage, prudence, justice, etc, stand those of the brave, prudent or just man Concepts of duty, on the other hand, are formed under the influence of the objective facts of moral action. Unselfishness, benevolence, liberality and the like are general notions derived chiefly from individual actions displaying the characters in question This fact, moreover, explains why the virtue-concepts should predominate in the earlier stages of ethical theory, while those of duties are added or substituted later Science here reflects the actual development of the power of conceptual thought In the realm of ethics, the individual personality leads to the formation of concepts much earlier than the character of actions does [1]

The fact that moralists were so long satisfied with classing moral facts under concepts that laid too exclusive and partial stress either on the motive or on the end of action is connected with the fact that these concepts were inaccurately defined and limited; and this vagueness, in turn, was due to their mode of origin. The ideas of the virtues are not wholly without relation to an end, nor are those of duties unrelated to the motives of conduct. the element lacking to each class of concepts is tacitly supplied in thought Moreover, of the two, the duty-concepts are proved to belong to the higher stage of development, because they indicate clearly not only the end to be sought, but the norm to be followed. Indeed, their relation to the norm is their most salient feature in the present state of ethical theory, as is shown by the sharper distinction now drawn between the theory of virtue, that of goods, and that of duties, a distinction that came into vogue with Schleiermacher Thus, the idea of duty is really the pure conceptual

[1] *Cf.* above, Part I., chap. 1, pp. 31-33.

## 552-3] *General Significance and Classification* 145

embodiment of the norm, while the end is distinguished from it under the separate designation of the moral good Further, 'duty' and 'norm' have become transformed into ethical concepts, whose relation is like that existing in the realm of law between legal ideas and the legal principles whence those ideas are derived In fact, the analogy holds still further, in that the norms are undoubtedly prior to the duty-concepts The only influences that operate directly on our moral conduct are the commands and prohibitions that guide the will under the guise of the various imperatives of conscience But the analogy fails, on the other hand, when we remember that the priority of the principles of law with reference to the concepts derived from them is external as well as internal The principles exist ready-made in the legal norms or in the laws of common usage, while the derivation of the concepts from the principles is a purely scientific task that has to be accomplished later. The priority of moral norms, on the other hand, is for the most part purely internal. It is only in the rare cases when, as, for instance, in the Mosaic Decalogue, certain moral precepts assume the form of laws, that the norm appears as both externally and internally prior As a rule, however, where the task of translating the inner command into an outward form has been left to science, the stage of the norm has been dropped out The method adopted has been purely descriptive, embracing certain fundamental characteristics of the moral personality in the concepts of the various virtues, and, later, certain facts of moral action in the concepts of duties The search for the original norms comes as the final stage of the investigation. Not until the time of Kant and his theory of the moral imperative does ethics really enter on this last stage

It is not only because the tracing of derivative concepts to their sources is always essential, that the discovery of the

L

146 *The Moral Norms* [553-4

moral norms is so necessary. It is because this is the most direct way of distinguishing the chief tendencies of moral action, and because the relation between the fundamental norms and their subordinate moral precepts can be made out more clearly in the norms themselves than in the derived concepts As a matter of fact, the customary mode of schematising the concepts of duties is highly unsatisfactory in this respect, and the case of the virtue-concepts is even worse For the former, a division of the various spheres of duty was so obviously indicated that it could not be overlooked. As for the virtue-concepts, on the other hand, an acceptance of the enumerations and divisions furnished by language was fortunately suggested by the example of Aristotle But the idea of making a distinction of values to correspond with the relation between fundamental and derivative norms, though in itself right enough, led to a perfectly arbitrary system of ranking the virtues. The so-called cardinal virtues of various moralists are indeed significant of the general ethical tendencies of their authors ; but they have, as a rule, no logical ground of division whatever, and in many cases lose sight of the essential distinction between general and particular These defects are closely connected with the nature of the virtue-concepts themselves. They are ideas of properties. Hence the conceptual determination of moral principles by their means is attended by two evils First, since it is the moral personality having the properties in question that is always in the moralist's mind, he is apt to make no distinction between the general and the particular ; sometimes he even neglects to separate the worthier from the less worthy attributes Secondly, the necessary result of such a system of property concepts, which refer wholly to external appearances, is that little regard is paid to the inner motives of morality and none whatever to the ends. Courage, veracity, prudence and the

554-5] *General Significance and Classification* 147

like are qualities that may be exercised from different causes and for the most various ends, occasionally even for those of an immoral character.

A tendency opposite in nature to this splitting up of morality into a number of disconnected virtues has often been displayed in modern ethics, since the introduction of the norm idea, namely, the tendency to establish one single norm as the sole decisive and fundamental one. Sometimes it is the idea of a particular end that is thus employed, as, for instance, the principle of utility, sometimes the moral imperative is comprehended in a particular prescriptive formula, after the manner of Kant and Fichte. Now we are perfectly right in demanding that all the special ethical norms shall be brought into a coherent whole and arranged according to a definite rule But if we try to force the most widely different spheres of moral life into the formula of a single imperative whose universality necessarily deprives it of all content, we do violence to the complexity of real life As a matter of fact, a plurality of norms is required by the very postulate that the norms must take into consideration both the motives and the ends of morality, for these latter cannot be reduced to a single motive or a single end ; so we must maintain their internal coherence, in the sense that no important motive and no one of the principal ends can be thought away without disturbing the security of the others This kind of coherence, however, is nowise different from that which exists among the various axioms of logic or the separate hypotheses of mathematical disciplines.

Another likeness between ethical norms and theoretical postulates is that in both cases the laws may be comprehended in simple concepts. We can transform the logical axiom of identity into the concept of self-identity, or the universal law of cause and effect into the concept of causality. And in the same way we may derive from the moral

148 *The Moral Norms* [555-6

precept, "Thou shalt respect thyself," a concept of self-respect. The ethical concepts thus obtained are no other than the duty-concepts There are just as many fundamental duty-concepts as there are moral norms When the practice of duty is thought of as a permanent characteristic, it becomes a virtue. Thus the fundamental virtue - concepts corresponding to the fundamental moral norms are identical in their essential features with the duty-concepts. The only thing that distinguishes them is the secondary circumstance that duty is concerned with immediate obedience to the norm, resulting from an inner decision and expressed in an outward action, while virtue is the habitual tendency of the moral personality to follow the norm Thus we may speak of the virtue as well as of the duty of self-respect. In virtue, duty becomes a living reality it has passed over from its objective aspect into the thought and action of an individual personality And this explains the fact that the concept of duty is more closely related to the objective end, while that of virtue has more bearing on the subjective motive of conduct.

But it is only in the case of the fundamental norms and their corresponding duty- and virtue-concepts that the agreement of meaning between norm, duty and virtue is so complete. Where the notions of duties and virtues are more closely adapted to the special conditions and phenomena of the moral life, their development is of necessity more independent. Hence those concepts which lay especial emphasis on the attainment of particular moral ends by means of certain actions come to have the specific character of duty-concepts, while those which take more account of the permanent conduct of life as a whole acquire the significance of virtue-concepts Thus we speak of the duty of self-sacrifice for one's country, and of the virtue of courage The former is not a characteristic that can be continually shown in our behaviour, but a difficult and hence

556]  *General Significance and Classification*  149

an unusual task, which many people may never be called on to perform. Courage, on the other hand, is a quality that may be exercised in the most various situations of life  It therefore marks a permanent trait of the moral character

All this is evidence of the primary character of the norm and the comparatively secondary character of the duty and virtue concepts  The increasing separation of the latter that goes along with this transfer to concrete facts and characteristics indicates very clearly the mode of their development, along divergent lines, from the original norm concept.  The defect of the older systems of ethics was not that they established the conceptions of duties and virtues,—such conceptions are in themselves just as necessary to ethics as the ideas of quantity are to mathematics,—but that they made these conceptions primary  whereas the more fundamental elements are the moral norms, which exist in concrete reality under the form of special moral precepts and maxims, the fundamental norms being derived from these by abstraction  The science of ethics, instead of choosing this direct method of abstraction, took a roundabout road, towards which it was urged by the processes of conceptual thought that had already begun in the speech of everyday life  Its attention was thus directed towards concrete moral qualities and actions earlier than towards the general laws upon which these concrete facts depend.  The virtue-concepts, which should in a systematic treatment of the subject come after the duty-concepts, were earlier developed ; and the latter, in turn, were made to precede the norms from which they take their origin

150 *The Moral Norms* [556-7

### (e) *The General Classification of Moral Norms.*

The method of classifying the moral norms will naturally be in accordance with the various spheres of life to which they relate, that is, will correspond to the various ends involved The first and most restricted of these spheres is that of the moral subject himself. Next, and occupying an intermediate position, comes the social circle, as defined in family life, in the life of professional associations and social organisations, and, above all, in political life Finally, the most comprehensive sphere of all is the community of universal intellectual interests, embracing all humanity, past and present Making our division in accordance with the three principal forms of moral ends, then, we shall distinguish individual, social and humanitarian norms. Moreover, this classification corresponds, in part if not wholly, with our division of motives. For the individual and social norms function more especially in the realm of the motives of perception and of the understanding, while the humanitarian ends always presuppose the activity of reason.

Further, in each of these three departments we may distinguish a subjective and an objective norm, with its corresponding subjective and objective virtue and duty concepts The subjective norm relates to the motive or disposition, the objective norm to the end, or the action itself Again, to every norm there correspond a duty and a right. The duty is directly expressed in the imperative form of the positive norm itself; the right, on the other hand, is more restricted in its application No man can claim from others as a right, without further ceremony, that which he himself feels to be his duty towards them Such a principle of reciprocity would seriously affect the spontaneity of moral action. It would, by making the fulfilment of duty dependent on external conditions, do away

557-8] *General Significance and Classification* 151

with one of the most essential characteristics of the fundamental norms, namely, their absolutely unconditional validity —unconditional, that is, save for such apparent exceptions as are necessitated by the conflict of norms. The sphere of moral rights is thus narrower than that of moral duties Right is not a correlate of duty in the sense that what is done as a duty is at the same time a right, but in the sense that the unhindered exercise of duty may be demanded as a right Hence duty relates to the subjective constraint of moral norms, and right to objective freedom in the following of the norm. The former, again, is based on free self-determination , the latter on the possibility that hindrances to such self-determination will arise as a result of the volitional activity of other free subjects

For this reason moral norms are purely subjective in their character. Everyone ought to follow them, but no one can be constrained to do so. Legal norms, on the other hand, form a system of objective precepts ; and they must of necessity use constraint as the means of establishing their validity The special formulation given to the legal norms may vary according to the historical conditions of their origin. But owing to their objective character, and to the fact that force may be used when necessary in their execution,—characteristics which distinguish them from the moral norms,—they are sometimes inadequate to the moral function assigned them, and sometimes exceed it, by reason of the tendency that constraint always has to extend the sphere of its power. But it is the fundamental character of law to ensure to every subject who recognises it the use of his freedom And since the moral norms are the rules that govern men in the exercise of freedom, the rules of law thus derive an ethical significance The peculiar relation existing between duty and right in consequence of this essential difference in the extension of the concepts requires that we

152    *The Moral Norms*    [558-9

should follow our discussion of the various classes of moral norms, which, as such, may be termed norms of duty, with a special consideration of legal norms or norms of right

### 2. INDIVIDUAL NORMS

The subjective duty that each individual owes to himself is self-respect.   It involves the following norm

'Think and act in such a way as never to lose respect for thyself.'

Thus conceived, self-respect is not only a virtue, but a condition on which all the other virtues depend   Its opposite is meanness, a quality that is in itself a subjective disposition ; though, like self-respect, it is reflected in the whole outward behaviour of the individual.   The source of meanness is lack of self-respect.   The antithesis between the two, however, is complete only where there exists in addition a spirit of self-seeking, guided by low motives,—which is, indeed, almost inevitably the case.

The individual's objective duty to himself is fidelity,— an unconditional adherence to the task he has set himself The following norm corresponds to the virtue of fidelity to duty

'Fulfil the duties to thyself and to others, which thou hast undertaken'

The opposite quality is forgetfulness of duty   This, again, is not a purely negative characteristic   Where the sense of duty is lacking, the direct outcome is merely a kind of reluctance to assume duties, usually the peculiar trait of lazy natures   But, as before, when egoistic tendencies get the upper hand, reluctance to undertake duties develops into a disposition not reluctant to forget the duty actually undertaken

The two individual norms here posited are the comple-

## 559-60]  *Individual Norms*  153

ments of each other. They are related as disposition to action. All attempts to discover further norms in either direction lead merely to further specialisation of those above stated, that is, to a more detailed consideration of either the various motives on which self-respect may be based, or the special duties to which we should adhere. And specialisation of this kind always takes us into the field of social and humanitarian norms. Thus we see that all other kinds of moral behaviour have their roots in the individual virtues of self-respect and fidelity to duty, just as their opposites, meanness and carelessness of duty, contain the germs of all vices

This brings us to a further characteristic of the individual norms. It is easy to see that they leave the content of moral duties wholly undefined. We do not learn either upon what qualities self-respect is based, or to what kind of obligations towards ourselves and others we should be faithful. The concepts of morality are really presupposed here ; and the norms themselves involve simply the formal prescription that these concepts should always be sustained in the individual's disposition and outward mode of life. The formal character of the individual norms, however, cannot surprise us when we recall the peculiar self-elimination of the ideas of individual moral ends,—a process whose result was the conviction that the individual cannot be his own moral end Now there is another fact which is the direct antithesis of this, namely, that all the moral motives refer back to the individual consciousness , for perception, understanding and reason, the three sources of moral grounds of action, are properties of that consciousness Evidently the necessary result of this reciprocal relation is that while moral norms are commands which hold good for the individual only, their content can never relate to the individual. It must always refer to those wider spheres of life wherein the individual is a moral unit.

154                    *The Moral Norms*                [560–1

### 3  SOCIAL NORMS.

The objects of social norms are the fellow-beings environing the subject, together with the ends for which they strive, singly or in common.  The whole, to which conduct directed upon the furtherance of these ends is related, is society with its various divisions, such as the family, the community, the State, professional and other associations

The subjective virtue or disposition which forms the basis of all objective social virtues and moral activities is love for one's neighbour.   And the corresponding norm is .

'Respect thy neighbour as thyself.'

The opposite of love for one's neighbour is self-love, which subordinates the welfare of others to that of self.

The objective virtue here has a far wider sphere than that of its subjective complement, since its reference is not merely to the individual, but to the totality of all those belonging to the same social community.   It is the virtue of public spirit , the undertaking and faithful performance of such duties as are imposed on the individual by the family, the State and other social relationships.   Hence the norm of public spirit is as follows :

'Serve the community to which thou belongest'

The opposite of public spirit is self-interest, which subordinates the interest of the whole to that of the individual, thereby regarding the community not as an end in itself, but as a means to individual ends.   Evidently the difference in comprehensiveness that exists between public spirit and love of one's neighbour does not hold between self-love and self-interest   Here, both subjectively and objectively, the self is the central point of all sentiments and endeavours.   Love of one's neighbour, on the other hand, as objectively exercised, is of moral worth only when it is not merely individual, but takes for its object our fellow-man as such

561]                    *Social Norms*                    155

aside from the special personal relations that make him an object of emotion. Thus the narrow sort of love for one's neighbour, which is summed up in consideration for and furtherance of the interests of our friends, relatives, or those who are bound to us by sharing in the same narrower interests, is nothing but extended egoism  Like the self-interest of a community, it leads only too often to the sacrifice of wider ends for the sake of individual, or at least of more restricted ends.  But it is a fact characteristic of the relation between motive and end that the subjective virtues are more limited in their scope, and have more of a personal tendency than the objective virtues  Real public spirit can never exist without true love of one's neighbour  But there is always about the latter a tinge of that individual emotion which binds a man, not to any or all of his fellow-men, but to some one in particular, with whom he is brought into touch through fulfilment of a common duty, through identical interests, human sympathy, or mere chance  It is only in the practical exercise of public spirit that the fulfilment of duty is freed from the personal tone of subjective feeling.  Love of country, in particular, is love of one's neighbour generalised through the reaction upon it of public spirit.  Yet even love of country tends, in the individual instance, to translate itself into feelings of a personal sort  What would become of it, if we were to eliminate the influence of all the ties that bind us to our associates, to those who speak the same language, enjoy the same intellectual advantages and the same memories with ourselves?  But here, again, the objective end transcends the subjective motive, and through its influence the feeling that serves as motive gains an intensity that is not to be explained as a result of any sum of personal feelings

In consequence, however, of these facts, there may easily be a certain lack of congruity between the demands of subjective and objective duty in the case of the social norms.

# 156 *The Moral Norms* [561-2

The virtues of neighbourly love do not always seem to harmonise with those of public spirit While the former are the virtues of weaker and more feminine natures, we are apt to think of the stronger and more masculine characters as the guardians of public spirit The statesman, whose public activity is inspired by the purest patriotism, may ruthlessly sacrifice individual to universal ends, and is seldom disposed to play the Good Samaritan. The solution of this apparent antithesis is to be found in the fact that in the subjective norm the motive is given especial prominence, while in the objective norm it is the end that is the important thing If the end has, through the conscious recognition of moral ends, gained the force of a motive, then the original motive may be the more readily subordinated for the time being It is not wholly destroyed, but suppressed in order to be more fully exercised Public spirit must sometimes disregard the immediate promptings of love for one's fellow-men, precisely because it is mindful of love's duties But in thus directing itself towards ends that transcend the immediate social motives, the virtue of public spirit tends towards the fulfilment of those supreme laws which have as their ultimate object the psychical community of mankind, free from the limitations of time and space.

### 4 HUMANITARIAN NORMS

The germ of the broadly human virtues is to be found in the virtues of individual and social life, for the individual and society are factors of different orders, which co-operate in the moral development of humanity. This is especially true of the higher manifestations of fidelity to duty and of public spirit, which always transcend the immediate sphere of duty to which they belong, and become humanitarian virtues. They can neither be explained nor justified, save as

562-3]        *Humanitarian Norms*        157

efforts to perform a task whose worth is infinite in comparison with that of the individual existence  Every act of faithfulness to duty, of neighbourly love, or of public spirit, that involves the conscious self-sacrifice of an individual or of a community united for the fulfilment of duty, far transcends the limits of the immediate conditions, individual and social, under which it is performed  The moral subject himself feels, under such circumstances, that in performing the finite duty he is sharing in an infinite task, compared with which individual interests, and even social interests of the narrow sort, are as nothing

Hence the subjective virtue corresponding to this consciousness of an infinite moral task is humility, and its norm is

'Feel thyself to be an instrument in the service of the moral ideal'

Any other kind of humility is a false virtue.  The objective virtue corresponding to this sentiment is self-sacrifice, which combines the highest degrees of fidelity to duty and surrender of self, since it involves the complete absorption of the moral subject in the ideal task set before him ; an absolute spending of self in the duty undertaken, which is the prerequisite condition of all great moral achievements  The norm of self-sacrifice is thus :

'Sacrifice thyself for that end which thou hast recognised to be thine ideal task'

The opposites of humility and self-sacrifice are arrogance and self-seeking  They deny the existence of the ideal, the one in the disposition of the agent, the other in the end sought  On the other hand, since the highest moral functions are the rarest and the hardest of all, we can see why disobedience to the norms of humanity should be held less injurious to individual morality than offences against the social norms  And yet it not infrequently happens that

## 158 *The Moral Norms* [563-4]

a single instant, in critical situations, lifts even the weak nature above the sphere of its ordinary interests, and renders it capable of moral achievements beyond the comprehension of its own calmer judgment. It is just here that the enormous value of inspiration lies, in the fact that it does away with the limits of individual existence, impelling the individual to acts that make him feel himself to be a mere instrument in the hands of an infinite power, to whose will he renders up his own

When we were discussing the individual norms, our attention was drawn to the fact that their character is purely formal, because the content of individual duties transcends the horizon of the individual himself. This is not the case with the humanitarian ends, since, on the contrary, they are the ultimate goal of all other ends. However, the notion of the ideal and the mode of its origin forbid us, as has been already observed in the case of the moral ends, to regard that ideal as something given. It is rather propounded as a problem. Thus the humanitarian norms, which represent the conception of the ideal in its practical applications, merely indicate the direction that we must follow in performing moral duties The special content of the action must be left to the influence of the developmental conditions governing every single moral act in the infinite course of the moral life It is, however, allowable to think of the ideal itself as unchangeable, in order that we may have a supreme regulative idea But our conceptions of it, which are all that is given to us, and hence all that can influence us, are subject to ceaseless development. This process of development is the ultimate moral end conceivable by our minds, the final outcome of all individual ends such is the postulate involved in the various historical modes of formulating the ideal problems of ethics Hence such problems are always relative ideals They represent something

## Humanitarian Norms

more perfect than the existing state of things, but never absolute perfection. Their comparative value is, however, sufficient to transform them into motive powers that must finally prevail, despite all disturbances and fluctuations in the ebb and flow of moral life If we were not sure of their final victory, moral endeavour would have no object, either ultimate or proximate, and the moral world would be transformed from a reality into the greatest of all illusions

A certain affinity thus exists between the ideal of ethics and the fundamental hypotheses of mathematical science They are not facts immediately demonstrable in experience, but postulates upon which we find it necessary to base our experience in order to make its coherence thinkable But how inferior in importance the theoretical postulate appears in comparison with the ethical ideal! If we were to abolish the former, while our desire for a coherent conception of the phenomenal world would, indeed, remain for ever unsatisfied, the world of our will, the moral world, would persist in undiminished reality. If, on the other hand, the moral ideal were done away with, each individual end would be a passing illusion, and the history of the world a disjointed comedy, forgotten as soon as the curtain falls Take away the moral ideal, and what would all our theoretical knowledges avail, however deep and broad, save to satisfy an idle curiosity, which sinks back into nothingness together with the ephemeral need it serves,—into that nothingness where the restless will itself, after exhausting its own being in the endeavour after imaginary ends, at length finds repose ?

160                    *The Moral Norms*                    [565-6

### 5. LEGAL NORMS

*(a) The Natural Law Theory and the Historical Theory
of Law*

We have already discussed, in our study of the general forms of society, the origin of the legal order as one of the most important facts of the moral life.[1] Like all the products of psychical culture, it is subject to the law of endless development. In the earliest conceptions of law we find the merest germs of our present ideas on the subject ; and in its further evolution, law, like every other intellectual creation, is affected by national tendencies and historical events. Even social, political and philosophical theories have not been without their influence on this development, since widely diffused subjective views react to a certain extent on objective relations.

In addition, there are special difficulties presented by the gradual separation of law from the kindred spheres of custom and morality, and by its dependence on the will of the State, which is not seldom influenced by heterogeneous motives.

Thus the questions as to the essential nature of the legal norms, regarded from the fundamental position which we have reached in ethical theory, and their relation to moral norms, cannot be answered, after the fashion of the old natural right theories, by deducing from the nature of man certain fundamental rights which are independent of all temporal and other conditions Nor is it possible merely to refer to the development of the structure of law, which is what the extreme historical theories do, instead of giving a real answer Man *in abstracto*, as assumed by philosophies of law, has never actually existed at any point in time or space. Law, like all psychical creations, and like the moral life in particular, is not invariable . it has been and will for ever

[1] *Cf.* Part I , chap. iii., pp. 264–6.

# Legal Norms

continue to be in a process of becoming. Certain legal norms may have come to be permanent acquisitions to moral culture at an early stage of this process of development; others may seem, to a more refined theory of law, inalienable possessions at least Yet not only are the more immediate conditions affecting the validity of such relatively permanent principles variable in character, but, what is more important, law itself would lose a part of its most essential groundwork, if it were restricted to such elements as were not expected to change A department of law that is in the highest degree important for ethics relates to the constitution and administration of the State And who at the present time would be willing to undertake the construction of a State that should represent the highest ideal of universal humanity, even for any attainable point in the future; not to mention one that should be valid for all ages and races? Do not the relations of capital and income, of labour and exchange vary, and with them men's views on the most fundamental relationships of private rights? Thus we see that law is as variable as man himself; and the attempt to include it in an abstract and absolutely valid system has about as much chance of success as the attempt to introduce an universal language Efforts of this sort vacillate ineffectually between an appeal to the few norms that have real permanence, such as, for instance, those of penal law; and arbitrary selections from some real or imaginary system of positive law.

While ethics gets little help from the theory of law that seeks to derive the whole content of the legal order from some conception of the nature of human personality, neither can it rest satisfied, when the question as to the relation of law to the moral norms is raised, with a general reference to the actual development of the legal order Rather it has to ask whether a certain regularity cannot be traced

162        *The Moral Norms*        [566 7

in this steady couise of development, a regularity that must be conceived as the really permanent element in morals, as that which persists through all changes in the content of particular principles. The fact is that just as the moral ends, while their details may vary in accordance with inner and outer conditions, yet ultimately point to ideal moral purposes which are themselves unchangeable, though our knowledge of them depends on the stage of moral development we have reached, so the changing conceptions of law may be regarded as the special forms assumed, in consequence of the existing state of moral and social cultivation, by the thought of law as it develops according to inviolable principles.[1]

In all these respects the case of law is similar to that of morality itself, the two are here, as elsewhere, directly connected. The only universal moral norms that ethics can reach are such as indicate, from the point of view of existing

---

[1] The view here expressed is somewhat akin to Lorenz von Stein's conception of the relation between law, the State and society (*System d' Staatswissenschaft*, II., *Gesellschaftslehre*, 1 *Abth.*, pp. 51 ff.) Stein contrasts with pure law, which he regards as the object of the philosophy of law, positive law, as the object of science He derives the former from the nature of personality, and makes it identical for all individuals and all times, though as a result of the constantly varying conditions of society it can never be made actual in this form, but is transformed under the influence of these conditions into positive law, involved in a continuous process of historical development Stein thus differs from the natural law theorists in expressly recognising the fact that abstract philosophical law or right can never be applied to reality His theory, however, resembles theirs in two respects First, he bases pure law exclusively on the free personality, which he assumes as existing prior to all historical conditions, while society, on the contrary, he regards as being wholly an affair of history In the second place, he removes pure law entirely from the flux of intellectual and moral development, making it an unchangeable object of abstract theory Against the former of these positions it may be urged, I think, that society is just as indispensable a condition of the existence of law as is the individual moral personality, and that the latter in its ends is just as much subject to the flux of historical development as the former. Against the second it may be objected that, because of this unceasing flux of moral development, we have in the case of law, as elsewhere, not a concept identical at all stages of development, but merely an ideal conceived from the point of view of the existing stage.

## Legal Norms

moral conceptions, the road towards the realisation of those ends which lie in the direction of the moral ideal, itself never to be attained  And so no legal principles can do more than furnish, whether directly or by implication, a broad outline of those more external ends which are necessary for the protection of society, and which express the conception of law conforming to the existing conception of morality. The priority of the philosophical norm of law, with reference to the positive norm, consists chiefly in the fact that it introduces into law moral postulates, which actual law, on account of the inhibitive influences that every process of historical development must encounter, has not as yet succeeded in expressing. The philosophy of law thus opens the way for its science and practice. Only, of course, we must not understand by philosophy the natural law of the schools, cramped by dogmatic prejudices. What is meant is rather that philosophical consciousness of law which lives in the science of law itself, and whose stimulus is drawn in the first instance from the motives of practical morality, and secondarily from the development of law as it has thus far progressed.

From this intimate connection of law with ethics, which, though sometimes frankly explicit, is often unconscious, we may infer that theories about the significance and basis of law are usually direct reflections of the corresponding ethical theories  The older conception of law, which still numbers many adherents among juristic savants, by reason of the conservative character which legal science owes to certain well-known historical conditions, was thoroughly individualistic in its point of view. In this respect it is a faithful mirror of the individualistic ethics. Where the latter makes the moral end the happiness of the individual, the former makes the end of law the protection of the individual. It is quite possible that these allied

# 164    *The Moral Norms*    [568-9]

tendencies in ethics and the theory of law may have reacted to strengthen each other, especially since they are in themselves concomitant expressions of one and the same theory of life. We find in our modern economic theories, with their principle of absolute individual autonomy, regulated only by the conditions necessary for the protection of all individual interests, a third embodiment of this theory of life, and one which is the most important of all for practical ethics. Not only has man's natural and, within limits, justifiable endeavour to secure his own freedom tended to support these views, but their logical clearness and simplicity have won them the approval of juristic and economic theorists Indeed, so much stress was laid on the logical advantages of the theory that its adherents required the practice of life to be ordered in accordance with its logical postulates,—one of the most striking examples that history has to show of the influence of theory on life

It is true that the science of law, whose association with history and tradition has always been closer than that of the constructions of political economy, has rarely attempted to carry its individualistic theory into the practice of public law The revolutionary political theories of the last century, which made this attempt in all seriousness, have served as deterrent examples. For the most part, one of two courses has been adopted. Public law has been left out of account altogether, as having nothing to do with the conception of law in general, which was derived solely from the comparatively unchanging relationships of private intercourse, together with those norms regarding the protection of persons and property which are indispensable adjuncts to such intercourse Or else the adherents of the theory have rested content with expounding the relations of political law by means of analogies drawn from private rights For instance, we find the unity of the State compared, quite in the spirit

## Legal Norms

of the old contract theory, with that of a private corporation; the management of the State's finances with that of an association's treasury, the State itself with a stock company or other "legal person," and the like

After what has already been said, no detailed proof of the untenable character of this purely individualistic view is necessary It cannot help involving itself in contradictions, for it must needs ascribe to the governmental authority powers that far exceed those necessary for individual protection And in thus defining the limits of public law, as well as in formulating the norms of private law, a certain influence is ascribed to historical tradition, whose tendency is wholly counter to the general postulate of equality of rights Just as the system of free individual competition, maintained by abstract economical theory, leads to individual monopolies, so in the case of private rights the theory of inherited rights or, as the enormous influence of inheritance on property relationships almost justifies us in calling them, innate rights, leads to actual inequality of individual rights, an inequality that contrasts most forcibly with the formal equality required by the theory Whatever meaning we assign to the latter, clearly we cannot make it a shield and cloak for the grossest inequality If the truth were really what individualistic ethics and the abstract theory of private rights assumes it to be, namely, that all law exists for the sake of the individual; if there were ultimately no rights but individual rights, and if social rights existed only so far as they were necessary to protect individual rights; then there would have to be a real equality corresponding to the formal equality But since real equality can be brought about only by governmental constraint, which would make the freedom postulated by the concept of right wholly illusory, the individualistic theory is again wrecked on its own consequences As Bentham postulated communism

166                    *The Moral Norms*                    [570-1

for the sake of principle, and later rejected it because of its injurious results, so the individualistic theory of law, in order to get rid of that omnipotence of the State which is the prerequisite condition of a real equality of rights, has to be satisfied with approximate equality of rights in a fraction of the members of the legal community Such are the absurd consequences of a theory that regards human society as a sum of completely isolated individuals, who are brought into mutual relations merely by external accidents, and whose moral function must thus be restricted to living, enjoying life where the conditions are favourable, and finally dying to make room for others

The broader conception of social life and historical relations that began to be current in later times necessarily influenced the conception of law as well. The schools of Hegel and Krause, with their doctrines of the philosophy of law, produced a considerable effect in this regard Hegel, especially, contributed more than nowadays he is ordinarily credited with towards placing the subject of public law in the forefront of interest. On the other hand, of course, his confusion of the legal with the moral and the historical was scarcely calculated to perfect the clearness of the conceptions Law and morality were similarly identified by Krause. But Herbart's derivation of law from "the aversion to strife" is a complete relapse into individualism At bottom it was simply the *bellum omnium contra omnes* of Thomas Hobbes, in a new form. This conception wholly fails of application to the most important department of law, namely, public law

But as this department of law, with its positive social problems, has come into prominence through the increasing activity of public life in modern times and the increasing claims of the State on individual functions, a twofold need has arisen On the one hand, the concept of law must be

[571-2] *Legal Norms* 167

made broad enough to include all these forms, and, on the other hand, it must be defined with sufficient precision and assigned its proper place in the general sphere of social and ethical concepts  There have been two attempts, in particular, to supply this need.  While both of them assert the most intimate connection between law and morality, they seek to establish certain marks of difference between the two  The theories are further distinguished by the fact that the one of them tries to define these characteristic marks negatively, the other positively  Law is marked off from morality negatively, when it is defined as that social ordinance whose end is the defence of society, as a moral community, against immorality.  On the other hand, it is distinguished positively, when certain parts of the totality of moral goods are singled out and designated as especially to be protected by law.  By reason of the great number of such goods, this selection, again, can be made only by including them in a collective idea, or by discovering a secondary mark whereby they may be known  Such a collective idea, for instance, is that of "the sum total of the conditions necessary to the existence of society." A secondary characteristic distinguishing the department of law from that of morals is the constraint which law may use in maintaining its norms

*(b) The Protective Theory and the Theory of Constraint.*

F J Stahl may be regarded as the chief adherent of the theory that maintains the negatively moral character of law [1] Every institute of law, in his opinion, represents a certain moral idea.  It is not the function of law, however, to realise

---

[1] We shall here neglect the specifically theological aspect which, according to Stahl, belongs to the concepts of morality and law  What has been said in Part II., chap iv. on the subject of heteronomous systems of ethics must serve as a critique of his views on this point

# 168 *The Moral Norms* [572

the positive content of this idea, but only to maintain the concept itself and prevent the admission of its opposite. "Thus, for instance, the law that personality must be protected does not involve a positive recognition of individuality, but merely the negative requirement that the concept of the person shall not be destroyed; for example, that one individual shall not receive bodily harm or injury from others The law of marriage does not involve the positive oneness and mutual self-sacrifice of the husband and wife, but merely prohibits polygamy, adultery, divorce on trivial grounds and the like, that is, it merely postulates the preservation of the concept of marriage. And the law of the State involves nothing more than obedience, the performance of functions, etc., it does not require that absolute interpenetration of the universal and the individual which Plato and Schelling demand of the political order"[1]

This theory starts with noting what is undoubtedly true, that the portion of the legal order which is most essential to the existence of society consists chiefly in prohibitions, that is, in negative norms. Thus positive penal law is largely comprised in prohibitions of certain acts, police control is exercised mostly, though not exclusively, in warding off and preventing certain disturbances; and even the law of private life protects its institutions chiefly by the method of prevention, the necessary means for which are supplied by the State. Yet even here the function of law is by no means merely negative Even penal law makes certain positive requirements, in the form of prescriptions that do not come under the head of universal ethical norms For instance, in certain cases it requires the individual to give notice of an intended crime that has come to his knowledge, and punishes neglect of this requirement The police deal with a number

---

[1] STAHL *Philosophie des Rechts,* 3rd ed., II, p. 205. A similar view has recently been maintained by A. LASSON, *Rechtsphilosophie,* pp 208 ff.

572-3]                    *Legal Norms*                    169

of positive regulations for the protection of health and life. And in the law of private life protection against breaches of the law is but the negative and reverse aspect of positive institutions, whose function as such is in no sense merely negative, which are adapted to protect and advance, not, indeed, the whole content of the moral life, but its most essential conditions. And how could one possibly restrict to purely negative functions the ordinances to regulate legislation and administration, which are the basis of all other forms of law? As a matter of fact, Stahl's own treatment of the subject soon carries him beyond the narrow limits that he has laid down for himself, for he calls law "the objective ethos," the external and living form of morality. And where he restricts this thought by saying that the whole of morality is not represented under the form of law, he does not really mean merely that law *prevents* disturbances of the moral order; but that it limits itself, in the maintenance of this order, to what is indispensable  In this connection he himself lays stress on physical constraint as the essential difference between law and morals[1]  Here his theory is in substantial agreement with that to be propounded below.

    Jhering has given clearest expression to the purely social conception of law in defining it as "the securing, under the form of constraint, of the vital conditions of society"[2]  Jellinek furnishes us with a modification of this definition, by subtracting the element of constraint, and defining law objectively as the sum of "conditions necessary for the maintenance of society", subjectively, as "the minimum of moral performance and disposition required of the members of a society'  Both aspects may be combined in the single formula that law is "the ethical minimum"[3]

---

[1] *Op cit*, p 197
[2] JHERING, *Zweck im Recht*, 1, p 434
[3] JELLINEK, *Die social-ethische Bedeutung von Recht, Unrecht und Straf*, p 42

170 *The Moral Norms* [573-4

It has been objected against the introduction of constraint into the first of these definitions, that law will still be law if we imagine a community of absolutely virtuous human beings, for whom constraint would be superfluous[1] But the argument is unimportant, for all law is human law, and its concept cannot be determined with reference to conditions under which it never exists

We must recognise, however, that constraint is merely a secondary mark of distinction, which, while its importance in the development of law, and especially in the gradual separation of law and morals, should not be underestimated, is yet simply a means to the maintenance of law, not law itself Hence its significance for the social theory of law is merely that of an accessory factor The point to be emphasised in the definitions which have just been advanced is that law, as "the ethical minimum," ensures the moral conditions indispensable to the life of society[2]

---

[1] TRENDELENBURG, *Naturrecht auf dem Grunde der Ethik*, 2nd ed , p 89

[2] What has been said above concerning the ethical content of legal norms has something in common with the views of Bierling (*Zur Kritik der juristischen Grundbegriffe*, 1 , p 153) Bierling also maintains that, in regard to their content, all legal norms may be considered as moral norms. Hence he thinks that the distinctive feature of law is to be sought not in its content, but in certain formal properties. He believes that the principle of universal recognition supplies a distinctive mark applicable to all cases (*op cit* , 1 , pp 12, 81 ff , and 11 , Appendix B, pp 351 ff ), understanding by universal recognition the continued assent of all individuals subject to the law in question Now, in the first place, it is clear that this criterion of recognition would necessarily bring under the concept of law all the norms existing in a given community, whether they were moral norms or the rules of a society formed for the furtherance of some particular interest. Such a state of affairs does not harmonise with the emphasis that Bierling puts on the moral significance of all legal norms Further, the theory finds itself compelled to have recourse to fiction, after a highly questionable fashion, when, for instance, it supposes unconscious and involuntary recognition of law on the part of children, insane persons, and those ignorant of the law In its treatment of the actual facts, the theory, which for the rest contains many acute discussions, is scarcely distinguishable from the contract theory This latter, like Bierling's, does not assume a contract actually entered upon, which would suppose a pre-existent law of contract , its hypothesis is rather that of an agreement, partly expressed and

## 574-5] *Legal Norms* 171

This theory, however, does not seem to meet all the requirements of the conception of law as it has developed in history. Just as the ordinary conception of the individual, which regards him solely from the point of view of private right, ignores society as a whole; so here, on the contrary, individuals seem to be lost sight of behind society Yet the theory remains individualistic, for it makes society consist ultimately in nothing but a sum of individuals The "maximum of happiness," the ultimate end in Bentham's ethics, is thus transformed into a kind of "minimum of happiness" The conditions essential to the life of society would seem to be assured when law protects each individual in his just rights, and where the forms of injustice that involve danger to each individual are held in suppression. But does the organisation of the legal community really terminate in such ends as these? Do they exhaust the actual content, more particularly, of the ordinances for the development and administration of constitutional laws? The truth is, rather, that all these institutions embody the idea of the State as not merely the representative of law, but as itself, together with the entire content of its moral problems, one of the chief ends of the legal order itself

partly tacit, which operates after the fashion of legal contracts subsequently made. Bierling agrees with the adherents of the contract theory, finally, in regarding the assumption of a social will as a ' fiction,' having no reality whatever But what does universal recognition amount to, if not a common tendency of will, that is, a social will? The only difference is that, if we acknowledge the reality of the social will, it is no longer necessary to make all the individuals in a society its representatives whereas the individualistic theory, which sees in society the mere sum of all individuals, must have the agreement of all, either under the form of contract or in some other form, to make its norms valid. Here, again, we see that the consequences of the individualistic view are always the same, whatever external differences may exist in its fundamental ideas

172                    *The Moral Norms*                    [575-6

### (c) Subjective Law, or Right.

If we start with the immediate subjective significance of the term law or right, every objectively recognised claim to any good, whether that good is a real thing, or an act on the part of some other subject, or one's own act, is a right Hence right, as such, is a privilege, not a norm , it is expressed by a permissive " Thou mayest," not by an imperative " Thou shalt " Thus the exercise of a right presupposes freedom of the will in the ethical sense of the term [1] Children, insane and weakminded persons may possess rights, but cannot exercise them. In general, the subject of a right may be an individual will or a social will The social will of the State is for the legal order at once the most comprehensive and most influential subject, since it regulates and protects all individual rights, and since, more particularly, all subordinate societies and associations derive from it their character as subjects possessing rights

To every right there corresponds a duty, which, in order to distinguish it from the general concept of moral duty, we term more accurately a legal duty As a rule, however, each right has not one, but many duties corresponding to it Further, the subject of the duties may or may not be identical with the subject of the right , or again, as is ordinarily the case, the subject of the right may have certain duties imposed at once on himself and on other free subjects by a given right Thus the political right of franchise is at the same time a duty The subject of the right is here identical with the subject of the duty, though according to our existing system of arrangements the duty is not one of constraint.

Similarly, the State's right of punishment is a case where the subject of the right and that of the duty coincide The

---

[1] *Cf* chap. i., pp. 37 ff

State is both : it not only may, but must exercise the penal authority And a series of secondary rights and duties, accruing to and devolving upon the judge, the executive officials, the culprit himself, result from punishment as exercised by the State It is the duty of the culprit, in particular, to submit to the punishment decreed by the State , and it is his right to demand that punishment The criminal may ask for mercy, but to thrust it on him against his will violates his acknowledged right.

The right of private property involves for its possessor the free disposition of the object that is recognised as his property For all other persons it involves the duty of respecting this right. But here, again, the subjects of the duty are not merely those who do not own the property A right that did not include any duty on the part of its possessor would be inherently absurd, an offence against that legal order which is based on a balance between rights and duties Really, the most conservative theory of property recognises the truth of this to a certain degree, for it tries to check the use of property for immoral ends, and in some cases even limits its useless expenditure. The scope of these duties is not a thing to be decided once for all it depends on existing theories of right, and especially on the moral spirit that inspires the theories in question Ethically regarded, property can never be looked upon as a good that exists for its own sake Its value will lie in the moral duties that it imposes on the possessor of the right. Apparently, it would always be a good thing if such duties, like the political duty of exercising the franchise, were to be kept free and voluntary so far as possible. But in both these instances such a course is practicable only where we can assume that the strength of the motives which operate without constraint is sufficient to make it safe for us to rely solely upon them ; and where it is apparent that the

174 *The Moral Norms* [577-8

moral disadvantages of constraint, which are undoubtedly great, can really be avoided through the influence of such motives. In any case, here as elsewhere, we must assert the truth that there is no subject of rights who is not at the same time a subject of duties, that rights exist only where an individual or social will can both exercise rights and assume duties  Doing away with private property would be accompanied by the gravest moral evils  It would abolish all the benefits to moral culture derived from the free intercourse of labour, from the spur to activity found in the effort to better one's position in life, and from the personal exercise of humanitarian virtues  In like manner the State, the community and other corporations must have property completely at their disposal to meet their collective needs

The narrowest form of a social will which is the subject at once of rights and of duties is to be found in the family  Under the conditions existing among civilised nations to-day, the family extends no further than the immediate circle of those dwelling beneath the same roof,—husband, wife and children.  Such institutions as the right of inheritance, that sometimes extends to collateral relatives who may never have seen each other in their lives, and who have, in any case, absolutely no community of moral duties, and the right of testamentary disposition, whereby the will of a person long dead acts as a constraint on remote generations, are anomalies in our existing theory of rights, and show the persistent triumph of abstract theory over the needs of life  They are in sharp contradiction to that principle which is of fundamental import to every moral system of law . the principle, namely, that there should be no rights where there can be no duties.[1]

---

[1] It seems to me that as regards this point, ethics in its turn cannot do better than assent to the conclusions, which are as moderate as they are unprejudiced,

## Legal Norms

It is duty that transforms the permissive rule of right into the imperative 'ought' Every man *may* use his property for whatever purpose he himself elects, but other people *ought* not to disturb him in the use of it. Offence against such a precept of duty is a transgression Hence it is not against the subjective right itself that one transgresses, but against the subjective legal duty implied by the right. When the duty corresponding to the right is not legal but merely moral, there can be no transgression, as, for instance, in the case of a monarch's right to exercise clemency, and the political right of franchise, which latter can be violated by others, but not by the subject of the right himself Similarly, property duties, *i e.* the duty of using property for moral ends, come under the head of moral duties. But where there is a positive *right* corresponding to the duty, we cannot draw any permanent distinction between moral and legal duties In such a case it is always a question to be decided by special considerations depending on time and circumstances, whether the system of law shall institute a legal right corresponding to the claim it allows, or rest content with a merely moral obligation.

### (d) Objective Right, or Law.

Subjective right, together with the legal duties dependent upon it, both those imposed on the subject of the right himself and those imposed on others, constitutes objective right, or law Here, too, we begin with particular rights My objective right of property in a certain thing means that I may use it for my own ends, and that it is the duty of everyone else to respect this right of mine. But the sum of the objective rights valid in a given community is

reached from the economic standpoint by Ad Wagner, in his investigation of the concept of property *Cf* his *Allgemeine Volkswirthschaftslehre*, 1 , pp 305 ff , 431 ff

176     *The Moral Norms*     [578-9

objective right, or law, regarded as a collective idea, and the sum total of the ordinances made for the maintenance of this objective right is the legal order   Of this order the State, the highest social will that can act as an unit, is the sole representative   Hence objective right and the legal order are acts of the State's will   As such they have binding force for all individual wills, and for all lower orders of the social will that fall under the State   Objective right comprises the ends that the will of the State sets before itself, the legal order comprises the means by which it seeks to realise these ends

Three conditions are accordingly necessary for the existence of every legal right   1   There must be a subject of right, a being capable of free moral volition, who may be an individual will or a social will.   2   There must be subjects of duty, for whom the same criteria hold good, and who may be identical with or different from the subjects of right   3   There must be a social will that takes under its protection all subjective rights, ensures the performance of the corresponding subjective duties, and is thus the representative of objective right and of the formulated rules necessary to its maintenance ; in other words, of the legal order.

### (e) General Definition of Law

Thus far we have been merely limiting the conception of law by means of certain formal definitions.   Since, however, we have postulated a free moral will as the representative of law, it is evident that the content of the concept will be thereby determined.   For the ends towards which such a will directs itself must be moral.   Hence the end both of subjective and of objective law must be thought of as moral   While this fact is not, as a rule, directly stated in the special formulations of law, it is expressed indirectly.   Whenever legal formulas have to be interpreted, we find the principle universally recognised that the will embodied in law must never be conceived as in opposition to the general norms of morality. We must, however, distinguish between law and the legal order on this point. The latter may contain many special ordinances that have no immediate reference to any moral end. The ordering of social life makes it necessary to have regulations with reference to certain needs that possess in themselves no moral significance. And ends that are really moral may be reached in different ways We have here an instance, in the realm of law, of the general ethical principle that moral means are always infinitely more manifold than moral ends, though the realisation of the latter may take on different forms by reason of the diversity of the former But no matter how many morally indifferent elements may be included in a given system of law, objective right, or law, as a whole, can have no other than a moral content. Nay, each individual right deserves the protection of law only in so far as it has moral value.

The fact that there have existed, and may still exist, particular laws, and even whole legal institutions, that cannot be termed moral, is, of course, no violation of this principle; any more than the actual immorality of many men proves that the life of mankind in general is without moral purpose. We are, however, too prone to forget the historical point of view, especially when we are dealing with institutions that once had moral significance, but have now lost it. Slavery, for instance, would certainly be an immoral institution nowadays But no unprejudiced person will deny that it actually did important service to morals in ancient times, and that the relation itself, in some cases, especially among the Greeks, was of value from an ethical point of view.

Since, then, law always has, or ought to have, a moral object, the spirit of morality takes possession even of those indifferent elements in the legal order which have in them-

178        *The Moral Norms*        [580-1

selves no moral import. They gain such import by being introduced, as necessary connecting links, into the structure of the system of morality

Bearing in mind the ultimate moral purpose of all law, we may describe objective right, or law, as the sum total of all those various subjective rights and duties which the moral will of society, the creator of law, ensures as rights to itself and its subordinate individual wills, in order to the fulfilment of certain purposes ; and imposes as duties, in order to the protection of the rights in question.

This formula does not restrict the nature of law to the protection of certain goods, or, what amounts to the same thing, the maintenance of the conditions necessary to the life of society. Besides protective rights and duties, the system of law embraces many institutions which may be termed promotive rights and duties The superintendence of instruction, together with certain positive regulations for the advancement of material welfare and of the most important interests of culture, are duties of equal weight with the protection of persons and property, ensured by political legislation , and they are directed only in part towards the protection of the existing conditions of life. Their aim is in equal measure the improvement of those conditions. For social life, like all life, is change and development. Law would be neglecting one of its most important functions if it refused to meet the demands of this ceaseless evolution Hence constitutional law makes comprehensive provisions for the alteration of existing law to suit new needs. But in addition to these arrangements for the origin and abolition of laws, the progressive factor can never be wholly absent from law as it actually exists Only it will assume various forms according to the current way of regarding the function of the legal order. In an age that ascribes the prime importance to individual rights,

581-2] *Legal Norms* 179

the chief task of the system of law will be to remove the hindrances that obstruct the free development of personal activities. On the other hand, when the social functions of the State are given a higher rank, the system of public law will contain a number of positive and promotive regulations.

This alternative, however, makes no difference with the question at issue · the only difference is in regard to the subjects upon whom the functions are imposed In the former case it is the individuals who assume the duties corresponding to the rights allowed them In the latter case the functions in question devolve upon the State itself, or upon subordinate bodies appointed for the purpose by the State. In general, here as elsewhere, the best division of rights and duties will be one that is dependent on the special historical conditions of civilisation only so far as its scope is concerned. For what the individual can, and as a rule will do, no co-operation on the part of the State is necessary. The functions that belong, or ought to belong, to the State are essentially those which the individual cannot perform, at least as well as the State can ; or those which, if he had the power, he would probably lack the inclination to assume.

### *(f) Justice.*

It is in the proper apportionment of rights and duties among the various subjects of law, an apportionment in accordance with the existing conditions which govern the life of society and humanity at large, that justice (*Gerechtigkeit*) consists , the virtue whose intimate connection with law (*Recht*) is expressed in the words themselves. Taken in this, its proper significance, it is wholly a public, not a private virtue ; though, of course, since public authority must needs have personal representatives, it is ultimately exercised by individuals acting in behalf of the social will But

180 *The Moral Norms* [582-3

the consciousness that the social will is the real power that exercises justice has led men to entrust the more important acts of justice, at least, to bodies of persons elected specially for the purpose, rather than to individuals

Thus the weightier cases in civil and criminal law are decided not by a single judge, but by a college of judges, and we often find the matter referred to other courts, in order to eliminate the possible influence of purely personal opinion within the college, while that uniformity in the pronouncements of the law which is essential to justice is sought by final agreement in a supreme court of appeal. The administrative court, the local assembly, the college of ministers, the privy council, whose influence on important questions is sometimes more far-reaching than that of the ministerial college, finally, the diet and representative assemblies having charge of legislation and general finance,—all these institutions express the idea that justice, in the different departments of government and public life, is the function of the social will. For the ultimate motive that leads us in all these cases to prefer the decision of a body of individuals to that of any one individual will is our conviction that the various interests, alike of society and of the individual, will be weighed with greater justice if the decision is preceded by an exchange of opinions, and if it is required to be the joint product of a number of wills. At the same time, this is why the decision of such corporate wills have more weight and authority; their impersonal character obliterates the individual influences that combined to produce them.

The fact that moralists have overlooked the impersonal character of justice is closely connected with the difficulties that they have encountered in the concept from the time of Aristotle to that of Hume. The reason why it is so easy to ignore this characteristic is because the will of the law is often really embodied in the volition of an individual

583-4]                    *Legal Norms*                    181

personality, so that its justice depends on the personal
characteristics of its representative. In this derived sense,
of course, justice has an individual character; and we may
speak, for instance, of one judge as more just than another,
though both represent one and the same social will But the
exercise of justice always presupposes a will that has power
to impose its standard of rights and duties upon certain
subjects of law. Where the decision is not accompanied by
this power, where, therefore, it is purely theoretical, or where
it leads merely to an act of subjective judgment, we are
really using the word justice to express another idea, that
of equity.

As justice is a public virtue, so is equity a private virtue
Justice indicates to the individual what is due to him by
right, after a careful balancing of all the rights and duties
involved. Equity indicates what, under the special circumstances in question, he may desire without infringing on
the rights of others. Equity may thus grant more than
justice does. The former is indulgent, the latter stern. Injustice, however, is always inequitable We should treat our
fellow-men with equity, not merely with justice, for it is not
the individual's place to constitute himself the judge of
others On the other hand, it is the function of the will
embodied in law to treat the subjects under its authority
with justice, not with equity. Its judgments must be made
without respect to the person or the particular case Equity,
on the contrary, takes special account of the person and
the particular case. Hence the man who is called upon
to exercise justice should not allow himself to be guided
solely by equity. Under such circumstances equity may
lead to injustice, because as soon as the decision is not based
on the sure foundation principles of law, it is only too easy
for conditions varying with every chance influence and
dependent on changeable subjective opinion to get control.

# 182 *The Moral Norms* [584

Thus we are guilty of a complete misunderstanding of the function of justice when we give certain institutions, *e.g.* the jury system, preference because we suppose them likely to furnish decisions in accordance, not merely with justice, but also with equity Such a view results from the perverted conception that regards public acts of law from the point of view of the private intercourse of individuals It would be in accordance with equity to judge a person who offends against a law he knows nothing about otherwise than a person who sins with knowledge. It would be equitable to grant more time to an accused person who, through a fatal talent for forgetting things, has forfeited the usual period allowed for filing his answer to an accusation. In both cases, however, justice would usually ignore such considerations of equity, in order to prevent injustice It is only under special circumstances, especially where there is no danger of violating any legal duties towards other individuals and towards society, or where the legal question is doubtful, that considerations of equity come into play alongside of considerations of justice , and at such times the legal formula itself often refers the judge to equity When it does so it leaves the decision entirely to his individual opinion, in accordance with the subjective character of equity.

### (g) *Fundamental and Auxiliary Legal Norms*

We may designate as legal norms all those norms which regulate the exercise of justice by establishing what rights and duties shall be assured to the individual by the will of society, and what consequences shall be associated with the breach of these duties. Since the immediate content of these norms consists rather in prescribing duties than in granting rights, they should, strictly speaking, be called norms of legal duty. As such they differ from the more comprehensive norms of moral duty, partly because their

## Legal Norms

585]

183

scope, depending as it does on the special conditions belonging to the concept of law, is narrower, and partly because, as we have seen, the essential nature of law requires them to include principles that have no directly ethical content Further, since the duties corresponding to certain laws are moral and not legal, we may make a second class of legal principles, namely, legal grants or privileges, in addition to the norms of legal duty, or, as for the sake of brevity they may be called, legal norms While the number of principles in this second class is extremely limited, yet it is evident that the correlation of rights and duties requires us to postulate as many privileges as there are norms. As a matter of fact, there is a privilege corresponding to every legal norm, though it is ordinarily left unexpressed The need of directly formulating the exact right involved is felt only when there is no norm of duty that contains it. Thus, while constitutional law finds it necessary to make an express declaration of the right of suffrage under definite conditions, penal law does not promulgate the protection of persons and property directly. It merely implies such protection by threatening to punish action directed against the security of either.

This fact, namely, that the system of law does not explicitly formulate all the principles contained in existing objective law, is based on a *lex parsimoniæ*, which must of necessity be adhered to in any field of thought where, as in the case of law, the prime object is not theory, but the practice of life. The system of law expresses what is absolutely indispensable; it leaves unexpressed what is self-evident or what is contained in that which has been already expressed. And where two principles stand related as the necessary complements of each other, it is generally the one which is of greater practical importance that is expressed. Certain phenomena, presented in every instance of the development of law, and of great moment with reference

184   *The Moral Norms*   [585-6

to one's conception of the essential nature of legal norms, result from these conditions

1. In the early stages of the development of law all its principles are self-evident   They are the foundation of inherited customs ; they are manifested in the habitual actions of men, and in the arrangements made for remedying or expiating actions that are contrary to the norms. Only gradually does it become necessary, on the one hand, to state the existing practices of law under the form of definite principles, and, on the other, to formulate explicitly new statutes having their origin in altered conditions.   Thus part of the legal norms develop into codified law, while there is always a remainder in the form of uncodified law, the law of usage

2. In this later development of law the prevailing need is for a codified formulation of the duties that law imposes. As a rule, the corresponding rights are not explicitly stated, except where no definite duty, enforceable by coercion, is involved, and where, morever, it is essential to the interest of society that the right shall be exercised.   By far the greater part of codified law thus consists in norms of duty, imposed by the State partly on itself, partly on subordinate social organisations, and partly on individuals.

3. Further, the norms of duty themselves are not fully expressed in codified law, which is rather restricted to the formulation of norms that relate to the maintenance of the legal order.   If, accordingly, we distinguish those rules of behaviour which must be directly observed by the community and its members as principal norms, while we designate as auxiliary norms those precepts intended to ensure the observance of such rules, and to avoid the disturbances that might arise from their non-observance ; then it is the latter that are for the most part expressed in legislation, because they alone are of practical importance in maintaining

586-7]                    *Legal Norms*                    185

the legal order: the principal norms are often left unexpressed. The various branches of law, however, are not
quite uniform in this respect. Generally speaking, when
the object of law is the *protection* of rights, legislation is
restricted to the promulgation of auxiliary norms. This
is especially the case where the rights to be protected are
based on universally valid moral norms, or have their source
in usage of long standing  Thus all penal statutes, and a
very considerable part of the civil statutes regulating private
intercourse, are auxiliary norms.  On the other hand, where
the State exercises the duty of *furthering* certain ends of
civilisation, as in administrative and constitutional law,
principal norms and auxiliary norms are both, as a rule,
expressed.  Here, moreover, we are dealing with developments in law that are of a more variable character and
exposed in a far greater degree to the influence of the
historical conditions of development.

4. In so far as it is a norm of duty, every legal norm
contains either a command or a prohibition.  Principal and
auxiliary norms may often supplement each other, the one
being positive and the other negative  Thus in the case
of penal law the principal norms are all prohibitions, while
the auxiliary norms, codified penal laws, are for the most
part commands.  This complementary relationship is based
on the fact that the principal norm, like the universal moral
norms, always has a command tacitly involved in its prohibition ; or, if it is positive in its nature, a prohibition involved in its command  And here, as elsewhere, the formulation of legal maxims follows the rule of expressing directly
only what is indispensably necessary.  Codified penal law
deals with murder, homicide, bodily injury; not with the
inviolable character of the person, though it tacitly asserts
the latter by forbidding the former.

It has remained for the modern science of law to direct

# 186 *The Moral Norms* [587-8

attention towards all those legal maxims which fall outside the scope of legislation, and are partly preparatory, partly supplementary to it, which have, however, great importance with reference to the continuous development of the legal consciousness. This has been done in two ways. First, uncodified law, whose actual exercise and recognition gives it equal normative force, has been distinguished from codified law. And second, codified law has been distinguished from the norm, which is often unexpressed. The two points are intimately connected, for the unexpressed norms may be regarded as a part of uncodified law.[1]

Less emphasis is usually laid on the fact that codified law always partakes of the nature of a norm[2] The real logical relation between the norm, ordinarily so called, and the formulated law lies in the fact that the former is a principal norm and the latter an auxiliary norm, which, of course, may, if necessary, include the principal norm either wholly or in part. While the principal norm expresses, positively or negatively, the object of a piece of legislation, the auxiliary norm contains the means through which this end may be attained Since the latter is the only thing essential to the maintenance of the legal order, it follows that the principal norms may ordinarily be left unexpressed, just as we ordinarily waive the consideration of the motives and grounds of the legal order.[3] Law as formulated contains no reference to the motives that might be assigned as reasons for its introduction. Such motives, indeed, are usually restricted to those which concern changes in previously existing laws. Legislative powers leave the investigation of

---

[1] *Cf* BINDING, *Die Normen und ihre Uebertretung*, 1, pp 1 ff, and *Handbuch des Strafrechts*, 1., pp. 155 ff.

[2] Indeed, the fact is often wholly denied. quite wrongly, as it seems to me. See especially ZITELMANN, *Irrtum und Rechts geschaft*, chap 111, pp. 200 ff

[3] *Cf* my *Logik*, 11, p 603.

588-9] *Legal Norms* 187

the broader basis of law to the science of jurisprudence; and the latter, when this investigation deals with the ultimate moral foundation of the legal order, hands it over to ethics

*(h) Fundamental Norms of Law*

Legal duties, the most important of which are simply particular applications of moral duties, are, like the latter, unlimited in number. This fact makes it the more necessary, in both cases, to reduce the innumerable special norms to certain fundamental ones  The latter, of course, are used in actual life only under special forms, directly in certain principal norms, and indirectly in the auxiliary norms that serve for the maintenance of the former.  Thus, in the realm of law as in the broader realm of ethics, the fundamental norms are simply abstract generalisations from the manifold of concrete legal maxims.  On the other hand, however, they may be regarded as the tacit presuppositions on which the whole structure of law is based; so that we have another instance of a relation like that between axioms and their applications in the realm of theory.  But it would seem at first sight that such a process of discovering fundamental norms must be more difficult in the domain of law than in that of ethics at large.  The efforts of ethical theory have for centuries been directed towards establishing those abstract principles, or the corresponding duty-concepts, whose various particular formulations are to be found in the special moral maxims and virtues  On the other hand, owing to causes not at all remote in nature, the attention of the science of law has been wholly occupied with the systematic working out of particular legal concepts.  Since it is the auxiliary norms that are most important in such a process, juristic investigation, properly so called, has been almost entirely diverted from the problem of the ultimate basis of the whole legal order.  As a matter of fact, the problem does not

188 *The Moral Norms* [589-90

belong to the science but to the philosophy of law, or to the former only in so far as it is both philosophy and science. And the philosophy of law must refer this very problem to the principles of general ethics.

Now we have already seen that every legal norm is a precept of duty  Hence the fundamental legal norms will be those precepts of duty which have just the same fundamental and universal significance for that external aspect of the moral life which is realised in law, that the moral norms have for the moral life in general.  Hence, again, it is clear that legal norms which have no direct moral content, but derive their moral significance from the fact that they form part of the moral system of law as a whole, can lay no claim to be considered fundamental norms.  The real fundamental norms of law will be related to the fundamental norms of morals precisely as the notion of subjective law, or right, is related to that of morality.  Now, as we have noted above, in the moral realm the concepts of right and duty are not correlatives in the sense that the individual may demand as a right from others that which he himself performs as a free moral duty, but only in the sense that each individual has a right to the practice of his own free moral duties, limited solely by the right of other individuals to perform theirs.  In this connection we must recognise as such a subject of rights and duties every form of the will, whether individual or social.  Hence it is an important function of every concrete system of law to make a just distribution of rights among the individuals and communities under its jurisdiction,—not excepting the supreme community which is the representative of the legal order itself, namely, the State.

Now since the special conditions on which this distribution of rights depends are variable, evidently law as a whole, together with the fundamental norms expressed in it, is involved in the ceaseless flux of historical development.

590]                    *Legal Norms*                    189

After all, though, the variability of the ultimate foundation of law is no other than that to which the realisation of moral norms is subject. What is moral is never completed ; it is always in the process of becoming. Hence our investigation of moral norms can never amount to more than the establishment of those fundamental principles which are recognised as valid for the existing stage of moral development. And in like manner, whatever fundamental norms of law may be discovered are to be regarded simply as those accessible to our present knowledge  This does not mean that their significance is merely ephemeral  Rather, the constancy and regularity of all psychical development are such that the present state of things is the ripe fruit of all the development that has gone before and the germ of all that is to follow.  But there are various stages in the subjective attitude of the mind towards a given product set in the stream of time.  At first, to the eye of prejudice, it seems eternal.  A more comprehensive survey shows it to be transitory, and it is therefore held to have no permanent value  Finally, to the far-reaching vision there is discovered an element of permanence in all that is transitory ; and what passes away is seen to have enduring value as the germ of future evolution.

In consequence of the great number of external aids that are needed to support the system of law, and as a result of the greater practical importance of particular precepts compared with the ultimate foundations on which they rest, even the special and individual norms of law are usually hidden from observation  Still more, of course, do the fundamental norms to which these refer escape attention  This is why in the realm of law what is variable and historically conditioned seems so preponderant.  Yet we must suppose that the fundamental norms of law are no more variable than the moral norms  For in the sense maintained

190  *The Moral Norms*  [590-1

above there is a subjective law or right corresponding to every moral duty. Hence, while the positive law at any given stage may possibly fall short of the legal norm postulated by the duties recognised in consciousness, no permanent contradiction of this sort can be supposed to exist  The subjective law, or right, postulated in the moral norms will be related to existing law as a postulate, which the future will seek to approach, according as the general conceptions of morality get control of the ruling social will which brings about the historical changes in law.  This view of the matter is not to be confused with the old theories of natural right, which sought to introduce eternal and unalterable primitive rights into the actual legal system ; thereby denying the possibility of development in men's conception of law, just as the corresponding tendency in ethics supposed moral ideas to be unchanging and incapable of development.  To take existing positive law for the realisation of the existing conception of law would be really the same as deriving all the moral postulates that have been produced in our minds by previous moral development from moral life as it actually exists.  The great motive force that governs the historical process of the growth of law is just the fact that the actual state of things never fulfils the postulates that must be maintained, and that their partial fulfilment is always producing new postulates, which in turn seek to be realised.

If, bearing these considerations in mind, we approach the question as to the content of the fundamental legal norms, there can be no doubt about the answer  The ultimate ends of law can be no other than morality itself.  Hence the content of the legal norms must ultimately agree with that of the moral norms.  But the latter seek to declare this content directly, containing as they do the precepts whose observance is necessary to the realisation of the tasks of

## Legal Norms

morality; while the fundamental norms of law, on the other hand, contain those precepts which the whole moral community subject to the legal order must observe, in order that all its parts, from the State down to the individual, may perform their free moral duties. Thus legal norms, like moral norms, are of three kinds. individual, social and humanitarian. But while in the moral realm the immediate subject of duty is the individual, the subject referred to in the commands of law is the social community. The individual is concerned only in so far as he fulfils the legal order upheld by the social will.

This fact suggests the question whether a third kind of legal norm is not conceivable, where the subject shall be the third member of the series of moral orders, namely, humanity As a matter of fact, the international regulations, to whose general observance those civilised nations whose historical function it is to lead humanity are pledged, may be considered as the beginning of such a higher realm of law. International law, however, exhibits in its mode of origin and acceptation noteworthy points of difference from the ordinary system of law, which is associated with political unity. Originating in various disconnected articles of agreement, some of them referring to the facilitation of intercourse, others to the protection of individuals beyond the boundaries of their own nation, others to the realisation of certain humanitarian requirements, many of these norms have gradually become a part of the law of general usage. The stage of formulated law, usually the concluding stage in the formation of law, is here wholly lacking. And for this reason the norms of international law have preserved a certain characteristic freedom that belongs to no other department of law, and is here based on the independence of the legal subjects, namely, the various states involved. The triumph of the ethical spirit manifested in the forma-

192 *The Moral Norms* [592-3

tion of law is the greater because of this very fact, that the universal humanitarian principles governing the intercourse of nations, in peace as in war, have begun to assume the nature of inviolable norms, whose sole but sufficient guard is the moral consciousness of civilised peoples.

## 6 THE NORMS AND THE DEPARTMENTS OF MORAL LIFE.

Moral norms are the outcome of a process of development that can be traced throughout all the facts of the history of morals. Once developed, their function is to react upon and direct the forms of actual life from which they sprang Where they have to yield to the ceaseless operation of checking and opposing forces, they are but the more insistent in raising the question as to how human life, present and future, shall be ordered in such a way that the ends which are so emphatically indicated by the normative ideas may be reached. And this question brings us to the field of practical ethics. While theoretical ethics directs its attention towards the past, the field of practical ethics is the future After the former has deduced from the history of moral ideas the norms that are to guide the development of the future, practical ethics seeks, on the one hand, to find what means give most promise of helping on this development, and, on the other hand, to infer what forms the moral life is likely to assume by reason of the moral laws immanent in it

This subject, inexhaustible as it is in content and scope, branching off into many independent fields of thought, we shall not attempt to discuss fully in the present exposition, even in regard to its most important and fundamental problems We shall merely glance at it, by way of appendix to the foregoing attempt at a development of the universal and fundamental norms of ethics.

The method to be followed in our investigation of prac-

593-4] *and the Departments of Moral Life* 193

tical ethics is already indicated by the ever-widening series of departments in which moral actions take place. The ultimate source of all moral effort is the individual personality. With the tendencies it derives from the common store of the society to which it belongs, and the forces which it produces independently, it seeks to react upon that society. Although the individual can never be thought of apart from the social ground of his existence, yet in a certain sense he is a world by himself. He proposes certain ends to himself independently, and uses for their realisation means peculiar to himself. These means are, chiefly, his property, his calling or profession, his position as a citizen, and lastly his intellectual culture, a circumstance less external in its character than the outward aspects of life, but reacting upon and influencing them all.

The next department of life is society. Though it is made up of purely individual wills, these produce in combination new moral ends in whose fulfilment a social will is exercised. Further, all the various organisations which are contained in society without any order or system, and which therefore, like individuals, often oppose the purposes of society, are brought into orderly union by the most comprehensive and most powerful of the phenomenal forms assumed by a social will, namely, the State. Finally, as in the preceding stage the individual forms a single unit in society, so the State becomes a social unit in the historical union of nations and races, humanity, with its supremely comprehensive moral ends.

# Part IV.

## THE DEPARTMENTS OF THE MORAL LIFE.

595–6]

# CHAPTER I.

## THE INDIVIDUAL PERSONALITY

### 1. PROPERTY.

THE moral basis of the possession of material goods consists in the double purpose that such possession may serve. First, it ensures the security of existence ; and, secondly, it affords the means for the external exercise of power. Without the preservation of life there can be no moral effort , but in order that moral effort may not succumb in the struggle for material needs, one's material possessions must represent a certain surplus over and above the necessities of life. How great this surplus shall be is a question of comparative indifference. The only thing desirable in the interests of morality is that the amount shall avoid the twofold extremes of deficiency and excess the former, because the surplus that exists when conditions are favourable may be transformed into a deficiency as a result of some chance disturbing influence, for which the individual is not responsible , the latter, because where the accumulation of wealth is excessive the ability required to apply it for moral ends transcends the limited power of the individual In the first case the moral worth of the duty imposed by material possessions is too small. In the second case it is too great , the duty can be fulfilled only under unusual conditions and by an individual of rare moral gifts.

The individual's power to choose or create the position in

197

198     *The Individual Personality*     [596

life that is his by virtue of inherited and acquired property
is very limited  For the most part this position depends
on external conditions, on birth and the fortunes of life, and
on the social and political circumstances in which he lives.
Especially is it true that his own merit and desert have
relatively little to do with deciding whether his position
shall approach the maximum or the minimum of existence.
This fact increases the moral responsibility resting on society
as a whole to establish protective regulations that shall
prevent, so far as possible, the occurrence of either unfortunate extreme in the matter of the division of property  Such
regulations, unless we are to risk seriously endangering
freedom in the acquisition of property—a condition indispensable to its moral function—must, of course, be indirect
in character.  They may consist partly of arrangements
which enable everyone who is capable of earning to profit
by his powers, and which insure him in the event of undeserved misfortune , partly in legal regulations operating
against the excessive accumulation of property in the hands
of individuals

The moral influence of property, like the end which it
serves, is twofold  The process of acquisition is a moralising
influence, because it incites the individual to work and to the
steady fulfilment of duty in the service of his calling  This
first function is exercised, if other conditions are favourable,
even where the state of a man's possessions approaches the
minimum of existence, and where his property, since it has to
be used for the necessaries of life as soon as it is acquired,
can be turned to no moral purpose  Hence this primary
effect of property, though it is almost wholly obscured by
self-seeking motives, is undoubtedly the most important.
It has done far more to maintain the moral order than wealth
has, with all that the latter has accomplished by its efforts
in behalf of society and humanity

## Property

Yet the importance of the second influence, that of wealth or property actually acquired, is not to be underestimated It would be a very undesirable state of affairs morally if governmental compulsion had to undertake everything that voluntary liberality and spontaneous interest now do for the intellectual benefits of life, and might do in far greater measure if the rich were as clearly conscious of their moral function as one could wish To compel the performance of such acts is surely as undesirable as the transformation of voluntary work in any profession into paid labour under public supervision In both cases the very element that is of especial moral value is lost, namely, liberty of production.

It is a necessary consequence of the division of property and the concomitant division of material and intellectual labour that the two moral effects of property are supplementary to each other. That is, where property once acquired furnishes an opportunity for the highest moral functions, the ethical influence of the process of acquisition itself is diminished. The rich man, while he may ennoble by his benefactions the wealth he has inherited, or has accumulated under the working of outside forces, cannot know the ethical influence of toil, whose effects are the blessing of the humble labourer It is only in a moderate station of life, where the individual's earnings are sufficient to allow him to use his property for moral ends as well as for his own needs, that we find both influences combined.

Precisely for this reason a moderate station of life is most favourable to morality. Fate, rather than any merit of its own, has made it least subject to the governance of immoral impulses. If a man is poor, and has to struggle for the necessaries of life, he easily loses the sense of pleasure in his work; and then, in seeking to find an easier way to obtain what fortune has denied him, uses immoral means. As for the rich man, the more easily his wealth rolls in, the

## 200  *The Individual Personality*  [597–8

more is he inclined to forget its moral value. He regards it as a natural right, without thinking of the duty which this right imposes. The poor man tries to get it immorally, the rich man to squander it immorally. Often enough the two stages approach each other, for in the play of fortune's favours, sought and unsought, the immoral acquisition of wealth and its immoral use go hand in hand. There is the more necessity that a society such as we must acknowledge our own to be, which favours the existence of extremes in the matter of property and of sudden transitions from one extreme to the other, by reason of the insufficient precaution taken against immoral forms of acquisition, should use stringent means to render departures from the average amount of wealth exceptional. Such measures, of course, would not be all-sufficient. In addition, a more moral conception of the value of material possessions must take the place of the thoughtless notion, still widespread, that property is a right to which no duty corresponds.

And this value consists singly and solely in the fact that property is the indispensable means to the production of moral ends. Hence that form of acquisition alone is moral which is in accord with such ends, and that form of possession alone is moral which is morally applied, either directly or indirectly (through the creation of that material substructure of existence which is essential to moral functions). Every instance of the frivolous or useless expenditure of wealth, every case of acquisition that is purposeless, or directed only towards the satisfaction of selfish wishes, is an immoral action.

It is noteworthy that the public conscience has always a sharper eye for immoral forms of acquisition than for immoral forms of use. We shut the thief up in prison; but the wanton spendthrift, who regards his wealth as a licence to spend money according to his will and whim, is some-

598–9] *Occupation* 201

times a highly respected person. This inequality in judgment is partly based on the consideration, to some extent justified, that it is a graver offence to do wrong than not to do right. In part, however, its source is surely to be found in the belief, not only that the right of property is itself inviolable, but that the right of its possessor to use it as he likes is also inviolable,—in fact, almost removed from the sphere of moral judgment.

### 2. OCCUPATION.

While the possession of material goods is a necessity of conscious life, and hence of moral life, which is bound up with sensibility, it is no less a moral postulate that every man should have an occupation, that is, that he should regard the regular fulfilment of certain moral ends as his life-task.

Ordinarily, material possessions and a man's calling or occupation are so far connected that the latter furnishes the means of acquiring the former. This connection, however, is not a necessary one One may follow an occupation without getting anything in the way of possessions thereby, and even in such a way as to involve a sacrifice of material possessions. The greatest moral benefactors of mankind did not make their calling a source of support, and many a material benefactor to his needy fellow-men has made a profession out of the benevolent use of his property. For the man of average moral capacity, however, one of the best possible features of the social order is that it does not leave the choice of a calling wholly to individual preferences, but regulates it, aside from the influence of example and custom, by the necessity of earning a living

The moral significance of occupation, like that of property, depends on the ends that are served. Every calling is moral

## 202 *The Individual Personality* [599-600

that furthers moral ends; whether directly, by immediate participation in the moral interests of humanity, of the social circle or the state to which the individual belongs, or indirectly, where the ends subserved by the calling help to create the material or intellectual substrate that is essential to moral culture. In this sense every calling that is in any way useful, even that of the labourer struggling for the necessaries of life, is moral; it is a part of the great machine of moral forces that go to make up the moral order. Moreover, it is evident that we must not take too narrow a view here of what constitutes useful work Not only is everything that contributes to intellectual interests a most valuable means of developing moral capacities, but, in a still more especial sense, art, which elevates and refines the emotions, and even play, which by relaxation and rest tempers the mind to severer work, may become the objects of an occupation that is of great value in the total of human functions. From this practical point of view morality and utility have sometimes been identified. After what has been said on this point, we hardly need to remark that the holders of such a position confuse means and end. An occupation may serve as a more or less subordinate means to moral ends, where the ends it aims at directly are not in themselves moral [1]

Hence an estimate of the moral worth of a given occupation depends on two considerations first, what it does objectively for the ends of the whole, and secondly, what it does subjectively for the agent himself, in the moral effects it has on him. As regards the first estimate, of course, the various kinds of occupation will form an infinite series of gradations, from those which aim directly at the realisation of moral ends, down to the lowest activities of daily life,

---

[1] Compare on this point the critique of Utilitarianism in Part II, chap. iv., pp 170, 171

which can serve only as remote aids to morality. The case is quite different with the second or subjective estimate This depends simply upon fidelity to duty, manifested in the individual's chosen occupation, no matter what that may be, so long as it is moral. There are few aids to individual moral training and self-education that can match this in importance And precisely because such is the case, one needs a natural moral tact to estimate a man's moral worth, not by the importance of his occupation, where external fortune may help or hinder him in so large a measure, but by the fidelity he exercises in whatever occupation fate or free choice has assigned him

Again, as regards their subjective aspect, the various kinds of occupation differ widely in their fitness to exercise a moral influence. And we find that those which are higher in the objective scale are precisely the ones most lacking in that moral incentive which operates with almost mechanical certainty to strengthen the feeling of duty, and with which the most external and material of all occupations, manual labour, is especially blessed. The more the work of the artist or scholar is left to the free inclination of the moment, as regards the mode of its exercise, the greater is the tendency to govern action by whim and caprice, rather than by real fidelity to duty. That disciplining of the character, which the mechanic in large measure owes to the nature of his occupation, must often, where the individual life-task is determined by a freer exercise of the creative power of mind, be gained through a weary battle of the will,—a battle where many a life succumbs that might not have failed of success had it trodden the plain path of a simpler calling Thus, of all occupations, it is manual labour and office work, which has other points in common with manual labour, and which resembles it in being the fulfilment of everyday duty with mechanical punctuality in a

## 204 *The Individual Personality* [601

moderate or even an inferior station of life,—it is these occupations that bring with them a sense of pride in one's calling, whose happy effects are unsuspected by the courtier or artist in the high places of life. The moral order has thus its own justice Where the objective moral results that the individual can produce are but small, it ordains that the subjective moral values and the moral satisfaction that goes along with them shall be greatest. How short-sighted is the judgment of the crowd, which looks only at outward results, on the happiness and unhappiness of existence! The great artist pays with his own peace of soul for the immortal creations which in happy moments he wrests from his genius And the man whose occupation is severe and simple labour feels, in his enjoyment of a work of art, the real happiness that the artist can create for others, never for himself.

One of the worst moral features of our present state of society, a feature, moreover, that goes along with certain other evils, is the tendency nowadays to do away with manual labour, that bulwark of the spirit of honourable toil, or, where manual labour is allowed to continue, to pervert its moral influence by loosening the ties between fellow-workmen, especially between the independent artisan and his assistants, and by organising all labour after a purely mechanical fashion It is doubtful whether manual labour will ever be able to free itself from these conditions, which in their present form are morally indefensible. Perhaps the government official, whose field of work is constantly widening as the scope of the State's functions increases, is destined in time to take the artisan's place in the moral economy ; and the private sense of the dignity of his calling, once the labourer's peculiar possession, may thus be strengthened by the sentiment of public duty

While a man's occupation is thus so powerful an educative

601-2] *Occupation* 205

force in the moral world, want of occupation is equally powerful as a cause of immorality. It is the worse in this respect because it is by far the most frequent cause. And we may note, as a fact of moral import, that want of occupation is ordinarily found under the two most dangerous property conditions, the maximum and minimum of existence. The needy man is driven to idleness by despair and the degeneracy that comes with want, the rich man by satiety and the spirit of pleasure-seeking that grows with the means of satisfying it. The matter seldom stops there The impulse to activity, deep-rooted in man's nature, joined with necessity in the case of the poor man, and acquisitiveness, increased by satisfaction, in the case of the rich, gives rise to immoral occupations. These, while they may differ in form according to the agent's situation in life, are alike in their final outcome, the production of crime. It is an inevitable consequence of his position that the poor man should be, as a rule, the first to come into conflict with the legal order. The rich man has at his disposal so many means of satisfying his immoral desires, in ways which are allowable, or at least not punishable, that for the most part nothing but the inexorable consequences of his own moral guilt can drive him to actual crime Nor can we defend modern society against the charge of an injustice in its moral judgments here, like that which we found in its judgments concerning the immoral acquisition and use of property. Perhaps it is an unfair proverb which tells us that men hang the little rascals and let the big ones go free Real crime, thanks to the more liberal sentiment of law in our times, is nearly always prosecuted with justice, and, where it is discovered, visited with punishment. But our conscience is as yet all too dull where moral offences are concerned whose nature is such that they cannot be punished, because they violate no expressed

206 *The Individual Personality* [602-3

law. The most effective means of sharpening the public conscience in this respect would be one that must be used with care, if the blessings of liberty are to be preserved: namely, legislative enactments against the immoral use of liberty. If usury and gambling are punished, the usurer and the gambler will cease to belong to that society which is called respectable, often by a curious perversion of the term In such cases it is really not so much the punishment as the fact of legal taboo that exerts a purifying moral influence

Another important regulation, adapted not so much to check immoral occupations as to prevent the immoral conduct of modes of acquisition and employment that are right in themselves, is the transfer of such employments from the control of private individuals to that of public corporations, the State in particular. This method must be regarded as a final and radical means of reform, to be used especially where the form of occupation, as is often the case with manufacturers, tempts the individual who enters upon it to make immoderate and therefore immoral profit out of the powers of other men ; and where public supervision and protection are not sufficiently practicable. Forms of occupation that, when carried on by individuals, inevitably bring about immoral results should cease to exist as forms of individual occupation

### 3 CIVIC POSITION.

Every member of society who has entered into the full and free possession of his rights has, besides his personal occupation, a public calling. Ordinarily we speak of public occupations only where the personal profession is one that serves the ends of public life, as, for instance, in the case of the head of the State, or of State and district officials, parliamentary representatives, and the like. To a certain degree, however, it is a part of the occupation of every independent member of the community to exercise the civic rights and assume the civic duties that belong to him

A man's position as a citizen, which is thus seen to consist in certain social rights and duties, depends in its general features on his property, and in its details on his personal occupation. In the present social order property is of decisive importance, for society to-day is, in many of the features of public law, as well as in its customs and usages, still governed by the principle that the individual's rights and duties should depend on the power to perform public services of a material character that remains to him after he has performed the social duties imposed on him by his occupation. Where all a man's labour is exhausted in satisfying daily needs, there is little room left for public interests Hence, at least for a long period of political development, the citizens of a state are divided, according to the amount of their property, into two classes those who have political influence and those who have none Within the former, again, we distinguish the governing class, though the line of distinction is not very sharply marked ; and the personal occupation of the governing class is, wholly or in part, a public function of supreme importance.

It is natural, however, that a division of classes on the basis of property should not be permanent. Those who have no influence try to get it So long as this effort is unaccompanied by any improvement in their financial position it is a source of social discords, whose gravity is increased by the fact that the claimants are unable to perform public services proportioned to the influence they seek Hence it is only by a general improvement of property conditions that the lower classes can gradually

208          *The Individual Personality*          [604-5

attain a situation in life calculated to give greater weight
to their political claims. Meanwhile, however, the original
scale of civic position, dependent wholly on property
relations, is attacked from another quarter. At the present
time the majority of the ruling class are men of moderate
wealth   This means that occupation has already proved
more influential than property in determining a man's
position as a citizen. And if, as we may hope it will, the
future sees a still closer approach to equality in the matter
of property, at least in the sense of doing away with the
minimum of property, which is morally the more dangerous
of the two extremes; then in all probability the mode of
determining a man's position as a citizen which makes
property the sole test will be completely superseded by
another, where the test is solely occupation. Our present
system of society bears distinctly the marks of a transition
period, in which, however, there is already a prevailing
tendency towards a classification based on occupation.

That a man's personal calling determines his position as
a citizen, and that consequently certain differences in both
will continue to exist, is as inviolable a law of human society
as that law of the physical organism, according to which
different organs fulfil different functions, and hence exert
different influences on the whole   And it is a man's personal
occupation, far more than his property, that influences his
capacity for public function, because upon it depends his
possession of the information and powers required to judge
public affairs and to take an active part in them if necessary

We see, then, that the standard which determines the
general nature of the rights and duties that belong to an
individual by virtue of his civic position is variable, and
to be determined by the capacity for political function
possessed by a given kind of occupation, rather than by
any abstract requirements   Similarly, the sentiment of

political duty, with the moral effect that it exerts on the personality, cannot be absolutely constant. It is naturally most developed where a man's public occupation and his private occupation are the same. Hence positions of this nature are especially fitted to keep the sense of duty and public spirit constantly alive, and the more influence and responsibility a man has, the greater the moral effect upon him It would be absurd to expect from the humble labouring man, or the artist living in a world of fancies, the same incessantly active interest in questions affecting the general welfare that is the bounden duty of public officials and politicians

The development of political virtues through the influence of certain professions thus appears to partake of the nature of a special privilege belonging to certain favoured individuals It is the more important that there should exist certain duties and rights which are common to all citizens, and which from time to time recall his public function to each individual. We find the rule holding good here that the greater the duty imposed on the individual, the stronger will be the tie of moral sentiment that binds him to the object of his duty. This rule is strikingly confirmed by the enormous differences that exist in the ethical influence exerted by the various civic rights and duties on the development of public spirit and patriotism The exercise of the franchise, the payment of taxes, the duty of assuming certain honorary offices have ordinarily, aside from the fact that they are for the most part restricted to certain classes, a doubtful influence, because many of these duties are merely temporary, while others, like taxation, emphasise the personally onerous aspect of duty So that it is certainly a mistaken speculation that expects an increase of patriotism to result from imposing on the poorest classes the duty of paying taxes.

P

210 *The Individual Personality* [605-6

There is but one civic duty that possesses in the highest degree the property of arousing, by the kind of activity it requires, sentiments of self-sacrifice that are strong enough to restrain the opposite inclinations, which, of course, are not lacking even here. This is the duty of military service for one's country, and it involves one of the greatest of political rights, that of protecting the State and of using force as a necessary means to this end, a means forbidden to the peaceful citizen. Of course, however, military service exerts this influence only where it is an universal duty, whose burdens and dangers are shared alike by all citizens, whatever their other occupations.

Whether the dream of eternal peace, which will do away with this duty, is ever to be realised, need not be here discussed.[1] This much, at least, is certain, that the production of such a state of things would be hardly desirable, unless we could find some other means of filling the lack in the education of the patriot that would be produced if serious military service and constant readiness to fight for one's country were to be done away with. It is indeed earnestly to be desired that such a means may be gradually produced, as the nation's moral and political education gains in breadth and maturity. So long, however, as such an ideal education does not exist, we must acknowledge that the evils of war are probably of less weight than would be the loss of the most powerful means of producing the sentiment of patriotic duty. It may be that here, as elsewhere, the end will vanish when the means becomes unnecessary. If eternal peace is realised, the heightened sentiment of law and justice that is presupposed by such a state of things will surely be accompanied by a more universal sense of political duty, which can flourish without external means of education.

[1] *Cf* on this subject below, chap iv., 2

## 4. INTELLECTUAL CULTIVATION.

Like his position as a citizen, a man's share in universal intellectual interests is largely determined by his property and his occupation A surplus of material goods over and above what is needed to support existence is indispensable for the development of any intellectual interests whatever And a man's occupation must not absorb all his time and energy, if the intellectual life is not to be starved despite the existence of a surplus of material wealth. From the point of view of the individual, then, the social order must meet a certain requirement if it is to be a moral order It must assure to everyone who does not wilfully abstain from honest labour the possibility of an existence not devoid of the intellectual blessings of life. Not only must the State take care to preserve to those in its own employ the freedom requisite to a share in intellectual interests: it must exercise this kind of protective supervision over private labour as well.

Intellectual cultivation, however, like property and employment, must differ for different men Differences of disposition, of property and of profession have their say here. Thus, in general, the moral worth of intellectual interests consists not in their scope, but in the energy with which they are applied to the formation of character Intellectual goods are like material goods in this respect Just as the humble labourer is often more content in the enjoyment of his moderate income than the millionaire merchant whose cares and duties increase with the amount of his possessions, so the man who is physically and intellectually poor may get more uplift from devotion to the simplest religious ideas than the rich man in the high places of life gets from his treasures of art and literature. Not *where*, with what comprehensive breadth and in what fields,

212 *The Individual Personality* [607-8

the individual shares the intellectual life of humanity, but *how*, with what earnestness and inner fruitfulness,—that is the question that decides the moral worth of his culture. For upon this alone depends the moral disposition, and hence the happiness that results from his share in intellectual goods.

It is from this point of view that we must judge the stages through which man's partaking in general intellectual interests, like the intellectual life itself, develops  The first and most universal of these stages is that of the religious interest.  It is under the garb of religion that mankind first encounters ideas and problems which transcend the limited horizon of daily life  Religion, moreover, is always the point where the man who is debarred from all higher interests of intellectual culture can meet his fellow-men.  Hence, except where it is made to serve worldly and foreign ends, religion intentionally sets aside all barriers between the rich and the poor, the high and the low, the learned and the ignorant  It preaches to every mind that truth beyond which science can never go, namely, that the individual lives not for himself alone, but that his individual existence belongs to an universal psychical commonwealth, that his finite ends serve infinite ends whose ultimate fulfilment is hidden from his eyes.  It expresses this truth veiled in symbols for the most part ; yet the impression would be no more certain if its speech were that of fullest knowledge.  Hence, if religion ever finishes its mission in the moral education of mankind, it will still be indispensable to cement the intellectual union of humanity and to promulgate the greatest of all moral truths, without which no life would be worth living

Next to religion in the series of intellectual interests stands art.  Here, again, we have, in the simpler forms of art, an influence that may be widely diffused and affect men

608-9] *Intellectual Cultivation* 213

of all professions and occupations, though certain specific conditions of preparatory instruction, which are not equally open to all kinds of occupation, do count for more in art than in religion. While, then, we must regard it as a public duty, unfortunately too much neglected in our age, to make art the common possession of all so far as possible, yet, as a result of the immense variety of forms assumed by creative art, from the simplest to the most complex, a variety which makes the conditions of its understanding and enjoyment extremely diverse, not every work of art can be enjoyed by all. Foremost among the kinds of art that appeal to everybody are those which are associated with common religious ideas or with the common stock of national memories. Subjects taken from religion and from the nation's history have another advantage . the true work of art in this field appeals to all stages of intellectual culture. It arouses in all individuals feelings of similar tendency, by reason of the nature of the object represented But each man gives to these feelings a form suited to his own degree of cultivation A higher grade of culture adds much that is lacking to the less cultivated artistic sense. On the other hand, the latter has a freshness and force of feeling that richly compensates for any loss incurred through ignorance

The third stage of intellectual interests is that of science. The nature of science makes it the most exclusive of all means of intellectual cultivation. Whole departments of science require a degree of intellectual exertion and a concentration of labour that limit even their receptive appropriation to a small minority of persons. The disadvantage of this state of things is not only that it excludes many people altogether from certain fields of intellectual interest. What is perhaps still worse, the exertion required in scientific work has a tendency to make the practice of science as a profession rather a form of manual labour than

## 214      *The Individual Personality*      [609-10

a free intellectual activity. Now the objects of universal intellectual interest—religion, art, and science—cannot bear being turned into manual employments without losing their true value. Religion becomes a trade, an external formalism; art and science are transformed, the first frankly and openly, the second secretly, into actual manual labour. As such, they may be useful in furthering the exercise of intellectual interests in everyday life, scientific manual labour especially, because of the help it furnishes to real science, but they have no true share in these interests themselves. The fact is universally recognised in the case of art, but our estimate of science still labours under the influence of an utilitarian conception of life. The worst effects of this conception are to be found where it invades the realm of education and instruction. Their object is supposed to be not the development of the child into a man and a citizen, but his equipment from the start, so far as possible, with the powers and skill necessary in his future occupation. Such equipment is, indeed, an indispensable result of education, but it should never be the chief aim of intellectual cultivation. The true object of education is to make the individual participate, so far as he has the capacity, in the intellectual treasures that have been produced and stored up for future development by the intellectual labours of humanity as a whole and of his own nation in particular. When instruction thus supplies a basis of broadly human and national culture for the future superstructure of professional training, it has the power to make the individual a member of the moral community. Thus only can it further that identity of intellectual aims, which is a necessary condition of moral equality, and before which all differences in property, occupation and civic position vanish.

Many departments of science, like philosophy, the higher mathematics, and philology, are open only to the few. Yet

610-11]          *Intellectual Cultivation*          215

in science, as in art, there are certain objects which may
represent and further an intellectual interest that is common
to all  To have no conception of the course of natural events
in which he is himself involved, to be ignorant of the civil
order to which he belongs and its relation to other orders
of human society, to know nothing of the previous history
of his own nation and the whole past of humanity as
illuminated by the light of culture,—ignorance such as this
a man who laid any claim at all to intellectual interests
would feel to be unworthy of him  Natural science, political
science, and history are the three departments that should
furnish the basis of a true general culture.  The higher
grades of mankind, those who are called by their position
and influence as citizens to a more comprehensive mastery
of intellectual instruments, may add philosophy, philology,
and the history of civilisation.  These should, of course, accompany a deeper insight into the three most general departments of culture above named, especially the sciences which
lie nearest the individual's own profession or the field of
thought to which it introduces him.  Undeniably, even
among the so-called cultured classes, we are pretty far
removed from a state of affairs that is satisfying to the most
moderate expectations in this respect.  There are many
people, not only among the educated, but even among the
learned, who know little more of nature than what strikes
their senses directly; whose knowledge of the State is confined to what they learn from a hastily skimmed newspaper,
and whose acquaintance with history consists of their scanty
recollections of what they were taught in school.

The moral influence of these three fundamental departments of general culture is essentially different.  Natural
science, which leads the mind to trace the unbroken chain
of natural causality, arouses the sense of stern fidelity to
law and heightens the ethical aspect of the æsthetic influence

216    *The Individual Personality*    [611

of nature, since the impression of the whole is strengthened by intelligent attention to details   Political science gives a higher value to the duties of the citizen, which might otherwise be performed with the thoughtlessness of habit   It helps us to regard every personal function from the point of view of the wider purpose served thereby.   History, finally, extends the individual's share in the interests of the whole beyond the horizon of the immediate present   It gives us a glimpse of that supreme intellectual community in which all individual life and effort are contained   Thus each of these three great departments of knowledge is intimately connected with one of the three main aspects of the moral life.   The study of nature serves, where it is something more than an external and mechanical exercise of the memory and the understanding, chiefly to further subjective moral development.   Political science educates the sense of general social duty.   But history takes all the moral powers under its charge, for it brings before our consciousness the idea of the moral development of universal humanity in the midst of all the varying fortunes of individuals and nations.

The departments of knowledge that we have designated as the bases of higher culture, namely, philosophy, philology, and the history of civilisation, add no essentially new ethical elements to those contained in the necessary foundations of all intellectual culture, natural science, political science, and history.   But since they give us a more comprehensive and detailed picture of nature and intellectual life, they increase the force of its moral effect and bring to clearer consciousness the influences that were more instinctive in the earlier stages of culture.   Thus philology, both in itself and in the treasures of thought and artistic creation that it discloses, has the peculiar power of introducing us directly into the intellectual world of foreign peoples and remote ages. Through the history of civilisation—using the term in that broader and more exhaustive sense which includes the history of art and science—the picture of the world's past gains a richer background and a more lifelike aspect, and thus we obtain a deeper insight into the supremacy of historical laws. Philosophy, finally, leads contemplation to its ultimate height, from which the individual, without losing his significance as such, ceases to be a separate entity, and finds his place in a general ethical theory of the universe. Philosophy gives a conscious formulation to those truths concerning nature as a whole and the coherence of history, which were rather hinted at than really understood in the earlier stages of culture. Thus, while philosophy, of all sciences, is most distinctly a privilege of the few, it is yet indispensable to the completion of the highest culture And there is no more striking symptom of misdirected culture than the fact that the majority of educated people cultivate a form of philosophy which they do not themselves understand, or else a kind that is only too easy to understand,[1] while the so-called savants get on without any philosophy at all, which means, of course, that their occasional philosophising is done through the narrow little window from which they regard the world

Religion, art and science thus mark the three stages in the general development of the intellectual life, through which individuals and nations successively come into touch with intellectual interests. But we must not, of course, take this series to mean that the previous stage ceases to exist when the next one comes into being or reaches its fuller development. On the contrary, the history of civilisation shows impressively, not only that the later stage always draws the stimulus and incentive to its development from the foregoing

---

[1] Such philosophy sometimes goes by the appropriate name of fashionable philosophy. Who would venture to speak of fashionable physics or astronomy ? A more annihilating sentence could not be passed on any science than to treat it from the standpoint of fashion,—that most ephemeral, worthless and degenerate scion of custom.

218 *The Individual Personality* [612-3

stage, but that it reacts upon the latter as a helping and guiding influence. Thus art took its rise from the cult of religion, and is always deriving new and powerful motives from religious sources. Moreover, it has in no small measure reacted upon religious sentiments to ennoble and clarify them. Who could wish to dispense with the wealth of stimulus and feeling that religion has derived from architecture, music and poetry ? Similarly, while science originally sprang from religious soil, the intellectual recasting of religious problems is more than what it often seems to a superficial consideration,—one of the mightiest weapons against the bondage of religious tradition Religion and science have an immense positive influence upon each other, which is obscured by the strife against outworn religious ideas The whole mode of thought in modern metaphysics, from Descartes on, is affected by the theological speculation of the preceding age Anyone who can see the deeper meaning of conceptions through their outer form may trace the profound influence of the spirit of religious devotion even upon a thinker so independent as Spinoza. Only the man who refuses to recognise that religion is developing and constantly adapting itself to the other conditions of intellectual life can ignore the fact that religious feeling is always deriving new incentives from scientific thought. It is through the agency of science, and primarily of philosophy, that the continuous process of transforming religious ideas takes place The Reformation, the greatest manifestation of the influence of science to be found in modern times, is especial evidence of the truth of this statement.

We need hardly emphasise further the analogous relations of mutual helpfulness existing between art and science, for they are universally recognised. What immense fields for artistic creation have been opened by history alone ! And in understanding the inner connection of characters and events in history, the artistic form of conception anticipates with a sure instinct what later investigation can but laboriously confirm. Art, giving life and reality to nature and history, not only arouses interest in the object it deals with, but gives us a grasp of the whole; while the labour of the understanding is too apt to disintegrate the whole into its separate parts. Thus, in all regions of science where the purpose is the reconstruction of reality in an intellectual synthesis, and not merely the laborious analysis of perceptions and concepts, scientific activity is at the same time artistic activity. And even in the other departments of science, the man who does not experience a breath of artistic inspiration, at least in the representation of his discoveries, remains a mere manual labourer.

It is a noteworthy fact that, despite the undoubted existence of these reciprocal relations between religion, art and science, one of the three, religion, should be regarded as gradually disappearing from the intellectual life. It is held that the stage of intellectual interest which finds its satisfaction exclusively in the religious activities of the mind is dying out. Art and science, it is thought, are filling the vacancy thus arising, and will, of course, free themselves from the manifold relations that now bind them to the religious life. We need not here investigate the question as to whether such a result would not deprive art, especially, of its most valuable productions; whether church music, for instance, as a mere reminiscence of a feeling now become foreign to the listener's nature, would have a power at all comparable to that of the true sensation. Nor shall we go into the still more uncertain question whether such a state of universal artistic and scientific culture as is here assumed would be possible, and whether the "ideal state" thus contemplated would not mean in effect that we should add nothing to what the intellectually rich already possessed, while we took away from the intellectually poor all that

220    *The Individual Personality*    [614-5

he had. The essential point consists not in these results, which, however lamentable they might be, would have to be endured. The fundamental error is rather the opinion that religion is a primitive mode of thought destined to be supplanted by science. This is true only of the non-religious elements of myth, not of religion itself. Moral introspection shows that religious ideas, whose tendency to free themselves from their mythical garb, though slower in operation, is precisely analogous to that of scientific ideas, constitute an intellectual realm of independent and permanent value  Ethics, if it undertakes to trace out the ultimate and permanent sources of morality, instead of limiting its attention to the merely individual and outward phenomenal forms, must recognise that the most enduring of all moral springs of action, that which determines the direction of all individual and social efforts, is the striving after an ideal, towards which the reality created by moral action approximates, but to which it can never attain. The ideal thus becomes transcendent, yet always immanent in the human mind through the moral impulses. In the development of the moral spirit of humanity it approaches its fulfilment by an infinite progressus.

Now religion always represents the transcendent moral ideal in a form corresponding to the existing stage of morality and intellectual culture  Since religion belongs to the world of human ideas, it is necessarily subject to the defects that belong to the real moral world. But its ideal is always more nearly perfect than the reality ; and hence the common and inalienable characteristic of all stages of religious development is the thought that there *must be* an ideal to which reality never attains. Though philosophical ethics may end by holding that the only real significance of the moral ideal consists in the ceaseless effort towards it, yet the ideal itself is not thereby destroyed

## Intellectual Cultivation

Such a conception only serves to connect the living reality more intimately with the ideal world of religion, and thus to ensure to the latter its purely ideal value.

There are two principal and evident reasons for the unmistakable fact that religion, of all intellectual interests, is most in danger of being suppressed by the advance of other means of intellectual culture. The first of these is the tendency of artistic and scientific interests to become superficial It is precisely here that the closer connection between these various sides of the intellectual life is especially apparent. The deeper our certainty that true science and true artistic enjoyment lead back to religion, the easier it is to understand why superficial and half-way knowledge, and that misuse of art which makes it a mere plaything and pastime, should have the opposite result All reasonable educators, at least, though their practice is often much at fault, are theoretically agreed that polymathy and technical preparation for practical occupations are not the main object of scientific education But art, and especially that form of it which is most popular and has the greatest moral influence, namely, dramatic art, is treated, if not actually regarded, by the State and by private individuals as a mere idle pastime.

A second reason, deeper-lying and apparently harder to remove, for the alienation of religion from the other two departments of intellectual interest is to be found, not in the misuse of the latter, but in the way in which religion itself is conceived In the case of really great works of art, which furnish enjoyment and uplift to all, whatever their degree of cultivation, no one demands that all men shall feel and think exactly alike about them. While we recognise the moral significance of the study of history, as a branch of knowledge having the highest cultural value for men of all stations in life, it would be absurd to require

222    *The Individual Personality*    [616-7

that the man of science, who devotes thorough and critical study to it, and the labouring man who uses it as a means of rising above the sphere of his daily life, should regard it from the same point of view. Yet many people exclude from religion the principle that is self-evident in art and science, namely, the adaptation of the mode of conceiving a subject to the individual's grade of cultivation. Religion, it is thought, must be the same for all, not only in the fundamental moral ideas which are its basis, but in the special formulation that may be given to these ideas. Nay, it must be the same to-day as it was for our ancestors centuries ago. People are narrow-minded enough to think that religion might lose something if her ideas were to broaden and deepen as the intellectual horizon expands  Yet science and art show us how the enduring value of religious conceptions might be maintained without imposing on thought and feeling the burden of ideas themselves indifferent to the matter at issue  For science tells us that dogma is a mode of thinking which is variable, and has arisen under definite historical conditions, that the only germ of real value in it is the moral idea, which is the real impelling force, often long unrecognised, in religious thought itself  Art, on the other hand, leads us to the thought that religious ideas are symbols, dependent partly on æsthetic motives, partly on other considerations foreign to religion itself, that as symbols they give to religious ideas a form that is adapted to the existing state of belief and knowledge  Because religious ideas have this character, because, while the more naive way of regarding them takes them for realities, a higher stage of culture discovers their symbolic nature, there is suggested the possibility of uniting men of the most widely different degrees of cultivation into one religious faith without exacting a *sacrificium intellectus* from the individual.

617] *Intellectual Cultivation* 223

It is undoubtedly true that the significance of each of these four factors—property, occupation, position and intellectual culture—for the relation between the individual and society has varied. At first property determines everything, occupation and civic position are inherited along with property. These circumstances decide the amount of intellectual culture that the individual can acquire, in the sense that culture is the exclusive privilege of the well-to-do and influential. But there has been a gradual change in this respect, during the last century especially. The weight of influence has shifted from property to occupation, and in both of these from inherited to acquired advantages, though the old state of affairs still persists to a certain extent as a result of the inheritance of property and the influence of the family and of education. A second transition is already preparing that from the estimation of men according to their occupation to the estimation of them by the degree of intellectual culture they possess. This fact is evident from the rules that custom imposes on social intercourse. It is true, of course, that in such intercourse property and civic position play a not inconsiderable rôle even nowadays. Many an otherwise reasonable man counts it an honour to associate with the rich and those of exalted position, even when the rich man is a scapegrace and the eminent individual a dunce But the tendency that is developing in our estimates of our fellows should not be judged by such weaknesses as this, which everyone smiles at in others and fails to notice only when he himself is the guilty party It should be gathered from our observation of the sort of actions that we all respect. Such actions show that the degree of a man's intellectual culture has become the test that decides his claim to stand on a basis of social equality with others We find that while a man of learning might without misgiving invite to his table a subordinate official or clerk, he

224        *The Individual Personality*        [617-8

would hardly ask a day labourer or factory operative. Nowadays, however, the reason for this distinction would not be that the one kind of occupation is regarded as more valuable than the other, or even as intellectually superior to it,—as a matter of fact this would not be true in many instances,—but simply that the one occupation is ordinarily associated with a higher degree of intellectual cultivation than the other, so that in the former case there is a community of intellectual interests that is lacking in the latter.

There are certain projects for social reforms whose idea is to introduce social equality by reducing the labour necessary to support life to the level of a fixed amount of mechanical work required from each individual. Such schemes as these show that their projectors have not freed themselves from the tendency to estimate the worth of personality by property and occupation, a tendency which the development of social culture is gradually overcoming. The real goal of moral culture finds its best expression, not in these Utopian dreams, but in the longing felt by every clear-sighted and ambitious worker to increase the degree of his intellectual cultivation.

The truth is that the only kind of human equality conceivably attainable is not complete equality of intellectual culture, which would be neither possible nor desirable, but equality in the chief intellectual interests of life. It is also that towards which, despite opposing principles, the forces of morality and culture are striving.

618-9]

# CHAPTER II.

## SOCIETY.

### I THE FAMILY

IN the moral oidei of to-day the ethical value of family life is confined to the family in its narrower sense of a single married couple with their children. We have before pointed out the increased depth of moral significance thus gained by family relationships[1] By reason of the closer connection established between the members of a family, there has arisen an unanimity of purpose possible to no form of association outside of the family bond Every outward function of personal life gives distinct evidence of this fact

In the first place, the family represents a common stock of property and of earnings Husband and wife combine the property which they have inherited or independently acquired, in order to use it for common ends and transfer it to their children, either during their own lifetime or after their death. The custom which sometimes obtains under certain conditions, of having the wife keep her property separate or even carry on a business of her own, is contrary to the natural conditions of family life. It is the first step towards a division of interests, which cannot fail to extend to other departments of life, and hence must necessarily destroy the moral basis of the family by reducing it to its original level, that of a purely external sexual relation.

[1] *Cf.* Part I , chap iii , pp 236, 237.

226 *Society* [619-20

Where the money-getting is the function of the husband alone, as is the case in many kinds of occupation, and regularly in the higher forms, the wife has still an important field of activity in looking out for the preservation of the family property, and especially in applying it to meet the family needs. Upon her depends the prosperity of the common establishment and of everything the family is thereby enabled to do

As regards the second general condition of life, occupation, it is only to a very limited extent that the members of a family can aim directly at like ends. Actual community of employment can exist only under relatively simple conditions, and in forms of occupation that make it possible for husband and wife to have equal or similar shares of the work involved. These conditions are approximately filled almost nowhere save in the life of the small farmer. And the moral advantage of such community of labour is very slight. It does away with a division of functions that is adapted to the physical differences between man and woman and in so doing imposes tasks on the woman that tend to produce corresponding alterations in her nature. It is when the labours of husband and wife are complementary, not identical, that we find the truly moral family relationship. The woman whose occupation has rendered her masculine has lost those qualities of disposition that render her valuable to the family. Her work is no longer prized as the qualitative complement to that of man it is claimed as a quantitative assistance, like that of a labourer in his service

A complete antithesis to this state of affairs, where man and wife share equally in a common labour or business, is formed by the case where they follow wholly different occupations. In the lower forms of employment the pressure of hardship has long since made such a relation necessary.

620] *The Family* 227

We find it existing more especially in cases where the husband's occupation employs his own powers alone, but does not suffice, as well as might be desired, for the family maintenance  Under such conditions it must be granted that for the wife to co-operate in the support of the family by manual labour, or by the practice of some occupation suited to her powers and capacities, is, while not in itself desirable, an expedient grounded in the nature of her circumstances and conducive, since it ensures the maintenance of outward existence, to the realisation of moral ends.  Of late years, however, the effort of woman to secure greater independence has not infrequently led to the occurrence of this relation in the higher walks of life, where there is no financial necessity for it, and where only the desire to increase the pleasures of life by means of a double source of income, or, still oftener, the impulse of the more talented women to seek a life of greater outward activity and more varied interests, furnishes the motive for its existence.  Evidently, the result of this state of things is in many respects like that which usually follows from similarity between the occupations of husband and wife.  Just as the wife must fail to give her husband the best kind of help where she is merely the companion of all his labours, so the family threatens to become a purely external business association when husband and wife follow separate occupations and independent interests  Only in the latter case they may even lose interest in each other's work, since their own employments furnish them with full occupation and satisfaction  These are disadvantages from which the most important family duties, those of education and of mutual moral help, cannot fail to suffer.  All of which is not to deny that there are cases which do not come under the rule. In particular, where great artistic talent on the wife's part justifies her assumption of a more independent position, the

228 *Society* [620-1

life of the couple, devoted to different intellectual interests, yet united by mutual understanding, may produce a relationship morally fai above the average But the rules of the moral life cannot be shaped in accordance with rare exceptions.

There is one case, of course, where woman must be allowed the opportunity of getting her living by an occupation suited to her powers, and of making herself useful to human society The unmarried woman, denied the functions of wife and mother, must not be prevented from competing with men in the field of labour, wherever the kind of activity does not forbid The prejudice that the intellectual capacity of woman disqualifies her for certain higher kinds of employment is a particularly ill-founded argument. While the exceptions to it as a rule are isolated instances, their occurrence is sufficient to leave the decision of the question to the existing state of competition It would, however, be unjust to apply a rule which may suit the majority to those whom it would forbid the exercise of a profession suited to their powers and useful to themselves and others.

Two conditions only may be posited as absolute, since the cases which they do not affect are so contrary to feminine nature that they can claim no privilege Woman should undertake no employment that exceeds her physical force, and should avoid occupations to which her character is opposed. Kinds of work that require great muscular strength, extraordinary perseverance, suppression of the feelings, and great energy of will are not made for woman, whose physical organisation renders weakness and changes of mood an unavoidable part of her nature, if she is to remain woman. The existing social institutions ought not to deny to those whose gifts are above the average the right to pursue exceptional careers , but they cannot assume the task of making laws for exceptional natures. The

621-2]                    *The Family*                    229

occurrence of uncommon degrees of cowardice does not
excuse man from military service, and the reason is that
such cowardice cannot be presupposed to exist. In like
manner, the possession of uncommon courage on the part
of some women cannot be made a ground for allowing them
to take part in military service, for it is not a characteristic
that can be counted upon. The inspired Maid, fighting for
her country in the moment of its greatest need, is a noble
figure, though she transgresses the limitations of her sex   but
a regiment of female soldiers would be a repulsive sight.   For
similar reasons politics will never be a profession suited to
women   It requires a force of character which is not too
frequent among men, and which in women would indicate a
masculinity foreign to their true nature

This brings us to the third aspect of personal activity,
that of the citizen.   The effort to secure for woman an
independent position as a citizen is not the least important
of the ways in which the so-called movement for female
emancipation usually finds expression   And of all the
attempts at abolishing differences in the conduct of personal
life, none bears so clearly the stamp of falsity to nature
as this   For a woman to take an active part in the political
conflicts that agitate the State and society is as contradictory
to her character and disposition as bearing arms and doing
military service is to her physical nature.   Even the highly
cultivated woman, who is intellectually far superior to the
average man, must always, where questions relating to
matters of public utility and function are concerned, depend
on the stronger masculine character   She must take her
guidance from man, and, under favourable circumstances,
may support him in undertaking and carrying out his duties
by following him in the thoughts and sentiments which he
seeks to act out in his life, so lightening by her sympathy
the burden of his duty and increasing the pleasure and

230 *Society* [622-3

the productiveness of his work  Thus, while woman should not keep wholly aloof from political life, her attitude to it should be marked by that reserve which is imposed upon her by the avoidance of any personal share in public contests, and by the requirement that she shall preserve an harmonious moderation in her emotions

At no time and under no circumstances, least of all here, where the sphere of the individual's function has been indicated by Nature herself, can it be a postulate of freedom that all persons shall be permitted to do all things  Everyone should be what Nature has made him.  If she has excluded women from many departments of life, she has opened to them others where they have a better right than men.  One of the noblest of these is the profession of educating the coming generation into capable human beings.  Few people have the opportunity to influence public life directly  And among the many forms of indirect influence, which are all that the civic position of most men allows, there is none greater than that influence on the living representatives of the future which it is the function of the family, and pre-eminently of the wife, to exert

While civic duties are a department of life in which woman has only an indirect share, the realm of intellectual culture, on the other hand, is as fully open to her, on the whole, as to man, though with a certain difference, it is true.  This is especially the case in the simplest conditions of human life, where the struggle for existence absorbs nearly all the husband's efforts, and where religious motives are almost the only influences that tend to unite the individual with the intellectual life of society.  Here, where the circumstances are favourable, it is especially the wife who cultivates the intellectual side of life and transmits it in education to the coming generation as their most precious heritage. Moreover, the sentiments of filial piety felt towards a mother,

623-4] *The Family* 231

sentiments that have something of religious reverence about them, are often the surest safeguard of morality in such stations of life, which poverty renders most dangerous to morals.

Other intellectual interests come into play at the higher stages of culture, and such interests now become an object of pursuit to the husband as well as the wife, whether in the leisure intervals of his proper occupation, or as an aid to it, or even as his own profession. This gives greater opportunity for a division of interests, corresponding to differences of disposition, and thus both husband and wife get a stimulus that they might otherwise lack. Scientific study is more in accord with the active character and the wider range of practical interests that belong to man ; or if he applies himself to art, either receptively or creatively, he uses scientific methods in its pursuit. For the wife, on the other hand, art is usually the prevailing intellectual interest, because in art her attitude may be wholly receptive, and she may gain the most varied stimulus for her more fully developed emotional life. Hence women, even when they are intellectually creative, for the most part pursue art and not science. And in the pursuit of art they cultivate forms and kinds of creation which are the direct outflow of feeling, or which depict reality without the aid of a mode of representation requiring study Thus, to confine ourselves to the realm of poetry, women have excelled in lyrical verse and kindred forms of emotional expression, and in the psychological novel, but they have never gone beyond mediocrity in the epic, the drama and the historical novel. As for science, centuries of experience compel us to maintain that it is not the true province of the feminine mind. The tendency of woman in scientific study is towards matters that appeal to her artistic sense in some way, like the observation of nature or history, and towards an individual

232                    *Society*                    [624

and biographical, rather than an universal treatment of
the latter. The sciences with which she has least affinity
are the pure sciences of the understanding, such as logic,
mathematics and jurisprudence. As yet there have been
no great mathematicians or jurists among women. Even
Shakespeare's Portia arouses our admiration less by the
juristic acumen of her judgment than by her splendid
speech on mercy, which is conceived in a truly feminine
spirit.

Property, occupation, civic position and common intellectual interests form a bond which joins the members
of a single family into a solid unity. They are the basis
of an unique social organisation, which is, moreover, the
most effective school of unselfishness and sacrifice. This
latter aspect of the family bond is especially prominent in
the relation of parents to children  The element of
reciprocal service, otherwise so valuable, interferes with
the development of perfectly unselfish impulses between
husband and wife. But the child is at first entirely helpless,
and for a long time afterwards is dependent on its parents
at least for the chief necessities of life and for its intellectual
training. The only return it can make for all it receives is
the pleasure of witnessing its progress. Hence childhood
has probably done more to combat barbarism and self-
seeking than all the influences of outward culture. Even
the mother who is morally a savage is at times stirred to
impulses of pure self-sacrifice by her child  And here is
where the wife has an infinite advantage over the husband.
For all these motives operate more strongly upon her, and
hence the pleasures that grow out of such feelings are
stronger and more permanent in her case. But no darker
shadow can fall upon the moral condition of any class than
the reversal of this relation of pure giving and receiving
between parent and child, the misuse of children from their

earliest years as sources of income, or the planting by parental example of the germ of crass selfishness in the child's disposition. The instances not infrequently met with of hardened and habitual criminals, who conceal their unhallowed trade from their children in the hope of shielding them, at least, from crime are far more praiseworthy than such wretches as these, who are often clever enough to avoid actual conflict with the law

No government, within any conceivable period of time, will reach the point where individuals will cease to be led astray by want of occupation, poverty and the spirit of pleasure-seeking, thus necessarily involving their families in physical and moral ruin. It is one of the gravest aspects of crime that it is not limited to the criminal himself, but disturbs the moral life for generations through the progressive influence of example and defective moral education. Such evils, of course, cannot be wholly obviated while the individual causes that produce them are in operation. However, we do not consider that society has fulfilled its whole moral duty by punishing the criminal, but regard it as still under obligation to furnish everyone who desires to earn his own living by honest labour with the opportunity to do so. And in like manner the endeavour to destroy, by providing a helpful system of public education, this silently maturing germ of immorality ought to be regarded, far more than is at present the case in our customary modes of remedying public evils, as a duty that society owes to itself and to the future.

## 2. SOCIAL CLASSES.

We have already discussed, in considering the civic position of the individual, the way in which social divisions take their rise in the diversity of property relations, and the gradual change from the predominance of this factor to that of occupation [1] Along with distinctions of property and occupation there go differences in intellectual interests, and from the totality of these conditions there finally arise those divisions of society which we call social classes.

The simultaneous and to a certain extent independent working of all three of these factors is a peculiar feature of modern society And their co-operation is the chief reason why social problems have become so much more serious and urgent, morally as well as in other respects. Property relations, which originally determined the social order in the simplest manner, by the use of an external standard easily applied under any circumstances, are now complicated in all kinds of ways by the other two factors. The more influential occupations have long since ceased to involve more extended material possessions, and, moreover, the tendency of intellectual culture, one of the most powerful instruments even of external influence, is always to elevate its possessors above the level of their fellows, and thus to render class distinctions elastic.

For a long time these equalising forces were hindered by the social ordinance, deep-rooted in the moral and legal order, which made a man's birth the test of his rank as a citizen The division of society into the nobility and the *bourgeois*, and of the nobility into higher and lower orders, was itself originally a distinction involving differences of property and occupation But when the *bourgeois* and the noble came into competition as landed proprietors, and

---

[1] See above, chap. i., pp. 206 ff

**626-7]**        *Social Classes*        235

existing property distinctions were done away with, usually to the disadvantage of the former owners, when the law abolished the most essential legal privileges of the aristocracy of birth; and when, finally, the levelling influence exerted by the increased esteem in which natural endowments and intellectual culture were held, had destroyed almost completely that last stronghold of inherited privilege, the exclusive right to certain occupations,—then the effect of birth was more and more restricted to those influences which must always be exercised on a man by the position of his parents and the nature of his education. From these facts it follows that the criteria which used to divide society into rigidly distinguished classes have now fallen into disuse. Almost the only question as regards property now is whether a man has or has not enough to ensure him a competence, this assured, an official or a merchant has the same social position, whether he is rich or very moderately well off. Even distinctions of occupation are becoming less sharply drawn A man's occupation is almost what he makes it : the commonest manual labour may be ennobled by an intelligent and lofty mode of performing it, and the worker with his hands may win for himself by culture and ability an honourable position as a citizen. Thus the balance of influence gradually shifts in the direction of the factor of intellectual culture, though the other factors, especially in so far as they determine intellectual culture, preserve a certain weight.

And so the only universally valid division of society turns out to be the distinction of an upper and a lower class, between which it is useful for many purposes to introduce a middle class, obtained, however, merely by subdividing the higher class. This division is sufficiently vague to allow for the great variableness of the standards according to which such distinctions are nowadays drawn, and also for

## 236 *Society* [627-8

the fluctuations which make it always possible for the individual either to rise above or to fall below the limits of the social class to which he belongs.   If we distinguish two classes only, the upper class will include those property-holders, persons engaged in the better forms of occupation and persons of influence as citizens, who pursue intellectual interests   The lower class will comprise those who are nearly or wholly destitute of property, who follow lower forms of occupation, and with whom intellectual interests are of less moment   If we divide the upper class, again, into a highest and a middle class, the test for the former is partly direct participation in the government and partly certain external circumstances, which, although connected with the historical tradition of an hereditary nobility, otherwise falling into abeyance, still preserve a certain influence   Thus the highest social grade will consist of the governing class, and of those with whom it has, or may have, social intercourse.

It is probable that the fluctuations which are already obliterating the boundaries between social classes, and which are in particular cases continually bringing about the rise and fall of individuals in the competition for position and culture, will increase.   The individual will soon owe his rank, far more than is at present the case, to what he is in himself rather than to the station in which he was born   But social classes will not cease to exist   For differences of occupation and intellectual culture must always exist, and differences of external position must result from them.   If they were to be forcibly abolished, they would tend to re-establish themselves through the occurrence of variations in natural talents and moral endowment,—above all, through the moral needs of society   Universal equality is desirable only from the point of view of that extreme individualism which regards society as merely a sum of individuals, and hence sees in its

628-9]                    *Social Classes*                    237

complete dissolution the ideal of a so-called social order. As a matter of fact, if the individual were really the sole end of all moral effort, little objection could be urged against an ideal of this sort. But the nature of man distinctly vetoes any such proposal to do away with the social order, and thus indicates plainly that society, like the family, has independent moral ends, which it can attain only through its division into different orders of occupation and culture While these orders originated in part from other considerations, they are emphasised and protected by the moral ends which they serve. Since we have already discussed (pp. 207 ff.) the moral influence that membership in a definite social class exerts on the individual, we need merely glance at the moral effects of the social order on society itself

Division of labour is the vital condition of all the more comprehensive forms of intellectual effort. The family pursues moral ends which the individual cannot pursue, and which the family could not attain unless every one of its members had his own indicated and peculiar tasks, based on his natural endowment and intellectual development. Just so in the case of society, a division into definite classes is an arrangement essential to the ends of the whole and hence to the morality of the individual as well We have found the fundamental assumption in all intellectual life to be that while the individual is on the one hand borne along on the current of the ideas and endeavours of the society to which he belongs, on the other hand he reacts upon society through his own ideas and tendencies of will. In this ceaseless process of action and reaction the creative function belongs wholly to the individual consciousness : society merely conserves what individuals have won. But the only way in which it can make its intellectual treasures available for future development, and thus bring about that continuity of the intellectual life which is essential to all progress, is

238 *Society* [629

by entrusting them to a representative that will outlast the individual.[1]

Now, in order that society may execute this important task, it must divide itself into an active element, whose immediate function is to increase the stock of intellectual wealth, and a passive element that absorbs and preserves the new thoughts and germs of will But all intellectual states are absolutely continuous in their development; and, moreover, these new intellectual acquisitions are made up of an enormous number of individual products, many of which lie hidden in a heterogeneous mass of phenomena, and fail to show themselves in their true nature as co-operative factors and conditions Hence the individuals upon whom the active rôle devolves do not always stand out distinctly from their environment, and the process of reciprocal influence must be arranged for in the divisions of society itself. This is increasingly the case, the more complex the society is and the more widely disseminated the capacity to do active service for the moral life In primitive societies it may well be that divisions are unnecessary, a few leading spirits ranking far above the rest. But with the intensive and extensive growth of moral culture, such a state of things becomes less and less possible. It now devolves upon a greater sum of individual forces to do what was formerly done by a few Along with increasing complexity of function there is increased necessity for a division of labour. The weaker minds must labour in the service of the moral ideas , the stronger ones, while they may indicate the path of moral development, cannot determine it in detail There is no realm of intellectual creation where this rule does not hold, from the province of the statesman, the man of science and the artist, down to the affairs of practical life, serving as they do ends that are merely transitory. All these in-

[1] *Cf.* above, Part iii., chap 1 , pp 34 ff

## Social Classes

tellectual realms are, however, directly or indirectly, aids to moral culture or elements in it.

Thus we see that the process of social development does not consist in a reduction of society to homogeneous elements Rather, the progress of the moral life and the demands of the growing multiplicity of moral problems and efforts, lead in the direction of a completer and complexer division of society into classes. As the development of the living organism does not do away with the differentiation of organs, but increases, while at the same time refining it, so the process of perfecting the social organisation proceeds from the simpler to the more complex, and not in the reverse direction. What sometimes gives rise to the opposite illusion is simply the fact, itself quite independent of this process, that the influence of inherited qualities other than personal merits on the individual's social position is decreasing, while that of acquired qualities, especially of intellectual culture and the development of character, is increasing

To the constitution of society out of active and passive elements there corresponds a division of its members into two classes First, there is the higher class, which furnishes conditions for the production of active intellectual leaders of social life Secondly, there is the lower class, which serves as the receptive social consciousness and allows the creations of the active element to gain the necessary fixity and security by their effect on the social will Clearly, such a relation between the classes will be successful in proportion as social position is decided by intellectual culture and moral energy of will, that is, in proportion to the ease with which the individual can raise himself from a lower to a higher social class, or obtain a more influential position in the latter, by his own merits.

These considerations offer a basis for the division of

240 *Society* [630-1

society into two classes only. The distinction of a third and supreme social order is based on other conditions, which, if they are not its originating causes, at least constitute the grounds for its preservation As the limits that formerly marked off social classes from each other are gradually effaced in the free competition for social rank, it becomes desirable to offset this continual movement and flux of society by creating a more permanent and stable class, which shall include the representatives of the supreme power in the State The leading motive here is identical with that which impels us to preserve the State from the disturbances attendant on competition for the highest places, by limiting royal authority to a single family, and to regard the permanence of such authority as an outward sign of the permanence of the political order. Naturally, this motive will govern the social order as long as any importance is attached to the corresponding political theory Hence the highest social class tends to disappear with the introduction of republican forms of government.

While, as all this shows, the social order is not a creation existing merely for the sake of the individual; while it need not seek its justification in the services it does to individuals, yet we must not neglect the fact that here, too, social ends react to the advantage of individual ends, and that the individual gains more from the division of society into classes than he could gain from a dissolution of the social order and a levelling of all distinctions. Aside from those features of the moral life already mentioned in our discussion of the individual's position as a citizen, which are peculiar to different stations in life, and which would, of course, vanish if social differences were abolished, the individual's effort to advance his station has introduced into the civilisation of to-day a certain factor that, while it involves its own dangers, like every new aid to morality,

631-2]                    *Social Classes*                    241

must yet be regarded as one of the most effective and indispensable forces of intellectual and moral development.

The chief reason why the social problem is at the same time a moral problem is because in the strife of individuals to secure social position, besides much that is objectionable and directed toward transitory ends, there co-operates a moral factor whose right cannot be gainsaid. It is this · the equality of social rights for which the masses deprived of such equality strive is a prerequisite to moral equality. For not only does the social regard enjoyed by the individual react upon his self-respect. Without it he is incapable of sharing in those common intellectual purposes whose pursuit unites the members of a moral community.

The great ethical superiority of Christianity over ancient civilisation consists in its thorough application of the principle of moral equality   At first it sought this equality only in that intellectual realm where its application to the moral life is still most fruitful : it believed that all individuals bear the same relation to the ultimate grounds and end of human existence   As the power of Christianity grew, however, the influence of this doctrine of equality, at first conceived with reference only to the future life, necessarily extended into the sphere of the present, and finally resulted in the demand for a common possession of the most important intellectual goods.   If we may deduce from the past and the present the direction of future development, the law seems to hold good that the sphere of those who share by their own efforts and with a clear consciousness of the ends they seek in the advancement of social culture will become wider and wider, and that its extension will become essential to the furtherance of moral ends.

While the sphere of intellectual culture is thus the only one where relative equality of individuals is at once attainable and necessary to ensure the moral worth of personality,

    R

242                    *Society*                    [632-3

intellectual equality cannot fail to react upon the other conditions that determine a man's social status. Personal property, as an aid to free personal activity, will probably always be indispensable on moral grounds. In order, however, that its influence may be restricted to the limits thus established, the extremes of wealth and poverty, which involve so many disadvantages to morals, must be gradually done away with. The society of to-day tends in many ways to regulate itself in this regard  For instance, there is the increased estimate, moral as well as material, put upon all kinds of useful work, and the diminished toleration of wealth acquired without labour, together with the tendency to depreciate the moral status of such wealth. The influence of the State is even stronger than that of these regulative influences which operate within the sphere of personal activity  As the State itself, local or district governments, and those associations which are under State supervision enter into competition with individuals in the production of material goods, there grows up an economic order where public property has increasing importance and private property gradually tends to be restricted within the limits indicated by the moral ends that it should serve  When the equalising of property relations has made the phenomenon of prosperous idleness an exception, it will no longer escape the contempt it deserves, though it will probably never disappear, any more than that of crime and dishonour Again, on the other hand, the more uniform distribution of goods that will be effected by individual and collective regulations will result in a tendency to estimate the social worth of personality chiefly by humane and intellectual interests and by the moral energy with which these are pursued

The two extremes within which the material postulates of a satisfactory social condition vary have been designated

633-4]                    *Social Classes*                    243

as "the right to a full equivalent of labour" and "the right
to existence."[1]  These formulæ suit the social movements of
the time, which are still almost wholly directed towards
the securing of material goods  They are also significant
of the way in which egoistic and altruistic motives are
intermingled, and of the insufficiency of all such efforts
to reform society without referring to the ethical principles
of the social order.  True, the fundamental law that labour
should be rewarded according to its value has a moral basis.
Hence even in the most ideally moral society there will be
differences of property and position corresponding to individual differences in capacity.  Communistic society is
as far removed as possible from the social ideal, precisely
because it does away with such differences.  But the demand
that every man shall receive a full equivalent for his labour
pushes this principle, in itself right and just, to the extreme
of reckless egoism, where the individual does everything
for himself and nothing for others, and a moral order of
society becomes impossible  While the first of these principles thus demands more for the individual than the moral
community, upon which the very existence of individuals
depends, can ever ensure to him, the second, which claims
for him the right to exist. demands too little.  The task of
a truly moral order of society will always be not merely
to render the individual's external existence possible, but
to make it possible in such a form that, whatever station
in life he occupies, he can share the intellectual interests of
the community and thus attain that social equality which
is the first condition of complete moral equality  Yet the
demand for the possibility of mere existence may serve
as an ethical minimum.  However meagre its content, it is
not wholly superfluous in a state of society where even

[1] A MENGER, *The Right to the Whole Produce of Labour*  Trans by M E
Tanner.  London, 1899.

## 244 *Society* [634

undeserved poverty is sometimes abandoned to hopeless ruin.

But, aside from the fact that they are partly one-sided and partly inadequate, all these maxims are defective, because they take account only of the material side of existence, which, ethically regarded, must be merely a means, not an end in itself The same error reversed affects all Utopian ideals of society, from Thomas More to Bellamy and others They depict ideal relationships of property and economics which are wholly lacking in historical continuity with the civilisation of to-day. The fact that in order to bring about such prodigious changes men themselves must become other than they are is entirely ignored. This is an inversion of the only true causal relation. Men are not supposed to create institutions, but institutions are supposed to create men. Of course, the social order may produce good as well as evil But to develop an order that will produce good, the forces in operation must ultimately proceed from individuals. The Utopian ideals, however, conflict with personal freedom, which is the very life-atmosphere of moral development, for they are conceivable only on the basis of a forcible reconstruction of things, and hence either frankly or tacitly introduce the element of constraint into the description of their ideal. Thus the ideal, applied to men as they are, is no ideal at all, but an institution for suppressing all independent moral impulses And it is the very opposite of an ideal for the ideal man it presupposes, since the reign of force is the most unpropitious and inadequate form of life that a society of moral beings can choose for itself. Thus if the Island of Utopia should be actually discovered, everyone would wish to get away from it; the good because they would have no opportunity to do right on their own motion, and the bad because even in the future they will prefer liberty to the house of correction.

634-5]                 *Social Classes*                 245

All reform schemes of this sort, which hold that the cure for moral ills is to be found in distributing the good things of life equally, or on the basis of a calculation of desert, overlook the fact that man's happiness, like his moral worth, does not depend on such an equality of so-called goods,—an equality that is essentially incompatible with the inner as well as the outer conditions of life. If the means to happiness could in the long run be distributed with approximate equality, unhappiness would not cease to exist, nor would crime, though certain occasions for it might be removed To bring about a progressive diminution of external occasions for unhappiness and crime, the first requisite is a social order that undertakes to prevent the occurrence of morally bad property conditions, and to produce that kind of social equality which arises out of the common pursuit of the highest intellectual interests. At the same time, it must not ignore the fact that the interests of life and occupation are manifold, and that the happiness of the individual, no less than the welfare of the community, depends upon this variety of interests, for the individual's happiness is not external, but internal. It springs from that consciousness of moral capacity, the possession of which makes a man who is true to his own nature unwilling to change his personality for that of another.

### 3  ASSOCIATIONS

An important supplement to the division of society into classes, which is based on the property, occupation, intellectual interests and general position of the various members of society, and which rests in part on obsolete historical conditions, is formed by the innumerable associations that originate from the free will of individuals. In such associations we have a combination of forces to bring about

## 246 *Society* [635-6

ends that the isolated individual would find it difficult or impossible to accomplish. While a man's own will is not wholly without influence in determining the social class to which he belongs, yet a long time must elapse before it can effect a change in his position, which is dependent on external causes. But the association is wholly a product of the free choice of its members Hence the life of an association brings into the historic fixity of the social order, which that order will never, perhaps, wholly lose, a freer play of social forces, and allows a wider scope to individual activity. Corresponding to this we have the fact that social classes, though individuals may sometimes pass from one to another, are mutually exclusive ; while the various kinds of associations and societies blend in a great variety of ways. A man may belong to many associations, but not to more than one social class.

Associations are always the product of a community of interests. While the word association or union (*Verein*) indicates that individuals are brought together into a unity, the bond that unites them may be closer or laxer according to the importance of the ends for which they strive in common, and the greater or less similarity of their positions in life. The general term association is usually employed to indicate the loosest form of union Associations, in this narrower sense, may include among their members men of the most widely different social classes, occupations and positions. There is a closer bond of union in societies that are formed for the pursuit of a single definite end, which presupposes a more permanent interest on the part of the members of the society Business or trades unions come next, membership in which usually implies a unity of endeavour that extends to other departments of life. Last of all comes the corporation, the union of whose members is outwardly manifested by its claim to be regarded as a legal unit, to have external representation, and the like A society presupposes that its members belong to the same social class, and have common material or intellectual interests, a guild or union is based on similarity of employment, while a corporation determines the civic position of its members, and often their occupation as well.

This external classification, between whose divisions many intermediate forms occur, is less important morally than the classification of associations according to the ends for which they exist Broadly speaking, such ends may be humanitarian, social or individual; or they may be complex, combining different orders of ends Especially do we find such combinations of social and individual, or of social and humanitarian objects. A trades union, for example, affects the individual's interests in the first instance, but its endeavour is to reach certain social ends as well by bringing together those engaged in the same occupation. The object of a benevolent association is humanitarian; but in so far as it is restricted to definite spatial limits and local needs, its ends are social

This broadly ethical principle of division is crossed by another principle, of preponderant importance for the immediate moral result of associational activity. It divides associations according to the sphere of personal life towards which their efforts are directed in the support and furtherance of certain ends Following the classification of the various directions of personal activity which we made above, we may distinguish property associations, associations based on community of occupation, citizens' unions and associations for the promotion of intellectual culture. All the divisions of the previous classification may be included under the present one; indeed, the two sets of categories almost coincide Property associations are exclusively concerned with individual interests, the interests of professional or

## 248 *Society* [637-8]

trades unions are partly individual and partly social, while citizens' unions for the most part address themselves to social problems, though they may aim at humanitarian ends as well. For instance, benevolent associations are, as a rule, bodies of citizens brought together by certain local and political relationships Even here, however, individual ends have a certain amount of influence. Most associations of a beneficent or political character would soon die of inanition if their members, and especially their leaders, were deprived of the hope of getting influence and position So long as the general object remains in the ascendency, such a co-operation of egoistic motives is not necessarily objectionable ; but, of course, it involves a danger that should not be underestimated, and that must be counteracted, in himself and in others, by every member of such an association Finally, all spheres of human interest are comprehended within the scope of societies for the promotion of culture Such societies, if we understand the word culture in its broadest sense, may take for their objects all kinds of intellectual interests, those of religion, art and science ; and their activity is usually directed towards the realisation at once of individual, social and humanitarian ends.

Property associations form the lowest grade in the series. Their immediate aim is always egoistic The individual hopes to find a more effective way of getting rich by associating himself with others and applying the common capital to some profitable enterprise Social advantages may be indirectly gained under some circumstances, for such collective undertakings are not infrequently directed towards matters affecting the public welfare In particular, they sometimes aid and sometimes prepare the way for the public activities of the State. But it is evident that the natural condition of affairs where such enterprises are started is for the persons who are associated in the scheme to be

## 638-9] *Associations* 249

themselves its projectors, and to aim at increasing their property by working together  In such a case the property association becomes a society based on community of occupation, and should be treated as such  On the other hand, there are grave moral objections to be urged against the formation of purely financial associations, whose members have no common interest outside of the effort to get more wealth, and may pursue the most diverse occupations and even belong to wholly different social classes, as is actually the case in our joint-stock companies.  The only thing that gives any moral worth to an association, aside from the special ends at which it aims, is lacking here  namely, co-operation for a common object, and the resulting education in activity for the common good.  In a society of this sort every man's sole object is his own profit.  Often he does not even know his associates, and in extreme cases his activity is reduced to participating in a general meeting, where nothing interests him but the question of dividends. Hence such associations are associations only in appearance  They are the undertaking of a few speculators, who seek to make the property of others serve their own ends  Loss and gain in such enterprises are quite outside the sphere of moral industry  The man who tries to get rich without expenditure of labour ought not to complain if he becomes a victim to chance or fraud.  Since the individual does not always have sufficient insight to see the social and moral objections to this misuse of associational activity, the watchful guardianship of the State is essential here

Of course, those associations whose prime object is merely the protection of property, especially of small properties, rather than the aggrandizement of large properties, are quite a different affair  Savings banks, subscription societies, and building and loan associations, while they exist simply for the interest of individual property owners, are useful

250 *Society* [639

and even beneficent aids to the security of existence; hence they have a value which, though subordinate, is not to be underestimated in its influence on the conduct of life. It is therefore entirely proper that such associations for the disposition of small capital should not be dependent on the chance honesty of individuals. They should be placed under the public supervision of the community or the State.

Associations based on community of occupation are of higher grade than property associations. It is usual to apply the term brotherhoods or guilds to them For here, more than in other associations, the members are comrades, occupying the same status in life, having the main objects of their existence in common, and associating themselves either in the pursuit of some special interest of their calling or for the benefit of the profession as a whole. Such associations may accordingly be divided into various classes, which in their relation to each other reproduce to a certain extent the divisions of society at large. In the first place, a few persons pursuing a common occupation may associate themselves, either for the general purpose of doing their work with united means and forces, or in order to enjoy in addition the benefits of divided labour. Next, those persons living in the same place, whose occupations are similar or kindred, may unite and undertake to further either special ends, in the way of business, law or culture, or the interests of their profession as a whole Finally, the most comprehensive form of such organisations is where all the members of a given trade or profession in the State are associated

Since, generally speaking, the moral value of associations increases with the degree to which its members are united in their moral endeavours, associations based on community of occupation are distinctly pre-eminent among

## 639-40] *Associations* 251

those forms of union whose object is to serve the material needs of life. They become harmful elements in society only where egoistic interests get the upper hand in them, so that the association aims to secure the advantage of its members merely by injuring other kinds of occupation or classes of society ; or where different associations or individuals among those engaged in the same business, as, for instance, masters and journeymen, manufacturers and workmen, come into conflict  Cases of this latter sort are, of course, usually symptoms of deeper moral evils. They indicate, especially, that the bond of a common occupation which should unite the warring elements is lacking, or only apparent, that *e g.* the manufacturer, or the workman even, has been transformed either wholly or in part into a scheming capitalist who is trying to use the labour of others merely as a means of increasing his own capital. Immoral conditions of this sort necessarily influence the various professional and trades associations, which may be divided by a conflict of interests just as they are drawn together by community of interests

Apart from such cases as these, unfortunately not exceptional in our day, professional associations are among the most important agencies of social morality. They strengthen the feeling of professional honour, and educate the individual to take his part in activity for the public good and to subordinate his own interest to that of the whole. There is no doubt that their importance for the social organisation is greater than that ascribed to them at present, measured by the amount of political influence they enjoy. But in this age, of course, when the will of the State has reached so great a degree of power, there can be no question of allowing them the autonomy they formerly had, as represented in the constitutions of the guilds and the legal privileges accorded to other corporations. Yet

252                    *Society*                    [640-1

it may be doubted whether such associations have not a far better claim to consideration in State or district assemblies than that of wealth or local interest, which last shows its influence in the practice of forming electoral districts.

While associations based on similarity of occupation are thus in some measure an educative influence, teaching men how to act in common and arousing them to efforts for the public good, this character is still more marked in the case of civic associations  Such unions have one great advantage : their broader purpose subordinates at the very outset that egoistic aspect which is never absent in professional or trades unions, and which is often frankly recognised as their basis  Political societies and associations for the public benefit may be of the greatest support and assistance to the community and the State by suggesting useful regulations and by preparing public opinion for necessary steps in the way of progress  Of course, it is best for such societies to co-operate with public institutions  We should certainly regard a state of affairs where all the political societies were working for the opposition as neither normal nor desirable  Yet here as elsewhere unusual conditions justify unusual procedure  Where the only way to introduce a necessary progressive measure is by an important transformation of the existing legal order, the life of such societies may so prepare the way for change that violent political agitations may be avoided, or their effects moderated

Finally, the most comprehensive, and in many ways the most important class of associations based on interest embraces those whose object is culture.  All societies aiming at the cultivation of any kind of intellectual interest come under this head  Here the end pursued rules out egoism altogether, or when there is egoism, individual interest is involved in its noblest form, where it serves the ends of universal culture,—the form, namely, of an effort to promote

641-2] *Associations* 253

one's own intellectual development    Hence societies for the advancement of culture, if they do not wander into wrong courses and become subservient to political or egoistic motives foreign to the ends of culture itself, are the most effective aid to the morals of society and humanity

One distinction naturally assumes greater importance in this class of associations than in the others    the distinction, namely, between societies established to further the personal ends of their members, or ends in which the members can have a direct share, and those where individuals unite in the pursuit of objects that do not affect them personally    Other kinds of associations, especially those based on property relations or on occupation, belong, as a rule, to the former class    For such societies to assume the second form would involve them in the exercise of a kind of protective benevolence that would not exactly conduce to the interests for which they exist.    The case is otherwise with societies for the promotion of culture    While associations for the advancement of religion, art and science may exist to serve the personal ends of their members, they usually involve a broader purpose as well    And in many cases the members have no direct share at all in the object to be realised.    The association simply tries to further general culture, either in a given population or a given professional class, or, it may be, to promulgate religious doctrine    In such cases it is almost the rule that the members co-operate to bring about results which affect them either indirectly or not at all.

By reason of this peculiarity two important ethical corollaries follow from the existence of such societies.    First, they involve, more than any other kind of associations, motives to altruistic action which indicate clearly the general social and humanitarian goals of moral culture    Secondly, their altruistic and utilitarian character makes them especially appropriate objects of public institutions, either wholly or to

254                    *Society*                    [642-3

a considerable extent under the supervision of the State or the community Where for any reason the interests of culture must be left to private enterprise, the State should at least maintain the right of a general supervision over them, since their public importance is so great.

Considerations of this sort apply especially to the two most important educational bodies, the Church and the school. The interests involved in these institutions, namely, the education of the young and the cultivation of religion, are so pre-eminently important that the State must do for them far more than it does for other associations, where its function is merely that of general supervision and the protection of lawful interests The Church, which represents the most universal of all intellectual activities, is a power that the State must respect if it would pursue its own objects undisturbed At the same time, it must require the Church to respect in turn those general moral duties that belong to the province of the State Thus there has grown up a relationship between the two, according to which, while the State does not give up its right to exert a general supervision over all the corporations within its bounds, it must be prepared, on account of the important interests involved, to allow the Church more rights than it could ever give to any other association. On the other hand, the function of the school is recognised to be so pre-eminently political that the State has taken under its own guardianship even those educational associations which have arisen as a result of private enterprise, and has thus withdrawn the whole system of education from the ordinary system of associational activity. Of course, this does not mean that educational societies may not support and co-operate with the State.

643-4]                    *The Community*                    255

### 4 THE COMMUNITY

While individuals are led to associate themselves through the various interests of life, economic and financial, professional and intellectual, there is another force operating in the social order, which, though external, is yet of prime importance because its influence is so constraining  It is the fact that human lives are lived in spatial proximity to one another  Formerly, when the social sentiment was still restricted within the limits of immediate spatial contiguity, it was natural that the State and the community should coincide  As the national life became more comprehensive, the community gradually lost its original significance  But it preserved all those interests which depend on the close association of individuals, and to a certain extent these needs can be more adequately satisfied by reason of its narrower sphere of duty.

Within its limited sphere, the function of the neighbourhood or community is to protect and further all those departments of life which require the immediate co-operation of individuals.  The restoration and support of trade, the proper construction of dwellings, the maintenance of public order, the protection of important professional interests, care for the general culture,—all these are, it is true, partly under the supervision and charge of the State, but they are also in part important problems for the independent exercise of the functions of the community.  In all such matters the community stands for a subordinate social will, which is represented by an organisation analogous to the State's constitution ; while at the same time, since its organisation is a fixed part of that of the State, it is itself dependent on the State

This association of individuals living in spatial proximity into a kind of state within the State is ethically important

256 *Society* [644

chiefly in two respects. First, along with its many ways of looking after the outward needs of life the community really assumes moral duties as well. Where the ends it serves are themselves morally indifferent, still the general rule holds good that they must not conflict with moral norms, but must, wherever possible, advance the moral life, indirectly at least  In order that the community may keep this duty constantly in mind, it is especially important that it shall be governed by the will of the State, which is still more comprehensive, and hence less accessible to egoistic interests. Thus it is not desirable to allow communities too great autonomy.  Large cities, though for other reasons they have many moral disadvantages, have one advantage · the spirit of their government is more apt to be like that of the State. This tendency is materially strengthened by the fact that in the more fruitful social medium of such communities it is possible to provide more adequately for the interests of culture

There is another aspect of community life that is important for morals  The life of a community furnishes to the individual an immediate and present type of the life of the State. It is a necessary result of the more comprehensive nature of the State that the national consciousness tends to be lost in those individuals who are removed from a direct share in political problems.  They feel the burdens and duties imposed on them by the State, but never realise the necessity and the great moral importance of the State's existence  The community is the very thing that can represent to them in visible form the benefits of united activity. It gives them an opportunity to practise the virtues of public spirit for which their position in life offers but a limited scope.  The effects of this practice extend far beyond the sphere of its origin.  Their interest for the common concerns of the neighbourhood arouses in them a broader public spirit,

644-5] *The Community* 257

through which they learn to regard the State and the nation as the more important and higher unity, whose prosperity is essential to that of all subordinate spheres of life. In order that life in the community may really furnish such an education for life in the State, it is, of course, necessary not only that the organisation of the community shall be such as to produce a lively interest on the part of the citizens, but that the constitution and administration of the State shall establish a bond between its life and that of the community, which shall show the citizens of the community that they are first of all citizens of the State.

[645

# CHAPTER III.

## THE STATE.

### I THE STATE AS A FINANCIAL AND ECONOMIC COMMUNITY

THE State may be regarded as a financial body in two senses. First, as a community made up of citizens banded together into an economic unit, it is itself a property holder; its right to dispose of its property being as independent as that of an individual Secondly, it is the power that regulates all the property relations existing between individuals or subordinate corporations, and decides in doubtful cases. It orders the conditions on which commerce and the exchange, both internal and external, of economic products depend We must consider the ethical aspect of the State's functions in both these directions

It is a necessary consequence of its independent existence and its actual needs that the State should be a property holder. Since it surpasses all its organs and subordinate parts both in the degree of its independence and in the scope of its needs, it has a natural claim to be regarded as the first of all property holders, transcending by virtue of the extent of its property all others in power and influence The nature of its possessions is determined in part by its own nature and in part by that of its needs The State includes not only the generation now living, but the whole people as an unity, in its history and in that future for which the life of the present is preparing Hence there is an

258

## 645-6]    *The State a Financial Community*    259

especial fitness in entrusting to State guardianship those kinds of property which must not be expended on objects of merely transitory value, unless the permanent interests of the nation's welfare are to suffer   Further, whenever the conduct of business is so important for the good of society that it cannot be left to the casual charge of individuals, the State must intervene, either directly or indirectly, by means of communities and associations acting in accord with it and under its supervision.  There is, finally, a third department, whose limits depend on time and circumstances, where the State may exercise special business and economic functions  An interest may be in urgent need of protection, either to avoid a degree of competition that involves too great a strain on human energies, or to stand in the way when the strong threaten to make profit out of the weak, and small property owners are in danger of becoming the prey of a few schemers  Under such circumstances as these, with their various combinations, the State has to possess itself of more or less real estate, and it has also to take charge of the more general branches of industry, especially the management of all the institutions of commerce.

In all such cases the State is the first of property owners and managers.  As it sometimes usurps or delegates to private activities forms of business that may be carried on by individuals, so its legal status is that of a single subject among other individuals or corporate subjects   At times it has to protect its own rights against those of others, and at times it must yield, when the legal order which it has established recognises the rights of individuals as superior to its own.

From this relation of the State to individual citizens is derived its further relationship to individual property.  It is not merely the first of property holders, but it has a power of far greater importance,—that of regulating all property

260 *The State* [646-7]

relations and, in so far as they are in accord with the order it has established, protecting them. In so doing the State assumes sovereignty over all property. It asserts this right with especial force by claiming, wherever it deems such a proceeding essential for the interests of society, the privilege of appropriating property itself Thus the right of expropriation, which belongs directly to no corporation but the State, is a plain intimation to the individual that with all his earnings and possessions he is working in the service of the whole

The economic life of individuals is in like manner under State governance. Here the attention of the State is directed towards the welfare of the nation as a whole, to whose interests the individual must subordinate himself. With this in view, the State seeks to regulate internal and external commerce. In governing the former it tries, as far as possible, to further individual freedom, since this is the vital condition for the best development of economic forces. Its regulation of external commerce is governed by a regard for the demands of the public welfare. Thus, despite the many ways in which economic forces oppose each other within the State, externally it is an unity under whose protection and restraining supervision the individual carries on his own private enterprise.

In all these ways economic life, if it involves a proper balancing of individual interests against those of the whole, tends to develop that sentiment of public spirit which is an indispensable basis for the performance of the higher tasks of the State. But physical life, for the State as for the individual, is but a means to an end, not an end in itself And the truth of this finds unequivocal expression in the legal order of the State, which, embracing all departments of the State's activity, everywhere asserts the moral nature of the social will embodied in the State.

## 2 THE STATE AS A LEGAL COMMUNITY.

As the State is the foremost of property holders, so it is the chief of legal persons  At the same time, it is that which gives to all other persons their legal rights  It thus represents, to itself and to individuals, the system of objective law. Wherever the State owns property or undertakes an enterprise it subjects itself to the system which it has itself founded. It concludes contracts, performs undertakings, and files claims; and wherever opposing claims develop in the course of its relationship with other persons, it enters into legal contests with individuals and submits itself to the decision of its own appointed courts. Thus in what it does and undergoes it realises to the highest extent the principle of justice  it voluntarily subjects itself to the judgment of its own organs. Justice of this sort, whose ruling motive is to seek the right for its own sake and not for personal interest, can be manifested only by a collective entity like the State. The individual may thus find in the State an ideal example of the spirit in which rights should be contested.

It is only by the exercise of justice without regard to persons, or even to its own advantage, that the State can undertake at once to decide legal contests between its members and to establish the norms according to which such contests ought to be settled  This fact is especially important as adding moral force to the reason for giving the State jurisdiction even in cases that do not involve injury to individuals, but rather a serious breach of the moral law in general. We have already seen how the right of punishment has been gradually taken out of the hands of the party injured, though it is still regarded as involving a private grievance.[1] The idea that it is the State

[1] *Cf* Part I., chap. iii , pp. 269  fl.

262 *The State* [648-9

alone which has the right and duty of avenging a breach of the moral order has grown up along with recognition of the fact that, even in a contest between individuals, the State, rather than the individual, has the function and the power of exercising justice. But the exercise of the right of punishment is better adapted than any other department of the legal order to arouse and intensify the consciousness of the State's moral tasks. Further, the high moral value of the State, as a moral community standing above the individual, is expressed in the fact that it ranks assaults on its own stability, or against the person of an agent representing any one of its manifold functions, on the same plane with the gravest moral offences

As the life of individuals needs external aids and laws, which in turn must have a certain order and regularity to prevent the occurrence of disturbances that might have a bad effect on morals, so the life of the State cannot get on without similar aids and regulations. In fact, its need for them is far more urgent than the individual's, because its functions are more comprehensive, and because it lacks the immediate unity of self-consciousness and will that the individual personality possesses  Matters that in the life of the individual are left to custom and habit the State prescribes by laws and enactments, whose non-observance involves either punishment or some other disadvantage Under this head we have, first of all, the whole police system. On the one hand, in the regulations it makes for the protection of public security, it trenches on the ground of penal law. On the other, it undertakes to preserve health and facilitate life in general by means of certain useful precautions. It is thus a helpful and controlling factor in the activity of private individuals and of communities.

The State exerts a similar kind of external regulative function when it requires that the execution of the norms of private and penal law in lawsuits shall be subject to certain rules for the investigation and establishment of rights. The individual may sometimes feel a certain sense of injustice in cases where the outcome of a lawsuit is influenced by the outward forms of the civil process, which are based on arbitrary enactments, rather than by a regard to the objective facts of the case. Undeniably such cases do often result in the assertion that something is just when it is not really just, and when the assertion can be maintained only by assuming certain facts which perhaps have no actual existence, or by neglecting other facts which did not find expression in the course of the transaction, as, for instance, when the defendant fails to avail himself of the legal delays in proceedings, or to produce certain evidence that is at his disposal. But precisely because the State makes it the duty of each individual to look after his own rights, it must now and then do what is not objectively right for the very sake of right and justice. If when there is a legal contest between individuals the State itself were to produce the evidence *pro* and *con*, it would have a difficult business on its hands, and one where the investigation would be exposed in many ways to accidents, for the nature of these relationships of private right withdraws them from publicity. But since it is the highest interest of both parties to present all the evidence at their disposal, and since they themselves are in the best position to adduce such evidence, the State has ordained that all civil processes shall be conducted on the principle that the parties themselves shall present the evidence, and that proofs not adduced by them shall be treated as non-existent, though the judge may have private information that such evidence exists The only way of realising justice in such matters is for this rule to be maintained without exception, the decision of the judge being entirely uninfluenced by the accidental possession of know-

## 264 *The State* [650-1

ledge which it is equally possible that he might not have had Moreover, the principle that every man must look out for his own rights is a powerful educative influence in developing the sentiment of right. If the individual's subjective rights were a gift bestowed upon him and accepted by him from without, with neither help nor hindrance from himself, a great part of their moral worth would be lost. By associating certain legal disadvantages with the neglect of one's rights, the law makes it a duty to fight for them While it cannot directly punish the omission of this duty, neither can it reward such omission by giving the individual advantages he has not striven to secure Thus along with the other duty imposed by every right there goes the duty which devolves upon its possessor to protect it Only when this duty is universally acknowledged can justice have its fullest sway. Where the individual's weakness and carelessness lead him to surrender his right without resistance to the claims of others, injustice triumphs.[1]

Evidently other principles must govern the trial of cases where there has been a violation of public rights or of the law itself. Here the State is the party immediately concerned, and hence must do all it can to bring to light the true condition of affairs. And just because it is directly concerned, it recognises its own obligation to place at the disposal of the accused all possible means of defence. Here, where the law is itself, so to speak, a party in the case, it makes no difference whether the accused is or is not aware of his own rights The State gives him a counsel, who is

---

[1] R. VON JHERING (in his work *Der Kampf ums Recht*, 7th ed., Vienna, 1884, 5th ed , trans by J J Lalor, Chicago, 1879), is quite right in opposing the widespread tendency that leads people to give up their rights for the sake of avoiding the inconvenience of bringing a lawsuit. Of course, however, as Jhering himself points out, the struggle for one's rights ceases to be a duty where the right violated has no ethical significance, especially where there has been no slight cast upon the personality.

651]                    *as a Legal Community*                    265

thoroughly versed in the matter, and whose duty it is to protect his client's right to the best of his power. Here, again, we have an expression of the thought that when the rights of the State are concerned, it must exercise justice even against itself.

In all the departments of law hitherto discussed the State exercises its function as the protector and upholder of the moral order that it has established. On the other hand, it fulfils the task of furthering all the material and intellectual interests of life by means of the administrative organisation that it creates  And it expresses the need of regulating in some definite fashion the division of functions required for the various manifestations of the State's will by means of its constitution. The latter encompasses the State with certain special regulations that guard it against violation from any of its organs and against changes of a precipitate nature which ignore the gradual character of the State's development.

The administrative and constitutional functions of the State presuppose the activity of manifold agencies. It is even more important here than in the other departments of law, that the individuals and corporations whose interests are affected should be enabled to take an active part in affairs as far as possible, not only because the real need of society will thus be best served, but even more, perhaps, because there is no other way to develop in the individual a livelier national sentiment, and to make him share in the spirit of universal progress, so that he may be led to look beyond the narrow horizon of personal and transitory interests There is more chance and more demand for this kind of personal participation in the system of administration, since the various gradations of the system itself come into touch with the workings of communities and other more limited spheres of interest. By the nature of the case the in-

## 266 *The State* [651-2]

dividual's share in the legislative and constitutional functions of the State must be remoter and less direct. For the majority of citizens it is limited to the exercise of the right of franchise, and the activity of political societies, which grows out of this right and supports it. There is in addition the fact that each citizen is enabled, by reason of the publicity given to the proceedings of representative assemblies, to understand the real state of legislative matters and of political affairs in general. Such publicity is a just and natural compensation for the very limited extent to which the citizens of a state can take active part in this most important of the State's functions In many instances the publicity given to legislative transactions may be of more use, because of the interest in State affairs which it awakens, than the content of the transactions themselves. A doctrine quite the reverse of this is the theory, based on ethical and political individualism, that the representative assembly is, actually or potentially, the opinion of the whole nation, and that the essential meaning of the representative system is a realisation of the *imperium omnium* This fiction rests on the idea that the State is merely the sum of its members, and that in consequence representatives really, as their name indicates, deliberate and decide in the stead of the whole nation If such a view were correct, they would be obliged to decide in every case according to the opinion of their constituents. This notion of the constant dependence of a representative on his constituents is justly repudiated by all constitutions, which take more account of the State's independence than do many theories about the nature of the State Constitutions always make it the duty of every member of a legislative assembly to vote in each case according to his independent conviction

As the State is not identical with the sum of its citizens, so it is not to be divided into a number of independent

652-3]                 *as a Legal Community*                 267

powers, cohering only by virtue of the fact that they influence the same individuals. Such a division is often made by the adherents of a theory closely akin to the one just stated . the theory of "separation of powers." Though the State assigns different functions to different organs for good and sufficient reasons, because, as the most comprehensive of all corporations, it cannot dispense with the principle of the division of labour, this does not mean that it abandons its essential unity. Hence it is especially erroneous to call this division a separation of powers. In accordance with the objects for which it exists, the division of functions is carried out most completely in the subordinate organs of the State's life, those devoted to the less comprehensive tasks. But all departments must be ultimately combined in the government. While there may be, even in the case of the government, division of labour with regard to minor problems, such division is no longer possible where important affairs are concerned, since matters of this sort have more or less influence on all departments of the State's activity. The series of authorities culminates in the person of the Sovereign, who unites in himself the legislative, executive and judicial powers, in that he gives his sanction to the laws and assents to all the more important administrative regulations and to the organisation of the judiciary.

It is of the greatest importance, not only for the State's own efficiency, but for the development of a national consciousness among its citizens, that the essential unity of the State shall thus appear to be comprehended in a single personality. By reason of the comprehensive nature of the State, a maturer moral insight is needed to understand its real nature and subordinate the individual will to the social will from motives of pure respect to the moral worth of the latter. But, in order to develop such a disposition, the power and dignity of the State must first be represented to the individual

268 *The State* [653-4

in an individual form. This is why it is so desirable for the person of the ruler to be withdrawn from party controversy and the variable results of elections. As the State itself is above all changing interest, so should be the personality of him who is called upon to embody, under a form directly apparent to the senses, the unity of the State in the unity of his own being.

But, of course, the Sovereign remains an individual man, and as such can never be quite free from the prejudices and propensities of his environment. Hence it is not desirable that the development of national consciousness should never proceed beyond this individual form. The earliest means to political education should not be the final fruit of political culture. As public sentiment and a love for the benefits of a common intellectual life, so far transcending all individual interests, increase along with the development of insight and the growing participation of individuals in the tasks of national life, men must come to realise that while an individual embodiment of the national consciousness is of value because it is a symbolic form that can be appreciated by everyone, the worth of the symbol is less than that of its significance. At this higher stage of development the universal character of the State will be felt as a characteristic that increases rather than lessens its value for individuals; for the whole worth of those supreme goods to which man dedicates his life rests on the fact that he does not think of them as individual like himself. All sacrifice demands the yielding up of self. And this, in its purest form, is possible only where we have not to do with another self.

### 3. THE STATE AS A SOCIAL UNIT.

The State and society are equally primitive The conditions on which the unity of the State is based are identical with those from which the union of different ranks, different financial classes, and forms of occupation into one society has resulted Nay, the two unifying processes themselves are not to be thought of as distinct. The parts of society originated independently of the existence of the State, out of the general conditions of life ; but their combination into a society is the work of the State, which is continually carrying on the process of unification, while its own regulations, in turn, are no less dependent on the nature of society.

In consequence of this reciprocal relationship, while the State and society have such close and immediate reference to one another, while the one can hardly exist without the other, they appear in the life of humanity as opposing forces which were for a long time in actual conflict Society is throughout governed by centrifugal impulses. Its tendency is to separate those who live in spatial juxtaposition and dependence by dividing them into various classes based on birth, property, occupation and interests, and into different circles according to the degree of their intellectual culture. Of course, such divisions themselves ultimately rest on that unifying tendency which always leads men to associate with those of their own kind But the influence of this tendency is at first felt within very limited circles, and hence it is the greatest possible hindrance to the more perfect union of the members of a nation in the State Each one of these small circles, so long as it subordinates national sentiment to its own narrower interests, strives to be an independent whole, and is unwilling to acknowledge a superior will.

The historical conditions of social development have been such as to render the origin and growth of these centrifugal

270                     *The State*                    [655-6

tendencies very gradual   In the early stages of civilisation,
either because social distinctions were too imperfect or the
authority of a few ruling classes too powerful, there could
be no such thing as the coexistence of different and independent social units.   In this sense the State existed before
society, and it is certainly fortunate that such was the case ;
that when the strife between the various classes of society
began there was already in existence a national unity based
on tradition.   Thus the conflict between classes at first took
the form of rivalry for the possession of the ruling power.
Often, indeed, as in the case of the German States during
the Middle Ages, it resulted in the coexistence of independent associations, whereby the unity of the State sank to
the level of a mere fiction.   Thus throughout the development of national life we can trace the conflict of the State
with society.   The State emerged victorious from this conflict,
but not uninfluenced by the disorganising forces of society.
In order peacefully to assimilate society, it had to adapt
itself to the divisions that society had brought about   Thus
social distinctions reacted to organise the State.   The division of social forces that originated in custom and the needs
of life gave rise to important political institutions, and in
turn derived security from these institutions   And so out
of the divisions of society there arose a completer division
of the functions of the State   This, again, made it possible
for the State to direct and guide society and to superintend
its various departments   The State is now, in one of its
essential aspects, the organisation of society

   With this result we have the conclusion of peace between
society and the State.   True, it is a peace that is still liable
to be disturbed by the strife between social classes, but strife
of this sort has now another significance from that which it
formerly possessed.   Its object is to bring about changes in
the social order by means of the State, or at least with the

656-7]                *as a Social Unit*                271

State's help, not to abolish the State or put it under the governance of a single class. If desires of this latter sort are not wholly wanting, they are concealed behind demands of a more general political character. Thus the supremacy of the State over society is recognised on all sides  Even the most impracticable of all political parties, Anarchism, requires the State to abdicate in favour of the individual, not of society, indeed, its project is to annihilate society first and the State afterwards, since the latter is a necessity at least until society has ceased to exist

Since the State is organised society, a co-ordination of all social forces into a single whole, evidently the organisation of the State must correspond to the natural divisions of society  Hence the attempt to put into force, without reference to existing relationships, constitutions and systems of administration that are drawn up after some philosophical model supposed to apply to all ages, is an attack made by the State upon society, and indirectly upon itself  But, of course, the law that the State exists for the sake of society must not be applied in its extreme and partial sense, as has often been the case.  The reverse is also true  society exists for the sake of the State.  Nay, the relation of the two is such that the State should be regarded as the higher aggregation of the forces of the national will, as that to which society owes its very existence, since without the State it would disintegrate into scattered parts.  Hence the State must be allowed the right to interfere with the existing organisation of society, especially when the tendency of such interference is towards a higher grade of civilisation  Thus, as a matter of fact, many distinctions of position and rank have been abrogated or weakened because the State took away privileges, removed restrictions upon liberty, or extended the sphere of political rights

The State performs a pre-eminently moral function in thus

272                    *The State*                    [657

seeking with a wise moderation and a due regard for the
conditions of historical development to reform society, or,
if necessary, to alter its whole constitution. It rescues social
structures from the hazards of their mode of origin and
adapts them to its own plans, which are guided by the moral
purposes of the whole. Society as such lives in the present
but the State is absorbed in the problems of the future, and
thus enlists the more transitory forces of social life in the
service of enduring ends. It must therefore direct its attention chiefly to the support of all those bonds of association
and union among individuals which tend to further a necessary division of labour and the participation of citizens in
the general objects sought by the State And it must seek
to obviate all those forms of friction between social classes
that operate to retard the moral functions of the whole.

### 4 THE STATE AS AN ASSOCIATION FOR THE ADVANCEMENT OF CULTURE

In the tasks that the State has to perform for society its
most powerful aid is intellectual culture, whose guidance it
recognises to be one of its most important duties. It thus
serves in the first instance the needs of the present, by
seeking to enable every citizen to pursue his calling, to look
out for his rights as a citizen, and to fulfil his duty towards
the whole. At the same time it directs its care toward the
future It tries to better the social position of the lower
classes by working for their intellectual elevation, and thus
to compensate for the distinctions between social classes, so
far as such a result is desirable, and in accord with the
demands of legal and moral equality and of the harmonious
moral co-operation of all social elements

Nowhere is the supremacy of the State's moral function

657-8]      *in the Advancement of Culture*      273

over that of the individual more strikingly expressed than in that general care for the interests of culture, which it claims as at once a right and a duty   Plato's demand that education should be entrusted to the State has been realised in the modern State, at least approximately   Of course, it is not realised quite as the philosopher conceived it, and yet here, as elsewhere, the fulfilment in a certain sense exceeds the fancied ideal   The State's education does not supplant that of the family, it supplements it.  The latter represents more particularly the individual, the latter the social aspect of moral education, that is, it prepares the individual for his occupation and position as a citizen

With this object in view, the first and chief function of the State as an institution for the promotion of culture is the superintendence of instruction   While, to avoid unnecessary restrictions on individual freedom, the State permits the formation of private educational societies, so far as they are not inimical to its own ends, and merely reserves the right of supervision over them, the fundamental idea of its educational system must be that of public instruction   For public instruction is not only the most practicable method, and hence the best for the individual, it is, in addition, the most effective way of securing that uniformity of culture which is so desirable, and there is more likelihood that it will be undertaken from motives of fidelity to public duty   Here the teacher exercises his office, not on the ground of a private contract based on mutual advantage, but in virtue of his sense of public duty ; and the importance of this fact is not to be underestimated. In addition, public education brings together members of various ranks in life, which is a good thing, especially in the education of boys.  We cannot begin too early to combat the spirit of caste that is the result of a narrow education based on class distinctions   And just here public instruction

T

274              *The State*                    [658-9

furnishes a wholesome counterpoise to education in the family, which is of a more exclusive nature

For these reasons educational societies or corporations, which have of necessity other functions, can at most never do more than supplement the educational work of the State Not only do private educational bodies lack the authority necessary to direct public instruction, which enables the State to compel children to be educated, if compulsion is necessary They do not make sufficient provision for the proper organisation of educational institutions, an organisation that shall recognise the political side of public instruction. When the authority of the State needs a deputy or an assistant, the community would seem to be the social body that is called on to serve, since, as a part of the political organisation, it is best adapted to work in accordance with the purposes and under the oversight of the State. However, the political importance of the instruction of the young is so great that here, as in other matters which transcend the sphere of community life, the State, which is primarily responsible for them, is also best fitted to undertake their immediate direction So that nowadays any kind of external assistance, even that of the community, should be regarded as merely an imperfect substitute for the direction of the State While in the larger cities, where administration is more far-seeing than that of smaller communities, the disadvantage of combining the more ideal ends of national culture with the predominant local interests of the community may be less, yet such exceptions do not alter the rule that all instruction, since the State has a far greater interest in it than any other body, is the proper function of the State.

The Church is still more unfitted than the community to act as a substitute for the State, or even as an auxiliary to it, in the sphere of education In the church or the religious society to which he belongs, the individual seeks to satisfy his religious needs, and at the same time to supplement the religious education of the young. Now religious instruction belongs by its nature to that part of education which is carried on in the family and the home, not in the publicity of the schools. This is not to say that the school should have no part in religious education. In so far as religious culture is an inalienable part of general culture, especially for the classes represented in national schools, it cannot be neglected in the school. But the object of public instruction is to make men and citizens, not adherents of any particular religious society. Hence it is especially undesirable that the State should surrender the charge of instruction into the care of the Church or the various religious bodies, if, as should be the case, its citizens belong to different religious societies according to their convictions. In such a case, where the Church gets control of education or even a decisive influence, it will naturally regard the religious side of instruction as of prime importance. Hence it will, as a matter of principle, admit only its own members to its schools, or tolerate those of other faiths only in cases of necessity. Education under the guidance of the Church means, then, a division of general instruction according to differences of church and creed. This means a division among the young in all those circumstances which should prepare them for their secular occupations and their position as citizens, a division of the intellectual culture of the nation in accordance with religious differences and such political views as are thereby determined. But the end at which the State should aim, in order to train its citizens into a national community, is unity of education, whereby at all stages of instruction the members of various classes and religious faiths shall be united.

276                    *The State*                    [660-1

Of course, if we are to hold to the postulate that the State should have a share in the religious education of the young, such an unity involves the supposition that those fundamental religious views which influence public education are, like the general and basal principles of knowledge, universally true And for our own State at present, and the civilisation it represents, there can be no reasonable doubt that these fundamental truths are those of Christianity[1] The small minority of freethinkers and Jews, who, while they reject the material of the Christian system, are open to its influence upon our religious and moral conceptions of the world, cannot be allowed to determine the education of the body of citizens as a whole. They may be suffered to care for the religious instruction of their young people outside of the schools, but to demand that the course of public education shall be decided with reference to such exceptional instances is out of the question. The case is otherwise with the various Christian churches and creeds. Since they all acknowledge in the life and teaching of Jesus that

---

[1] I must not omit to state that in making the above observations I have had German conditions chiefly in mind  I do not deny that other considerations may have some weight in other nations,—America, for instance, where, owing to the influence of a more developed sectarianism, the separation of Church and State affects the very heart of individual life much more than among us  But I doubt whether American conditions represent a desirable ideal in this respect. The complete exclusion of religious culture from national schools, which other nations seek to bring about, has yet to vindicate itself by practical tests  I do not believe that, in the education of the young, compendia of utilitarian ethics such as are introduced in France can ever take the place of that concrete embodiment of the ideal conduct of life which religious theory has to present  Aside from the glaring pedagogical error that they involve, such attempts at reform seem to me to conjure up the very evil that they ought to prevent  For the inevitable correlate of national education without religion is unrestrained licence for private or Church educational institutions, which, entering into competition with the State, endanger its influence on education  Reforms of this sort are meaningless, except where, against the evidence of history and human nature, the right of religion to existence is contested  If the intention is to carry on a war of extermination against religion, such a campaign would naturally begin in the schools.

661-2] *in the Advancement of Culture* 277

historical form of the religious consciousness which governs all the tendencies of our moral life, they must allow that life and that teaching, as it appears when separated from later dogmatic formulas and traditional elements that are opposed to the knowledge of the present day, to be the universal foundation for a Christian system of religious instruction The only basis for public religious teaching in a State that is Christian in all its civilisation, and yet allows free play to all kinds of Christian dogma, is an undogmatic Christianity, representing the common element in all Christian creeds The teaching of creeds and dogmas must be left to the discretion of the adherents of such creeds

There are a few people even to-day who, mostly with a sincere intent to serve religious interests, hold that religious instruction without creeds is of no value, and that a religious education that is not based on a definite confession of faith is the same thing as education without any religion at all. We must suppose, for the credit of those who calmly express such opinions, that they are unconscious of the import of their words For if what we call the Christian religion were really constituted, not by the life and teachings of Christ, but by the Confession of Augsburg or the Tridentine Decrees, probably the whole body of truly religious persons, as well as the whole community of thinkers, would turn from it What sort of ideas can a man have on the value of religious education, if he thinks it is derived chiefly from dogmatic structures, whose origin from the complex interaction of religious ideas and philosophic systems is well known, and which escape doing serious harm to the child's mind only because, as a general thing, they are appropriated by the memory and not by the mind? Surely the permanent moral worth of Christianity consists not in these artificial intellectual structures, wherein is displayed

278 *The State* [662-3

the theological acumen of centuries, but in the plain teachings of Jesus, which are accessible at every stage of intellectual development, and in the human part of the New Testament history, freed from the mythological alloy of a wonder-loving age.

For one thing is unmistakably true. That form of belief which makes the founder of the religion of humanity into a god, thereby in reality divesting him of his human and moral significance, has, along with belief in the Trinity and in miracle, lost its power even over those who still call themselves Christians with entire conviction And the number of those who are wholly alienated from the system of dogmatic traditions has increased among all classes and grades of enlightenment, in proportion as men have become generally convinced that this system is in contradiction with all the other elements of our intellectual culture Then shall our intellectual culture retrograde, in order that humanity may recover the simple and happy faith of earlier centuries? Or shall Christianity itself move forward, like everything else in history, in order to keep its value for the world of to-day? The answer to this question can hardly be doubtful. But our decision as to the proper spirit in which the religious part of public education should be carried out is independent even of such considerations. The broad, human foundation of the Christian view of the world is of value even to the man who is unwilling to give up the specific traditions of his church, and he is at liberty to supplement the former with the latter. On the other hand, if a man is convinced that a Christianity which is to survive can tolerate no element of mythology, we cannot wish to make him transmit as sacred truth to his children what he does not himself believe.

While the unity of the State's life demands uniformity of

663] *in the Advancement of Culture* 279

public instruction, independent of differences in politics and creed, this does not exclude the possibility of differences that are justified by provincial and other outward conditions, though such differences have but a transitory significance. In fact, even the distinction between town and country is not absolutely permanent in this respect. The growing mobility of the population involves increasing similarity of educational needs.

A more important distinction is one that is based on the separation of social classes, namely, the distinction between primary and secondary education, as we see it in the difference between national schools, properly so called, and *Bürgerschule* (grammar schools, *lit.* citizen schools), or *Realschule* (high schools), as they are less appropriately termed nowadays It is the function of the latter, as the name *Bürgerschule* indicates, to provide to a greater extent than the former all necessary aids to the education of a citizen. They furnish to all students of sufficient means and consequence an adequate degree of general culture, excluding only preparation for the learned professions There exists an unmistakable tendency towards equalising even these grades of primary and secondary education But certain distinctions remain associated with differences of social position However, as the latter is no longer dependent solely on birth and inherited property, intellectual gifts are beginning to secure more rights even in education, for it is becoming easier for one who has the capacity to obtain better instruction. And this facilitation of the passage from one grade of instruction to another is itself the chief means of securing that wholesome mobility in the social world which allows scope for talent to develop along its proper lines.

The dividing line drawn by the nature of different professions between the broadly humane culture that is sought

280 *The State* [663-4

in primary and secondary education and the scientific culture that is pursued in higher institutions of learning is more permanent   It is evident that neither kind of training should consist exclusively of technical preparation , at least not until just before the transition to practical professional work.   The influence of an age that makes too much of immediate utility has not always been favourable to the real needs of higher culture   We have forgotten that man must be trained, not only for his profession, but for his place as a citizen ; and that this latter makes certain general demands on his education, according to the station in life that he occupies.   His social position does influence these demands, but the special branch of business that has fallen to his lot in that position makes no difference.   We have already pointed out which departments of knowledge are adapted to serve as the general scientific basis of secondary and higher education.[1]

It seems to me that one of the unhappiest results of this utilitarian tendency in instruction is the partially successful attempt to divide our whole system of higher education into two branches, the one devoted to the realistic, the other to the humanistic disciplines.   This distinction does not greatly affect the practical needs of professional life   Everyone knows that both kinds of education produce equally able mathematicians, physicians, etc   Surely, however, it is most undesirable that the whole body of those who have undergone the higher education should be divided into two classes, whose interests, intellectual needs and general attitudes towards the world are partly dissimilar.   But here, again, the tendency on the part of the lower class to reach the level of the higher would seem to offer a method of bringing about uniformity   When each system has appropriated the best points in the other; when, in consequence, the differences

[1] *Cf* chap. 1., p 215

664-5]            *in the Advancement of Culture*            281

between the two have become so slight that no one can see why they exist, the distinction will vanish. And the result will not be unfavourable to the ends of higher culture as a single whole.

In directing the various grades of instruction, the objects for which the State works are primarily social, though at the same time it meets the needs of individuals On the other hand, it combines the interests of society with those of humanity at large, by seeking to further the ends of science and art beyond the domain of instruction proper, through the medium of public institutions. Private enterprise may do much in this sphere, but the best results must be left to the State, since it alone has sufficient power and means, while in many cases no private individual has time enough at his disposal Here the State fulfils a function whose consequences reach far beyond the sphere of its own narrower interests. Entering into competition with other nations, and supplementing with new achievements the treasures of the past, the nation shares in the intellectual life of humanity as a whole.

The State thus unites all the tendencies of national life · property and business, law and education. In so doing, the objects that it follows are more various than those of any other association of individuals. Only the individual personality resembles the State in this respect. Along with the manifold nature of its purposes, the State has also an entire freedom in the choice of new courses, such as belongs to no other entity but the individual For good reasons, it makes but a limited use of this freedom, extending its activity into new fields only by a gradual process of change. In this it follows the law of continuity in development, which must also guide individuals in the use of their powers. As the individual limits himself in his occupation and his endeavours

## 282 *The State* [665-6

after position and culture, in order that his work in his chosen field may be more thorough and more satisfactory to himself, so the State restricts its own activity by the legal and economic system that it has established, in order to allow more scope in the remaining fields for the work of individuals, of voluntary associations, and of those political organisations that form an immediate part of the State. It does this with a wise regard to the interests of society, as well as of the individual But the extent to which it sets bounds to its own activity depends on its own free decision, made after considering all the circumstances, to a greater degree than in the case of the individual; because when the collective will of the State is once directed towards a certain end, it meets far fewer obstacles in the accomplishment of that end than the individual will does. For this reason, in organised and civilised states all decisions of the collective will, especially such as refer to new objects not hitherto sought by the State, are made under conditions whose aim is to lessen the dangers that might arise from this power of the social will. The law averts the perils that threaten it from individual wills by means of regulations which usually follow the breach of law with punishment But the only way to avert the dangers that proceed from the social will is by means of measures that precede the action and subject the actual decision of the will to conditions which ensure its taking place only after due consideration. Aside from the relation between the origin and the results of volition in the two cases, the collective will of the State has equal autonomy with that of the individual. There is no other organisation between the individual and the State that can compete with either in this respect, or in the multiplicity of its functions. Societies, guilds, the community,—all pursue narrower purposes; and where they have autonomy in the pursuit of these

666-7]       *in the Advancement of Culture*       283

ends, either it arises from the voluntary union of individuals, and hence is really based on the autonomy of the individual will, or, as in the case of the community and other political organisations, it is derived from the State and is exercised only in the fulfilment of the general regulations of the State

It follows that no conception of the State could mistake its nature more completely than the individualistic theory that derives it from an actual or fictitious social contract, and thus identifies it either with society or with some association originating in society through the voluntary assent of individuals   We have here a complete reversal of the real relation between the State and society.   Instead of regarding the State in its true light, as the force that brings system and order into society, the adherents of this theory suppose that the State is an artificial creation made by society, or rather by the individuals constituting it.   The theory really regards the State, not as an organism, but as a machine, in whose construction various plans may be followed.   The best plan, because best suited to the supposed mode of the State's origin, is held to be that which restricts the object of the State from the outset to certain definite functions, necessary in the interests of the individual, but beyond the individual's power to perform alone   This conception is the source of a theory which was peculiar to the period of the Enlightenment, and which is not yet extinct. the theory, namely, which regarded the State as nothing but a great protective institution, whose moral function was at best the negative one of removing hindrances to the free exercise of the individual's moral impulses.   After all that we have said on this subject, it is unnecessary to remark that this conception accords neither with the actual development of the State and its functions, nor with its moral purposes for the

284 *The State* [667-8

future, which can be served only by further development in the direction hitherto adopted It is consoling, here as elsewhere, to note that while such obsolete ideas still influence theory now and then, they have been long since thrown overboard in the practical life of the State.

In the fact that its activity is not restricted to any limited number of ends, and in the autonomy of its will, the sole counterpart of the State is the individual personality But since these two characteristics—multiplicity of ends and autonomy of will—are the essential marks of the concept of a person, the State has the nature of a collective personality. It is the only association of individuals to which this character can be ascribed. All other bodies between the individual and the State lack it because they are always restricted to a definite range of purposes, and, moreover, have not the necessary autonomy; or at least their autonomy is only apparent, derived either from the State or from their individual members Hence such a more restricted social will acts rather as the representative of another personality or a number of personalities than as a person itself. Thus we must not confuse the concept of personality in the psychological and ethical sense with the notion of a legal person. The latter is the way in which jurisprudence expresses the idea that an association, a corporation, or even a foundation endowed for a specific purpose shares, within the sphere of ends where it is recognised as a legal subject, the same protection that the personal subject enjoys In this intentionally transferred sense every legal subject is a 'legal person.' Real persons, on the other hand, are those legal subjects alone who are self-conscious and free agents and of such there are but two, the individual person and the collective personality of the State The two are distinguished, again, by the fact that in the former self-consciousness and will are directly combined into a single

668] *in the Advancement of Culture* 285

whole, while in the latter they are distributed among many individual units, so that every volition presupposes a more or less complex interaction of individual persons And it is precisely this difference that makes the real significance of the collective personality far greater than that of the individual person.[1]

[1] In the first edition of this work I raised objections against applying the concept of personality to the State, or to any real existence other than the individual personality (1st ed., p 551). On closer consideration of the subject, however, I find that the character of immediate oneness of self-consciousness and will, which I formerly thought should be the test, is too inessential to counterbalance the fundamental agreement of the concepts On the other hand, I think it important to lay stress on those points where the individual and the collective personality are alike, in order to emphasise the great difference in nature and importance between the State and all other associations. For these reasons I cannot agree with O Gierke, when, in his admirable works on the nature of associative bodies, he extends the concept of personality to cover corporations in general The extension thus ascribed to the notion of a 'real collective person' may suffice for juristic purposes and may be of especial service in opposing the untenable fiction-theory. But it ignores the very thing that constitutes the ethical value of the notion of personality (O GIERKE, *Das deutsche Genossenschaftsrecht*, vol. iii , and *Die Genossenschaftstheorie und die deutsche Rechtsprechung*, Berlin, 1887.) For the rest, I can understand why the historian of German law, especially when considering the subject of mediæval corporations in Germany, should be inclined to efface the distinction between the legal subject and the real personality. *Cf* on this point the observations on the ideas of a collective organism and a collective personality, in my *System der Philosophie*, 2nd ed., pp 616 ff

[669

# CHAPTER IV.

## HUMANITY

### I  THE ECONOMIC INTERCOURSE OF NATIONS

WE know that the peaceful intercourse between nations which is a necessary condition of the consumption and exchange of goods reaches back to the earliest beginnings of history.  Commerce, which in old times not infrequently took the government itself into its service, has, in proportion as the need for it has come to be felt by all civilised nations, more and more stimulated the desire to secure peace.  Of all the factors that have furthered the development of humanity, economic intercourse is undoubtedly the one that has worked most effectually towards the establishment of a system of international law, and thus prepared the way for the conception of humanity as a whole, united in one common moral life

Of course, the bearing of traffic in material goods upon the development of the moral life is indirect only.  By securing the means and improving the conditions of physical existence it creates the necessary foundation for morality Moreover, it stimulates many impulses towards intellectual perfection, which in its turn helps ethical culture.  For instance, one of the most effective aids to moral development is that higher form of division of labour which is rendered possible by economic intercourse.  Since each nation can obtain from without the goods it does not itself

286

669-70] *The Economic Intercourse of Nations* 287

produce, and usually under more favourable conditions than if it did produce them, it is enabled to confine itself to those departments of industry where its character and external conditions make it most effective.

A new factor is thus introduced into this development. The greater the degree of international division of labour, the greater is the need for international commerce. Whatever interferes with it becomes a serious peril to individual existence  It is unnecessary to indicate what powerful incentives for the development in various directions of material and intellectual culture, and hence of moral culture, lie in this fact  There is just one point that deserves to be emphasised, because it is the first clear expression of the idea of international law  In the regulation of its economic intercourse with other states every nation is guided mainly by its own interest. Thus the question as to how and in what measure it shall govern the importation and exportation of products is decided wholly by weighing the individual interests of its various forms of business and the collective interests of its citizens  It sacrifices its own advantage only for the sake of a greater one. Unselfishness is essentially foreign to the realm of economic intercourse ; and it is so even more in the life of the State than in that of the individual  For the egoism of the State is more justifiable than that of the individual, because its ends are greater and more permanent. The State is an economic unit just like the individual or the family, only with more comprehensive functions and far more complex economic conditions  It is especially so in its external relations, where it seeks to obtain the most favourable conditions for its own material existence and that of its members. Nevertheless, the idea of equality before the law has penetrated even into this field  Not, of course, in the sense of the absolute economic identification of one state with another, which

288          *Humanity*          [670–1

would be incompatible with the unity of the State, but in the principle, which is more and more recognised, that every state should regard all others as having equal rights with itself. The value of this kind of international equality is not diminished by the fact that it is in each case a voluntary relation, expressed in the customary forms of economic contracts rather than in any universally acknowledged law. The "most favoured nation" clause would seem to have a meaning of this sort In proportion as it becomes a permanent form, it is equivalent to a guarantee of equal rights to all nations in their intercourse one with another.

### 2. THE LAW OF NATIONS.

On the basis of material interests and their demand for legal protection there has been gradually erected a structure of international law, which, extending its influence far beyond the sphere of its origin, is beginning to unite all civilised states into a higher form of legal community.

These norms of international law originated out of the need of individuals for security. As soon as any permanent intercourse between nations had been developed, the State was forced to undertake the duty of protecting the persons and property of its citizens outside as well as inside its own boundaries The principles of international law, thus established, soon extended beyond the field of individual ends, and invaded that of the affairs and interests of the states themselves. Hence our present system of government has two distinct organisations to serve these different purposes. There is the consulate, whose functions are chiefly to protect individual interests And there are the embassies to foreign nations, whose task it is to regulate affairs of state. For matters of special importance congresses and conferences of plenipotentiaries supplement the

671-2]    *The Law of Nations*    289

work of the embassy, and problems relating both to individuals and to the State are settled on a more permanent basis by international agreements and conventions. These latter correspond, allowing for the different conditions of their origin, to the codified body of laws that governs the affairs of the individual state. Finally, partly out of habitual practice in matters of detail, and partly out of principles that have been regularly agreed upon, there develops, as the last stage attainable by the united legal consciousness of nations, the law of international custom.[1]

Thus the legal commonwealth of nations does not lack its administrative organisation, and even has a kind of constitution  The autonomy of its various parts, however, gives greater freedom to both these organisations. International affairs are decided on the merits of each individual case, and the very organs for their regulation are constituted with reference to the needs of each case as it arises. Yet as these needs regularly recur, and certain views on the subject of international law come to gain wider and wider acceptance, a certain constant practice grows up both in legislation and administration, which may form a substitute for the constraint of codified laws. The freedom that attends the formation of international law may be a weakness from the juristic point of view, but it is an advantage from that of ethics. For a free moral action has always, for states as for individuals, greater moral worth. In any case, it is a characteristic too deeply involved in the very nature of the State's life ever to be thought or wished other than it is. The more the moral consciousness of the various nations develops, the more impossible becomes the dream of a " world-government." Free competition among material and intellectual interests is more and more coming to be the vital condition for the existence of the legal commonwealth

[1] *Cf.* on this point above, Part III , chap iv., p 191

U

of nations itself. Hence the idea of "a codification of international law" is one that can hardly be carried out, except as a purely scientific task, whose influence on practice is simply that exerted by all science as it clears up men's ideas on a given subject.

On the whole, however, it is probable that science exercises distinctly less influence on the general and permanent structure of international law than on the legislation of the individual state. This is partly because the effects of individual influence are more rarely met with, the wider the sphere of life concerned, and partly because international law lacks and must of necessity lack those legislative organs that are the substrate of individual influences. Possibly the development of international law may be delayed by this fact. But it is none the less certain that a form of government conditioned by practical needs will maintain the results of its endeavours with greater energy, and will not readily abandon them.

There is no more striking expression of that change of view which has led to the idea of an universal commonwealth of law embracing all humanity than the significance which the conceptions of war and peace have assumed in modern legal theory. War formerly meant a state of brutal oppression which one nation might impose on another at its own arbitrary will, without giving any account to itself or to others of the motives for its action. Even Hugo Grotius, though he is the first to speak of 'the law of war,' scarcely ventures to oppose this view. Peace in those days was simply the absence of war. One nation was at peace with another when the two were not actually at war. It is significant that treaties of peace are the oldest form of international agreement. They are also the most imperfect, because they usually express the will of the victor only. Nevertheless, they sometimes contained agreements for the regulation of intercourse between the parties, thus rendering the recurrence of war less easy. Hence they had in germ the idea of real international agreements, concluded with the free consent of both parties, and establishing certain positive regulations for the state of peace, thereby indicating peace as the normal condition of nations, war as a temporary interruption of peace Thus a total reversal of opinion has gradually come about. While the right to wage war was formerly the natural right of every state, which it merely suspended when it kept the peace, the latter has now become a positive legal status, protected by guarantees originating partly by contract and partly by usage War, on the other hand, arises from a conflict of interests where the existing guarantees are no longer adequate and new ones cannot be found by mutual agreement. If a solution cannot be reached through the mediation of other powers, war ensues as a process that either decides a contested point of international law or leads to the formation of a new code to take the place of an old one that has ceased to be of use to the common-wealth of nations In the former case the analogue of war within the limits of the state is the civil process by which legal contests between individuals are decided In the latter case it corresponds to the constitutional struggle that pre-cedes any change in the organisation of the state, a struggle that frequently has to be decided by force even in the indi-vidual state, where civil war arises.

These changes of view are especially apparent in the ideas associated with the sea and its use for navigation and commerce In former times the sea was the region of universal lawlessness Because it belonged to no one state it was regarded as an arena where everyone must be ready to defend his life and property against everyone else The pirate is the typical figure of this age Unlike that of robbers on the land, his profession was regarded as so far from dishonourable that whole nations were not ashamed to conclude alliances with pirates or to practise piracy themselves The idea of the legal commonwealth of humanity has transformed the sea into the great territory of the international commonwealth. Precisely because it is not the property of any one state, it is taken under the protection of all seafaring nations, which are jointly responsible for its security. Hence, in general, the rules that govern marine warfare are apt to be stricter and more inviolable than is the case with the more localised warfare of the land.

The preceding century looked upon war wholly from the point of view of the older conception that made it an act of pure violence, resting on the absolute irresponsibility of the autonomous state It was against this idea of war that the notion of "everlasting peace," which plays a leading rôle in the philosophy of the time, was directed Hence we should be regarding these philosophical endeavours after peace in a false light if we were to ridicule them as the offspring of an unsound cosmopolitanism, or as wholly Utopian dreams. Many of the conditions requisite for an everlasting peace that were first postulated by Kant in his "Preliminary and Definitive Articles," are now recognised by the public sentiment of law, while others are looked upon as ends that are at least worth striving to attain. With the firmer establishment of an international commonwealth of law, arbitrary breach of peace for dynastic or other egoistic interests is becoming less and less possible nowadays, for such a commonwealth strengthens the forces that make for peaceful action and against purely aggressive war, and increases the moral weight of public opinion. It may be, of course, that wars which arise out of irreconcilably opposed conceptions of law, or an insoluble conflict between political interests, whose settlement can be reached only by the adoption of new legal principles, will never be wholly abolished But the same auxiliary in-

675]    *The Law of Nations*    293

fluences that hinder aggressive war render possible a peaceful settlement of such differences. Thus the forces of the commonwealth of nations are directed towards producing a balance of power, which has an increasing tendency to prevent war and to strengthen the influences that enable nations to reach an amicable arrangement of their disputes. Hence the postulate that the relation between states is constantly approximating one of permanent peace is warranted not only by ethics, but by history, if we regard the future as a development out of the present rather than a repetition of the past. Ethically, war is always an expedient to be used only in times of extremest need, and the goal of every effort towards moral improvement must be the ultimate avoidance of such expedients  The course of historical development shows, however, that neither an international tribunal endowed with supreme power, nor a world-state such as Kant had in mind, is an attainable end, but that the efficacy of such voluntary arrangements as are in use to-day, for example, submission to the decision of an arbiter chosen by free consent, or peaceful alliances and agreements, will increase. And the most important factor that ensures the effectiveness of such institutions of international law is the increasing sentiment of moral responsibility for the serious consequences of a breach of peace.

War thus having become a method of solving irreconcilable conflicts in the social life of nations that is adopted only as a last resort, the means and conditions of its conduct have altered their character. The rules of warfare have become more humane, but this is merely an external circumstance. A more important one is the fact that, at least in the majority of civilised nations, military service is a duty so universally required that war is made a real contest of nations, where each throws into the balance its whole power, intelligence, and especially its political vitality, as expressed in its capacity

294 *Humanity* [675-6

for self-defence. Thus warfare is in a fair way to become a critical process in history, where the so-called fortunes of war count for less and less, and moral preparation is almost everything. The rule that might makes right will always hold in war, but it is destined to be amended by another, namely, that right makes might. Perhaps it would be dreaming of another Utopia to hope that such a goal can ever be fully attained  The struggle between right and wrong will not cease while moral development lasts, for it belongs to the very essence of such development.  And it is no less an inevitable characteristic of this struggle that wrong must occasionally win.  Here, as in the legal order of the individual state, the principle holds good that, if we are to get an idea of the nature of the moral progress, we must look at the changes in men's conception of law,—not at particular actions, which may or may not be in harmony with the law, and whose conflict with one another will never wholly vanish.  Yet in the international commonwealth it is easier for the conception of law that is universally accepted in theory to become the maxim actually followed in conduct, because of the comprehensive character of that social will which is represented by the power of the individual state in such a commonwealth  For here the spirit of wrongdoing is not a power lurking in secret places, ensnaring in its toils the individual will with all the fluctuating motives which determine that will.  It is an act of public violence, and hence regulations tending to prevent its occurrence may be made before the fact  These regulations will not always prove as effective as might be desired, because the commonwealth of nations lacks an organisation to combine the totality of its parts into a firm system.  In a measure, however, a substitute for such organisation is furnished by the alliance of civilised states  It is not a social unit like the individual state, but for many purposes it produces an equivalent social order

676-7] *The Association of Civilised States* 295

### 3. THE ASSOCIATION OF CIVILISED STATES.

As the division of society into classes originated largely from the natural conditions of social life, so the social union of states, international society, is a product of the play of like and unlike interests, where the relative power of the various states has a decisive influence

There is only one permanent difference between a society made up of individuals and the general international society of states. It lies in the fact that the latter is always directed by the free self-regulating power which is the universal condition of the origin of social life , and that in consequence there is a total absence of such influences as proceed from a superior social will. For humanity as a whole, a society will always be the highest form of union possible, at least within any future that we can now anticipate.

This higher form of human society, where the relations between states is like that between the citizens of a single state in the primary form, is wholly a product of modern civilisation. True, there have always been differences of power and consequence among nations, such as now form the basis of the international commonwealth But they had no permanent recognition Supremacy was maintained merely by the direct exercise of superior force in war, or by the consequences thus brought about. Such a condition of affairs is represented by the alliances and feudal relationships of former times, which were as far removed from an actual international commonwealth as the relation between freemen and slaves or serfs is from a social organisation Not until the rise of the modern commonwealth of states do we find the beginning of a condition where all states, the least as well as the greatest, are allowed the same freedom and equality that the State gives to its individual citizens , while at the same time a due regard is had to the differences in

# 296 *Humanity* [677-8]

political power and other circumstances that exist among the members of the commonwealth. We smile nowadays at the painful and laborious care with which the relative rank of princes and their adherents was ordered by the seventeenth-century codes of etiquette, and at the curious interest which even a man like Leibniz took in contests over trifling questions of external form. But we must not forget that such dull discussions of court ceremonial marked the beginning of this new and higher social order, the society of states, which is slowly working out its destiny and extending itself into an international society embracing all humanity

The circumstance to which such an international commonwealth, based on internal equality of rights, chiefly owes its origin and maintenance is the existence of a number of states approximately equal in power, each one of which strives jealously to guard against any encroachments that the others might seek to make upon it. Thus, instead of a higher system of law, we have a strife between various interests, which in the first place tends to keep opposing forces within bounds by violent means, and later gradually produces a sentiment of law adapted to become the strongest bulwark of order in the intercourse of nations as in that of individuals. Hence the great Powers, whose especial duty it is to carry on war between nations when a peaceful settlement of conflicting claims becomes impossible, are at the same time the proper guardians of the peaceful interests of nations  Not only must they watch over the security of their own rights they must guard those of the lesser states that cannot protect themselves. This means a certain preponderant tendency towards the eventual necessity of deciding questions by force , but it is evident that such a tendency is the inevitable result of the fact that along with the influence of the sentiment of law a conflict of interests persists. The capacity of a state to form alliances is thus the final test of its

678-9] *The Association of Civilised States* 297

capacity to exist. And the limits to the growth of a nation's power, thus defined, are significant also of the limits within which other factors, such as the common feeling of nationality, long political and intellectual association, may form the basis of political unity.

It is a well-known fact that the modern political commonwealth of nations, which in this latest form, that of a social balance of power, is largely the product of this century and of a reaction against the last great attempt to found a world-empire, has not always kept within the above-mentioned limits. With the avowed purpose of maintaining European order, many of the great Powers have felt called upon to interfere even in matters affecting the internal constitution of other states The latest step towards securing complete equality of rights here is the express rejection, by all the great Powers, of the fundamental principles involved in such a policy of intervention. This leaves the social system of nations free to follow exclusively its proper objects, the protection and furtherance of the common interests of civilisation.

It is impossible as yet to trace to their ultimate consequences the moral advantages of this highest form of civilised community, which is also, of course, the freest form yet instituted by humanity. An immediate result, though rather a negative than a positive one, is the greatly increased possibility of finding an amicable settlement where interests conflict. But there is another consequence of greater moment for the permanent common life of humanity. This is the powerful impulse given in all directions towards realising the positive ends of civilisation in material and intellectual intercourse. Among all the special consequences of the establishment of an international commonwealth, which need not be enumerated, there is one of the highest value. Such a concentration of the forces of civilised nations brings about

298 *Humanity* [679-80

a general diffusion of the consciousness of humanity's common ends and goods, a consciousness that in earlier periods of the world's history was at most the possession of a few exceptional minds. Thus, from being a merely potential unity, humanity begins to become an actual unity, upon which larger moral tasks devolve as its means grow larger

### 4. THE COMMON INTELLECTUAL LIFE OF HUMANITY

The idea of humanity is not primitive, but a product of gradual development, and still in process of growth. The intellectual life took its rise in isolated and disconnected beginnings The intellectual possessions created by one nation passed, through no volition of its own, into the possession of others Thus, preserved from destruction by being imparted, such possessions became the inheritance of new peoples called to civilisation. So the course of history became coherent, not because the human race was originally animated by a common intellectual life, but because from scattered fragments of the intellectual life a whole was gradually built up. For this reason the continuity of the intellectual life as displayed in history does not directly follow the course of events itself, but is evident only in retrospect.

Yet historical life labours without wearying to bring about a transformation of this original relationship. In the first place there is a more clearly conscious estimate of the intellectual heritage of the past as regards its value and the conditions under which it is obtained. Thus Rome even in its day delighted in the treasures of Greek learning and art, and during the period of the revival of ancient civilisation the traces of antique culture were everywhere followed with loving care. Yet even here the

680-1] *The Intellectual Life of Humanity* 299

eye that begins to see the continuity of the intellectual life is directed towards the past alone. Only in a few isolated minds there dawns the thought that now and in the future humanity is called to a common life. The idea of a commonwealth of humanity owes its increasing practical recognition in the establishment of universally recognised principles of law and the union of civilised states, not to art or to science, but to political life, whose problems are pre-eminently those of the present. The handmaid of politics in this task is history, which seeks to obtain from the life of the past conclusions about the future, and thus to enable the art of politics, drawing from the teachings of the past, to make sure of its results by absorbing those historical ideas to whose fulfilment it is called.

It is true that the metaphor, recurring in nearly all the theories of the philosophy of history, which compares the periods of history with the stages of development in the individual life, is in many respects inept. The unity of personal volition and action, in particular, is necessarily wanting in the life of history. Hence the latter is rich in simultaneous processes of development, where many things are produced at one and the same time which in individual life are necessarily successive. In one point, however, the illustration may serve to make clear the general course that the life of humanity as a whole has followed in history. At first the impressions out of which the individual consciousness builds up its ideas flow in upon it at random and unsought. Though its ideas enter into an internally coherent system, this is rather a passive process than the result of active volition. As the will matures, the relation is altered. True, outward impressions still exert their influence; but a new factor appears, at first subordinate, then increasingly predominant. It is the factor of preconsidered action, for

300                    *Humanity*                    [681

which the outer impression is no longer the determining
influence, but merely the material on which it must operate
and the condition under which it must take place. Thus
the life of the mind, originally the plaything of external
circumstance, beccmes more and more a self-formed product
of inner motives    The child *is* educated, the man educates
himself,—unless the immaturity of his character is such
that he remains a child all his life    So is it with the spirit
of history    Its first task is to unite disconnected ideas into
a single whole by allowing the fortune of events to transfer
to one people the fruit of another nation's labours, thereby
enabling the former to gain a fuller culture through the
means thus transmitted.    It lets even that division of
function, which is best adapted to serve the intellectual
ends of humanity, develop of itself through the force of
outward events and original national characteristics    Finally,
however, here as in the individual mind, what originated
without choice is transformed into something that is consciously willed    History itself is no longer merely that
which happens , it is made by men, that is, by nations, and
by those individuals whose function is to shape the civilisation and the destiny of nations.

It is true that the life of humanity as a whole, thus
originating by a gradual process and continually developing,
is grounded, like the individual life, on a material basis.
But just because its nature is more comprehensive, it is
more of an intellectual product than the life of the individual
The bond of material interests embraces only what is directly
contiguous in space and time    Such interests are, indeed,
the impelling forces which must at least co-operate in the
fulfilment even of intellectual ends.    Yet with increasing
distance in time their traces tend to disappear, and the
intellectual results alone remain.    The intellectual treasures

681-2] *The Intellectual Life of Humanity* 301

of antiquity are all that is left to us of its civilisation   Even as regards the past of our own nation, the material condition of former times affects the present indirectly only, through the medium of the intellectual culture that it allowed or forbade.   Thus the wider the sphere of the life of humanity, the more purely intellectual that life becomes.

The intellectual nature of the commonwealth of humanity is apparent in the fact that its conscious expression, the idea of humanity, was originally not the product of commercial and economic interests, but the outgrowth of intellectual forces.   As in the separate life of nations, so in their common life, religion is the primary source of the social consciousness.   Ancient civilisation having once actually created a common stock of intellectual possessions, it was Christianity that first postulated the existence of an intellectual commonwealth, in the form of a commonwealth of faith   As a result of its influence science and art became common possessions, shared by peoples and ages according to the functions devolving upon them by reason of their natural characteristics and historical conditions   Thus the intellectual commonwealth is really earlier than the material. And the strongest moral support for the latter is to be found in the sentiment of equality of rights produced by oneness of intellectual interests.   For centuries, however, peaceful intercourse was possible only between Christian nations, and common warfare against the infidels was one of the earliest occasions for the formation of international alliances, which were for the most part, of course, temporary in character.   Thus that political union of civilised states for the purpose of common peaceful endeavour, in which the problems of material existence occupy the foreground of interest, is the final and not the first stage of development.

302 *Humanity* [682-3

But it is a stage whose importance for the later aspects of the moral life is all the greater. As more lasting safeguards against hostilities allow of an unbroken development of intellectual forces, commerce begins to exert an influence upon nations like that experienced by the individual through social life. A peaceful competition of material and intellectual interests gradually gives rise to a division of labour in the material realm which is of service to the needs of the whole, while in the intellectual realm it brings about mutual aid between forces that are performing the same function, and even, to a certain extent, an interchange and balancing of opinions that is as good for the development of human nature in nations as in individuals.

It would, of course, be a mistake to expect or even to hope that this increasing unity of intellectual life should cause national differences of endowment and character to disappear  Culture enriches; it never impoverishes  That which tends towards an indefinite increase in the manifold development of character within the individual nation must surely bring about a fuller development of the characters of nations along their own peculiar lines, by producing a livelier exchange of ideas. The Middle Ages, under the powerful protection of the Church, made a remarkable attempt to extend into all other departments that unity of intellectual life whose first manifestation was in the unity of religious convictions. Art and science were associated with forms in which national distinctions were supposed to disappear. But the art of each nation soon followed its own peculiar tendency, despite the fact that the religious elements in the material with which it dealt were everywhere the same , and science gradually laid aside the common speech of the learned  For an age whose task it was to call a world-literature into life this common speech had an indispensable mission to fulfil,

## 683-4]  *The Intellectual Life of Humanity*  303

even apart from the fact that the various national tongues were then too little developed to be of service  Yet science as well as art has gained infinitely by the development of national forms of thought, while its unity, once established, has never been lost  The present age has a world-literature quite as truly as had the age when all the world wrote Latin; nay, in a fuller sense, so far as rapidity and scope in the interchange of ideas are concerned.  Yet it is a world-literature written in all the different languages of civilisation, and thus all the varieties in national ways of looking at things become the common possession of humanity

With the products of science, national in their origin, yet appropriated by all nations, there vie the creations of art. These, while they express the particular emotional tendencies of some one people, are transmitted to other nations, which appropriate them, and thereby develop further their own ' peculiar national characteristics  Finally, even the increase of personal intercourse between men of different races, and the broadening of individual views through knowledge of foreign lands and peoples, play a certain rôle in the increasingly lively exchange of intellectual values  While their effect is of rather an external character, it is not in-essential to the life and growth of this system of reciprocal intellectual influences  As humanity thus learns to unite temporally with its own life the intellectual acquisitions of the past, and to combine spatially the life of all contemporaries into a single great collective life; as it thus realises the idea of its unity, it imposes higher moral tasks upon those less comprehensive wills which labour in the service of the whole.  The man is more responsible for his acts than the child, because more is required of those whose capacity is greater  And so out of a wider knowledge of the tasks of humanity greater moral requirements arise  The idea of

304    *Humanity*    [684

Humanity, at first instinctively practised, rather than clearly conceived, in the various forms of personal benevolence, creates its own proper object through the consciousness of a common human life, directed throughout history towards the solution of moral problems. It thus finds an inexhaustible content, out of which there develops an international sense of obligation , and this in turn is at once the guide and the goal of all the functions of the individual moral life.

# INDEX OF NAMES AND SUBJECTS

Altruism, primitive character of, 27, 28, 79, 80; why preferable to egoism, 80

Apperception, nature of, 14

ARISTOTLE, 76

Art, as element in culture, 212, 213; in intellectual life of humanity, 303, 304

Associations, classification and moral value of, 245–55

Atomism, ethical, in Spinoza, Leibniz, Descartes, and Herbart, 29–31

AUGUSTINE, 54

BACON, 24

BENTHAM, 165, 171

BIERLING, 170, 171 *note*

BINDING, 186 *note*

Cartesianism, 29

Causality, psychical and mechanical, 39, 41, 44, 45; of character, 55–9

Character, causality of, 55–9

Christian ethics, method, 75; conception of individual, 82, 83; application of principle of equality, 241

Christianity, as basis of religious education, 276–8; as origin of intellectual commonwealth of humanity, 301

Church, relation to State, 254; in education, 274–9; in Middle Ages, 302

Citizenship, moral influence of, 206–10; of women, 229, 230; as basis of associations, 252 4

Commerce, 286–8

Community, moral significance of the, 255–7

Conscience, theories of, 59–64; imperatives of, 64–74

Consciousness, nature of, 4, 5

Constraint, motives of, 67, 68, 92; as essence of law, 169–71

Culture, moral significance of, 211–24; of women, 230–2; influence on social classes, 235; relation to the State, 272–81

DESCARTES, 31

Desire, relation to feeling and volition, 4

Determinism, error of ordinary, 41, 42; relation to indeterminism, 41, 42

Duties, concepts of, relation to virtue and norms, 143–9; individual, 152, 153; social, 154–6; humanitarian, 156–9

Economic conditions, relation to State, 260; international, 286–8

Empiricism, method of, 76

Ends, immoral, two sources, 91–3

Ends, moral, forms of, 75–7; individual, 77, 78; social, 79–84; humanitarian, 84–91; heterogony of, 66, 84, 102; hierarchy of, 88, 139

Enlightenment, individualism of, 29, 78, 246, 283

# 306 *Index of Names and Subjects*

Equality, possibility of social, 224, 236 ff.

Equity, relation to justice, 181, 182

Family, rights and duties, 174, moral significance of, 225-33

Feeling, relation to desire and volition, 4; to will, 6-8, æsthetic and intellectual, 8; in motives, 94

FFUERBACH, 35 *note*

FICHTE, 147

Franchise, right of, 172, 175

GIFRKE, O, 285 *note*

GROTIUS, 290

HEGEL, 34, 35, 166

HLLVEIIUS, 25

HERBART, 31, 166

HOBBES, 24, 25, 166

Humanity, as a moral end, 84-9; as an economic unity, 286-8, as a legal commonwealth, 288-98, as an intellectual commonwealth, 298-304

HUME, 26

Ideal, the moral, as motive, 69-72; as motive of reason, 104-8

Immorality, nature of, 108-17, individual forms, 112-16

Imperative, categorical, 62, 63

Impulsive action, 14, 16, relation to voluntary action, 16-18

Impulses, self-regarding, 99, 100, social-regarding, 100-4

Indeterminism, relation to determinism, 41, 42 · criticism of, 53-5

Individual, and society, 32, 37, 55-9, development compared with that of humanity, 299, 300

Individualism, of the Enlightenment, 24-6; criticism of, 27-9, in Hegelian school, 35, theory of social ends, 32-4, theory of immorality, 108-9; theory of State, 283, 284

Introspection, influence of external perception on, 3, 4

Intuitionism, on nature of imperatives, 65, 66

JELLINEK, 169

JHERING, 169

Justice, 179-82

KANT, 6, 26, 42, 54, 60, 62, 119, 145, 147, 292

KRAUSE, 121, 166

LAPLACE, 41, 49

LASSALLE, Ferd, 35 *note*

Law, relation to morality, 134-6; natural law, theory of, 160, 161, individualism in, 163-6, historical theory of, 166, 167; protective theory of, 167-9, theory of constraint, 169-71; subjective, 172-5; objective, 175, 176; definition of 176-9, codified, 182-6, relation to State, 261-8, international, 191, 288-98

LEIBNIZ, 14, 30, 31, 296

LUTHER, 54

Materialism, 50

Matter, nature of concept, 45, 46

Motive, relation to will, 9, 10, actual, potential, final, leading, and incidental, 11, 27, relation to effect of act, 12; to end, 87; to humanitarian end, 88, 89

Motives, immoral, 108-29; complexity of, 116, 117

Motives, imperative, origin, 64-6; of constraint, 67, 68, of freedom, 68-72, 92, religious form of, 72-4

Motives, moral, forms of, 94, 95; of perception, 95-8, of the understanding, 99-104, of reason, 104-8

## Index of Names and Subjects 307

Nominalism, 53, 54

Norms, legal, relation to moral norms, 151, origin and nature, 160–92, fundamental and auxiliary, 182–92

Norms, moral, fundamental and derivative, 130–2, positive and negative, 132–6, conflict of, 137–42, relation to duty and virtue, 143–9, classification of, 150–2, individual, 152–4, social, 154–6, humanitarian, 156–60

Occupation, 201–6, influence on civic position, 208–10; on culture, 211, of members of a family, 226–8; of women, 226–9, influence on social classes, 234, 235, as basis of associations, 250–2

Perception, motives of, 95–8

Personality, in individual and State, 284, 285

Physiology, relation to psychology, 51

PLATO, 24, 168, 273

Property, extremes of, 114, 115, 199, 205, 242–5, right of private, 173, moral significance of, 197–201, influence on civic position, 207, on culture, 211, relations in family life, 225, 226, influence on social classes, 234, 235, associations, 248–50, relation to State, 258–60

Punishment, theories of, 118–23, nature of, 123–9; right of, 171, 172

Reason, motives of, 104, 108

Reflex acts, voluntary origin of, 13, 17

Religion, conception of social will, 37, of moral imperatives, 72–4; of moral ideal, 36, 37 107, as element of culture, 212, permanence of, 219–222

Representative government, significance of, 266

Rights, relation to duties, 150, 151, nature of, 172–5

ROUSSEAU, 24, 25, 35 *note*

SCHELLING, 168

Science, as element in culture, 213–17, in intellectual life of humanity, 302, 303

Self feeling, as moral motive, 95, 96

Self-preservation, as moral end, 77, 78

Self-satisfaction, as moral end, 77, 78

Separation of powers, doctrine of, 267

SOCRATES, 68, 76, 84

Social classes, 234

Society, relation to State, 269–72, international, 295–8

Soul, nature of, 32

Sovereign, 267, 268

SPINOZA, 25, 30, 120

STAHL, 167–9

State, individualistic theories of, 25; relation to law, 172 ff; regulation of property, 242, relation to Church and schools, 254, 272–81, to community, 255–7, as financial and economic body, 258–60, as legal body, 261–8, relation to society, 269–72, as a personality, 281–5

STEIN, L. von 162 *note*

STIRNER, Max, 35 *note*

Sympathy, not identical with feelings of its object, 28, nature of, 96–8, relation to social-regarding impulses, 99

TRENDELENBURG, 170 *note*

Understanding, motives of the, 99–104

Universalism, theory of immorality, 109

Utilitarianism, 79

Virtue, concepts of, relation to duties and norms, 143–9, individual, 152, 153; social, 154–6; humanitarian, 156–9

Volition, relation to feeling and desire, 4; causality of, 52, 53

# 308 — Index of Names and Subjects

WAGNER, A , 175

War, mediæval and modern views of 290-4

Will, freedom of, 37-59

Will, relation to feeling and desire, 4, 6, 8 , nature of, 5-8 , relation to consciousness, 7 , motives and causes of, 9-12 , doctrine of a substantial, 9 , development of, 12-14 , relation to personality, 20, 21 , to external nature, 22 , to other wills, 22, 23 , in formation of character, 58

Will, social, 20 , relation to individual, 32-7, 58, 59 ; to immorality, 108-10 , to punishment, 118, 123-5

WOLFF, 60

Woman, position and education of, 225-32

ZITELMANN, 186 *note*

PLYMOUTH
WILLIAM BRENDON AND SON, PRINTERS

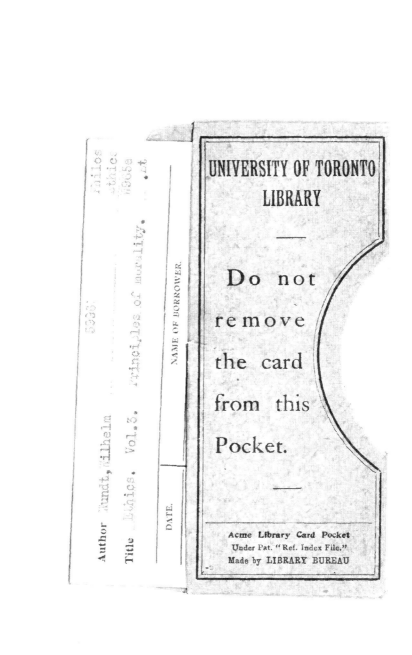

CPSIA information can be obtained
at www.ICGtesting.com
Printed in the USA
LVHW040846181222
735461LV00004B/124